Q & A SERIES INTELLECTUAL PROPERTY LAW

Cavendish
Publishing
Limited

TITLES IN THE Q&A SERIES

BUSINESS LAW
CIVIL LIBERTIES
COMMERCIAL LAW
COMPANY LAW
CONFLICT OF LAWS
CONSTITUTIONAL & ADMINISTRATIVE LAW
CONTRACT LAW
CRIMINAL LAW
EMPLOYMENT LAW
ENGLISH LEGAL SYSTEM
EQUITY & TRUSTS
EUROPEAN COMMUNITY LAW
EVIDENCE
INTELLECTUAL PROPERTY LAW
INTERNATIONAL TRADE LAW
JURISPRUDENCE
LAND LAW
REVENUE LAW
SUCCESSION
TORTS LAW
'A' LEVEL LAW

Q & A SERIES INTELLECTUAL PROPERTY LAW

Alan Murdie, LLB, Barrister
Department of Law
Thames Valley University

Cavendish
Publishing
Limited

First published in 1995 by Cavendish Publishing Limited, The Glass House, Wharton Street, London WC1X 9PX, United Kingdom

Telephone: +44 (0) 171 278 8000 Facsimile: +44 (0) 171 278 8080

E-mail: info@cavendishpublishing.com

Visit our Home Page on http://www.cavendishpublishing.com

Reprinted 1998

Murdie, Alan

Intellectual Property Law – (Q & A)

1. Intellectual property law – Great Britain – Examinations, questions, etc.

I Title

344.1'0648

ISBN 1 85941 274 2

Printed and bound in Great Britain

Introduction

This book arose from a perceived need and requests by students studying intellectual property law for a book which would demonstrate how to answer assessed essays and examination questions. It was not that students were inexperienced in writing essays and answering questions (it being a third year level subject). It was because they were finding it difficult to get a grasp of the scope, significance and range of intellectual property rights to set about answering questions about them with confidence.

The volume of material which intellectual property law textbooks succeed in covering and the erudite attempts that they make to discuss and reconcile complicated authorities can at times confuse students who are newcomers to the subject. The situation is not helped by the fact that a number of copyright cases are contained in obscure law reports (eg *Macgillivray's Copyright Cases* published in five and seven year intervals between 1901–45) and even when located can be exceedingly brief. Furthermore, reported decisions can be on obscure points of procedure and evidence, rather than the basic principles of intellectual property law which a student is seeking to grasp.

As a topic at degree level, intellectual property is unusual in that it requires a student to have a knowledge of remedies and an awareness of practical High Court procedures which are not normally addressed until the stage of studying for professional exams. For many students this means straying into very unfamiliar territory. To reach a correct answer it is often necessary to take into account factors which a court will apply in deciding whether to grant the most frequently sought remedy – an interlocutory injunction.

To an extent each case will turn on its facts, but a number of basic principles can be identified and applied, providing a student is clear on which particular right is involved. The problem for students is to 'see the wood for the trees'. The aim of this book, therefore, is to assist the new student in coming to grips with this wide ranging subject so that they can answer questions with confidence.

Topics covered

This book covers the most frequently examined areas; copyright (with a note on design rights), trade marks, passing off, patents, confidential information, malicious falsehood and character merchandising.

Intellectual property law is a statute based topic so access to a statute book (with or without commentary) is essential for reference and application. The statutes of prime importance are the Copyright Designs and Patents Act 1988, the Patents Act 1977 and the Trade Marks Act 1994.

This book seeks to give a core grounding in the most commonly examined areas within the context of intellectual property law as contained in domestic UK law. A work could be devoted to protecting intellectual property abroad, the growing effect of EC legislation and international conventions and agreements. Since most courses feature questions that can be dealt with by the application of domestic law it was considered best to concentrate on these.

Basic approach to questions

The questions which are set for examinations and assessed course work tend to be relatively simple and straightforward; the problem for students lie in extracting clear principles from the wealth of material and applying them in sufficient detail.

Most problem questions can be dealt with by the following approach:

- Identify the area of intellectual property concerned
- Identify any limitations on the right concerned arising from the law itself
- Identify the author or owner of the right concerned
- Set out all the elements that need to be proved
- Decide whether the defendant has infringed upon the right concerned
- Set out all the elements that need to be proved
- Decide whether the defendant has infringed upon the right concerned
- Consider whether there are any defences which a defendant can raise
- If a right of action can be established consider what remedies will lie

- If an injunction would be a suitable remedy consider the balance of convenience and any factors the court may consider when granting or refusing relief
- Advise the parties of their position

This approach provides the student with a checklist so that questions can be answered in a comprehensive way. Essay questions tend to require a succinct discussion of certain basic principles. The problem for students is to deal with a surfeit of information and to be able to condense it into clear, concise statements of law which can be contained within a reasonable word limit.

In order to grasp the significance of the law as it stands today, it is often useful to have an appreciation of the history of intellectual property protection. Earlier cases are worth referring to because they can state the law (as it then was) in detail and with clarity. A little knowledge of legal history will help students to understand the developments of such provisions as s 51 and s 52 of the Copyright Designs and Patents Act 1988. Older authorities may be of assistance because in many cases the principles are sometimes expressed in greater clarity than in modern decisions where the interlocutory nature of proceedings and the pressures of time often curtail the amount of judicial consideration devoted to points of law in judgments.

However, considerable care must be taken with older authorities. Intellectual property law is often policy led; industrial and technological developments lead to the re-writing of the law and there are fashions in judicial approach and interpretation which have prevailed and then retreated over the years. A judge looking at an issue in 1897 did so in the context of a very different technological world. The approach that the courts may take in one era may be different to that taken in another and earlier authorities may not be relied upon in every case. It is possible to find parties doing or believing exactly the same type of things a century apart leading one to believe that changes in human nature lag well behind technical progress. Certainly, the judiciary cannot be accused of being backward-looking in the field of intellectual property – see RSC Order 104 of the *Supreme Court Practice* (the 'White Book') which makes provision for interlocutory summonses in patent cases to be dealt with by telephone conferences.

Intellectual property law is a subject which continues to move forward and students should seek to keep abreast of new authorities by reviewing the new cases as they appear each month. As was said in *Caird v Simes* (1887):

Neath this starry arch
Naught resteth or is still

It is hoped that if students can grasp the basics then they will be well-equipped to confront new issues which are continually emerging in this subject, encompassing fields as diverse as the growth in information technology and the Internet, to the expansion of biotechnology and the disturbing attempts to patent life forms.

It is also worth remembering when answering questions that many intellectual property disputes take place in the context of frantically competing commercial interests who are striving to protect their market share or monopoly. It is rare for authors and artists to be concerned with aesthetics and non-pecuniary interests in intellectual property litigation. It is also rare for parties to be simply concerned with proving a point of law on principle. Furthermore, disputes which go to court often involve some of the more obscure aspects of the subject and the practice of non-contentious intellectual property law often bears as much comparison to the theory as conveyancing and property speculation do to land law. However, if the commercial factor can be considered by a student, it may be easier to understand such requirements as the balance of convenience which may be a factor in determining whether an injunction should be granted. The law is stated as believed correct at 1 December 1996.

Acknowledgments

In writing this book I would like to express particular thanks to a wide range of people. For assistance with word processing, arranging layout and technical advice my sister Rosemary and my friend Ms Sara Hill must come top of the list for my thanks for their invaluable help and support. I also wish to thank Ms Kate Aldridge and Mr Andrew James for vital computer support in the closing stages of preparing this work.

Thanks go to Mr Norman Baird and Mr M Ramjohn, lecturers with the School of Law at Thames Valley University, for their encouragement and interest in my writing this book. Much gratitude is also expressed for the suggestions and encouragement of a large number of students at Thames Valley University who have either studied or who are in the midst of studying this topic. Lastly, I must state a debt of gratitude to a number of people (not named herein) who have consulted me on practical issues of intellectual property law and who have allowed me to use their problems as inspirational material for certain of the questions and answers in this book. The fact that none of them have come unstuck on the basis of the answers I have supplied to date is naturally most encouraging.

Contents

Table of Cases

Table of Statutes

Copyright Designs and Patents Act 1988 (contd)

Chapter 1

Rights and Remedies

Introduction

In introducing intellectual property rights to students, a number of courses begin with a question requiring a student to identify the different varieties of right which exist and the major distinctions between them. Question 1 is a typical example of such a question, requiring the student to clarify the different categories of intellectual property rights that may subsist in a single item and outline the distinctions between them.

Once the range of intellectual property rights can be identified, the next stage is to clarify the different ways of protecting them – the remedies. A knowledge of remedies is necessary for two reasons. It is quite possible for questions to be set about interlocutory remedies alone, so detailed answers may be required on such matters as Anton Piller orders. Secondly, an understanding of remedies is necessary for answering many problem questions which usually require the student to consider the merits of an injunction and/or damages. Naturally, the methods of enforcing intellectual property rights are of great practical significance since, as is often stated, rights that cannot be enforced are ultimately meaningless. It should be remembered that the reason why many areas of intellectual property law remain somewhat unclear is that few cases ever go beyond the interlocutory stage. Questions that may be expected will thus be either essays on areas of practice and procedure, or problems where the student is expected to supply details of a specific remedy and its limitations in detail.

Checklist

Students should be familiar with the following areas:

- Sections 96–110 of the Copyright Designs and Patents Act 1988
- RSC Order 29
- *Anton Piller v KG Manufacturing Processes* (1974)
- *American Cyanamid v Ethicon* (1975)
- *Gerber Garment Technology v Lectra Systems* (1995)

- *Series 5 Software Ltd v Clarke* (1996)
- *Work Model Enterprises Ltd v Ecosystem Ltd and Clix Interiors Ltd* (1996)
- Damages
- Account of profits

Question 1

Whoosh! Slimming Products Ltd have developed their new 'fade to light' slimming powder to be added to meals. Advise them on the intellectual property rights which may subsist concurrently in a packet of the company's new powder which they plan to market. The powder is contained in a box with artwork and instructions for use on the outside and stamped with the Whoosh! trade mark. Short advertising slogans incorporating the name Whoosh! are written on the box.

Answer plan

A question which expects a student to demonstrate a knowledge of the range of intellectual property rights which may exist and which may be claimed by a party, and to be able to distinguish between them. Some precision is needed in identifying the boundaries between different forms of protection.

The issues to be considered are:

- CDPA 1988 – copyright
- Confidential information
- Patents Act 1977
- Trade Marks Act 1994
- Passing off

Answer

It is possible for a number of intellectual property rights to exist in the slimming powder produced by Whoosh!

Copyright

Copyright may subsist in the instructions and in the art work on the packet of Whoosh! The instructions on the packet of slimming powder are a literary work under s 1(1) of the CDPA 1988. In *Exxon Corp v Exxon Insurance* (1982), it was held that a literary work is one that conveys information or instruction. Copyright exists in the expression of the words, not the information itself.

The written details of the formula and the steps necessary to synthesise or produce the powder will be capable of copyright protection if recorded in material form, almost certainly as a literary work if it is sufficiently substantial. Copyright will not attach to the formula itself as copyright does not protect theories or ideas or information in itself (*Pike v Nicholas* (1869); *Harman Films v Osborne* (1967)).

Although effort and skill may have been devoted to coining the invented name Whoosh! it will not be capable of constituting a literary work because it is not sufficiently substantial (*Exxon v Exxon Insurance* (1982)). The name of the powder cannot be protected by copyright. There is no copyright subsistence in a name (*Taverner v Trexapalm* (1975) or in a title (*Francis Day Hunter v Twentieth Century Fox* (1940); *Rose v Information Services Ltd* (1987)).

In *Elanco Products v Mandops* (1979), instructions for use of a herbicide were protected as a literary work. Parts of the description for use may not be capable of copyright protection since they are part of the public domain and readily available. However, if the words are based on experimentation or research, a rival would not be entitled to copy these, but would be expected to confer their own labour effort and skill (see *Ladbroke v William Hill* (1964)) in order to confer originality in the new work. This could involve them having to conduct their own tests and experiments and obtaining data which could then be recorded in writing. In other words the rival would not be allowed to copy.

It is possible that copyright in any logo or art work incorporated into the name can be protected as an artistic work under s 4 of the CDPA 1988. Similarly, the surface decoration of the box may be capable of copyright protection as an original artistic work under ss 1(1)a and 4(1), irrespective of artistic merit. Artistic works are ones which appeal to the eye (*Spectravest Inc v Aperknit Ltd* (1988)).

A claim for copyright of the advertising slogans is likely to fail. Protection for advertising slogans was rejected in *Sinanide v La Maison Kosmeo* (1928). The more difficult question is whether the manufacture of Whoosh! powder from the formula will amount to production of the work as copyright infringement contrary to s 16 of the CDPA 1988. Under s 17, it is infringement of copyright to reproduce work in any material form, but the basis of such a claim is uncertain.

Confidential information

The formula itself may qualify as a trade secret. In *Saltman Engineering Co Ltd v Campbell Engineering Co Ltd* (1963), the Court of Appeal held that if two parties make a contract under which one obtains knowledge of a confidential matter, the law will imply an obligation to treat the matter confidentially. For example, technical material which is subject to a patent will be protected (*Cranleigh Precision Engineering v Bryant* (1966)). In *Faccenda Chicken Ltd v Fowler* (1985), Goulding J held that there were three categories of information: (1) publicly available information which cannot be classified as confidential; (2) information which is confidential but which remains in an employee's head and becomes part of his or her skill or knowledge and regarding which obligations of confidence may disappear when the contract ceases; (3) information so sensitive it remains confidential even when employment ceases. It is likely that knowledge of the formula for Whoosh! will qualify as a trade secret, protected under the equitable doctrine of confidential information under category (3). Employees with a knowledge of the formula or process may be restrained by a clause in their contract of employment, restricting them from disclosing it to third parties without consent.

Patent protection

Whilst the formula for Whoosh! cannot be patented in itself, a patent may be obtained for the chemical product or for the process for producing it. To be patentable, Whoosh! must fulfil the requirements of s 1(1) of the PA 1977. The powder or the process producing it must be novel, involve an inventive step, be capable of industrial application and not fall into one of the excluded categories. A discovery or a theory cannot constitute a patent under s 1(2) of the PA 1977.

Chemical selection patents are possible (*IG Farbenindustrie AG's Patents* (1930)). Since the stated use of the powder is as a slimming aid, it will also be necessary for Whoosh! to overcome the restrictions of patentability on methods of treatment. Section 4(2) excludes from industrial applicability any method of treatment of the human or animal body by surgery or therapy. However, as with contraceptive pills based on chemical products, patentability may be possible, as obesity is not necessarily a disease (*Schering's Application* (1971)). A new drug does not necessarily entail a method of treatment and can be patented together with the process that produces it. Under s 2(6), a substance that has previously been patented may be the subject of a second patent for medical use (*John Wyeth & Brother Ltd's Application and Schering AG's Application* (1985)). Experimental use of Whoosh! (eg laboratory tests in secret) will not deprive it of novelty. In any case it would be essential for Whoosh! to delay marketing the product until after they have made their application for a patent. In this way there could be no claim that the product or process has been made available to the public so as to disclose it.

If a patent is obtained by Whoosh! in the powder or process it will be valid for 20 years unless revoked (s 25 of the PA 1977). Any manufacture or use without licence is likely to be an infringement under s 60 of the PA.

Trade mark

Although the name of Whoosh! may not be protected by copyright, it will be capable of protection as a registered trade mark under s 1 of the TMA 1994. Section 1 states that a trade mark may be any sign capable of being represented graphically and which is capable of distinguishing the goods or services of Whoosh! from any other undertaking. Since a sign is capable of being a name, Whoosh! will fulfil s 1. The Registrar will consider an application for trade mark registration with reference to the absolute bars to registration (ss 3 and 4) and the relative grounds for refusal, such as conflict with an earlier mark (ss 5–7).

In *British Sugar plc v James Robertson Ltd* (1996), it was held that the protection conferred by a trade mark only applies to the use of the mark in a trade mark sense, in the course of business. Under ss 5 and 10, the reputation of the Whoosh! trade mark may also be protected in situations where it is applied without consent to goods or services which are dissimilar to those on which Whoosh! registers it. By these provisions Whoosh! will be able to protect any reputation associated with their brand name from dilution or damage to their reputation.

The advantage of trade mark registration will be that Whoosh! will be able to restrain use of the sign in the market place and any use of the mark without their consent. Under s 103(2), use is not restricted to graphical representation. An oral use of the name might amount to infringement in certain situations.

Given the wide definition of a trade mark (s 1(1)) it is also possible for colours or the shape of the box to be registered, provided that they are capable of being distinguished, and subject to the restrictions on functional shapes (TMA 1994).

Passing off

Related to trade mark law is the protection that is given to unregistered marks under the common law tort of passing off. Utilising these rights, the claim may exist to restrict misuse of the name Whoosh! In *Office Cleaning Services Ltd v Westminster Windows and General Cleaners Ltd* (1949), it was held that in the case of trade names the courts do not readily assume confusion between one trader and another where commonplace names or descriptive terms are used. However, with invented or fancy words the risk of confusion and deception will be assumed much more readily. It will be necessary to establish that the name or 'get up' of the goods has acquired a reputation, and trading for a limited period may be sufficient to confer goodwill. The packaging of goods and their appearance may be the basis of a claim for passing off, eg *William Edge & Sons v William Niccolls* (1911) ('Dolly Blue' washing powder). In *John Haig & Co v Forth Blending Co* (1953), a dimple whisky bottle was similarly capable of protection. The essential elements are the existence of good will, a misrepresentation and damage.

Question 2

'In intellectual property law, interlocutory remedies are more important than awards of damages at trial.' Discuss.

Answer plan

A question which requires a student to compare injunctions and Anton Piller orders with the remedy of damages. In answering such a question, a student must keep the question firmly in mind, whilst showing both sides of the argument.

The issues to be considered are:

- Injunctions
- Anton Piller orders
- Damages
- Problems with civil actions
- Monopoly nature of IP rights

Answer

Intellectual property rights are only meaningful if they can be enforced. Fortunately, the law provides a wide range of sanctions and remedies which are available when rights are infringed. Often, as the question suggests, interlocutory remedies are of greater importance than awards of damages on the basis that prevention is better than cure.

The intellectual property rights involved with copyright, trade marks, passing off and patents each involve the creation of either a total or a partial monopoly in their particular field. The preservation of such a monopoly is what gives the right its value, and serious damage may accrue if a plaintiff has to endure an 18 month to two year delay before trial, followed by the prospect of further delay for an appeal. Whilst statutory provision for damages is extensive, including for copyright (ss 96–103 of the CDPA 1988 and ss 61–63 of the Patents Act 1977); unregistered designs (ss 229–35 of the CDPA 1988); trade marks (TMA 1994) and Plant Breeder's rights (s 4(1)(c) of the Plant Varieties and

Seeds Act 1964, as amended by the Plant Varieties Act 1983), plaintiffs invariably seek an injunction at first instance when issuing proceedings.

The primary interlocutory remedy is the injunction. An injunction is an equitable and hence a discretionary remedy. It has long been recognised that 'the court will act to protect property alone' with an interlocutory award, as well as granting it as a final order at trial (*per* Lord Westbury in *Endelsten v Endelsten* (1863)). The injunction restrains the defendant from carrying out what the plaintiff alleges is an unlawful interference with his or her rights and from continuing with a course of wrongful conduct or a threatened wrong. The plaintiff need not prove damage but there must be a likelihood of damage.

An injunction provides a speedy remedy and can be obtained *ex parte*. In many cases it can be obtained almost as a right where the plaintiff can show a case, with certain exceptions such as infringement of the copyright of architectural plans by the actual commencement of building work based on the design (*Hunter v Fitzroy Robinson and Partners* (1978)).

Prior to 1975, the grounds for a the grant of an injunction was a *prima facie* case or, as it was put in *Harman Films v Osborne* (1967), the plaintiff had to show a case which was 'reasonably capable of succeeding'. In *Lyons Maid Ltd v Trebor Ltd* (1967), it was held that a further requirement for the grant of an interlocutory injunction was that the risk of damage (by diversion of customers) be direct and immediate. However, principles for considering the grant of an injunction were restated in a clear formula by the House of Lords in *American Cyanamid v Ethicon* (1975). In deciding whether an injunction should be granted, the court will consider: (1) whether there is a serious issue to be tried; (2) whether damages would adequately compensate the plaintiff; (3) whether damages would adequately compensate the defendant; (4) the balance of convenience. If the balance of convenience is equal the court should preserve the *status quo*. The preservation of the *status quo* is important to many plaintiffs since their existing rights in the market place will be protected at the expense of those of the newcomer defendant. Ultimately, an award of damages will mean that the defendant has remained in the market and in competition until a final injunction is granted at trial.

These principles have been subsequently reviewed in *Series 5 Software Ltd v Philip Clarke and Others* (1996) by Laddie J who held that when considering whether to grant interlocutory relief, the court should bear in mind the following: (1) the grant of an interlocutory injunction is a matter of discretion and depends on all the facts of each case; (2) there are no fixed rules; (3) the court should rarely attempt to resolve difficult questions of disputed fact and law. The major factors the court should bear in mind were: (a) the extent to which damages were likely to be an adequate remedy and the ability of the other party to pay; (b) the balance of convenience; (c) the maintenance of the *status quo*; and (d) any clear view the court may reach as to the relative strength of the parties' cases.

It can be seen that the potential inadequacy of damages as a remedy is recognised at the earliest stage by the court. Inability to pay damages due to financial weakness will be a reason for granting an injunction (*Missing Link Software v Magee* (1989)). An injunction is often essential to prevent the release of confidential, sensitive or valuable information at the earliest opportunity, since an award of damages might be of little consolation once the information has been released.

Interlocutory remedies provide the only effective method of curtailing the activities of pirates and infringers who have already blatantly infringed intellectual property rights. Anton Piller orders granted under RSC Order 29 provide a further effective interlocutory remedy in enabling a plaintiff to seize infringing copies which a plaintiff will not wish to remain on the market and to obtain further information about the identity of tortfeasors. An immediate remedy is essential, particularly where large profits are at stake.

A quick decision at the interlocutory stage may also have the added benefit of encouraging the defendant to settle. Having tested the strength of the case at an initial stage, a defendant will be more likely to abandon his activities completely or reach a licensing agreement with the plaintiff. The application for the injunction will also enable the plaintiff to obtain undertakings. The fact that an injunction is granted may paralyse a business and can effectively ensure that by the time the trial stage is reached there are no realisable assets which can be used to pay any sums awarded in damages.

There are further drawbacks to an award for damages. Apart from the delay to which a plaintiff is subjected, by the end of a lengthy trial there may actually be no ability to pay, the defendant having closed, gone bankrupt or disappeared. Although the aim of damages is to put the innocent party into the position that he or she would have enjoyed had the harm not been inflicted, this can in practice be hard to quantify. Indeed, it was observed in *Fenning Film Services v Wolverhampton Cinemas* (1914) that the assessment of damages 'must necessarily be to a large extent a matter of conjecture'. Although in passing off cases a court may award damages 'on proper proof' (*Spalding v Gamage* (1915)) and may infer some damage to the plaintiff without proof of special damage (*Draper v Trist* (1939)), the court may only award nominal damages such as in trade mark infringement cases. Proving the actual damage sustained by the plaintiff can often be very difficult, and indeed impossible in such matters as proving lost sales. However, in patent cases, the scope for damages has been extended to cover losses flowing from the original breach (*Gerber Garment Technology v Lectra Systems* (1995)). In copyright cases, claims for actionable damage have been restricted to the value of the parts taken rather than any consequences which might be argued to flow from the appropriation with the result that a plaintiff may only recover a relatively small sum (*Work Model Enterprises Ltd v Ecosystem and Clix Interiors Ltd* (1996)).

The statutory bases for many claims in damages allow for awards of additional damages in certain cases having 'regard to the flagrancy of the breach'. In *Ravenscroft v Herbert* (1980), it was held that flagrancy implied 'scandalous conduct, deceit and such like' including 'deliberate and calculated copyright infringements'. In *Noah v Shuba* (1991), it was held that if a defendant is careless rather than deliberate in infringement and the profit is small, additional damages are not justified. Such flexibility, however, opens up the scope for legal argument and hence uncertainty in the outcome of awards that a court may make. Alternatively, a plaintiff can claim an account of profits from the defendant but this is also a discretionary remedy and a plaintiff cannot enjoy the benefit of both (*Potton Ltd v Yorkclose Ltd* (1990)).

Litigation or even the prospect of it taking place can be damaging to a business interest, particularly in the areas of patents and trade marks which can be readily traded in the market. The risk of damage to a business caused by the threat of litigation is recognised by s 70 of the PA 1977 and s 21 of the TMA 1994, which make groundless threats to sue actionable.

The commercial value of any asset which is subjected to protracted litigation will obviously degenerate, and if issues can be resolved at an early stage this will be all the better. This is particularly true in the case of a plaintiff who seeks to exploit a particular fashion or craze (eg *Mirage Ltd v Counter Feat* (1991) 'Ninja Turtles').

The abundance of reported decisions which go no further than interlocutory proceedings indicate that the preservation of a monopoly at an early stage is of far greater importance to the owner of intellectual property rights than the uncertain recovery of damages and costs at the end of a lengthy trial.

Question 3

Outline the principles upon which the courts award damages in intellectual property cases.

Answer plan

A relatively straightforward question which requires a student to show a knowledge of the principles on which damages are awarded with regard to different intellectual property rights.

The issues to be considered are:

- Tortious measure of damage
- Patents
- Trade marks
- Passing off
- Statutory provisions in copyright
- Additional damages
- Confidential information

Answer

The courts have often been faced with fundamental problems in assessing the quantum of damages in cases involving intellectual property rights. Like most intellectual property rights, the provisions for damages are largely the creation of statute. Since intangible property rights can be hard to define and involve creations which may be individually unique and susceptible to the uncertainties of the market forces, the courts have not sought to define exact formulations. English law has never been wholly comfortable with purely economic torts and many cases turn on their facts, a situation that is hardly conducive to the development of anything more than broad principles. Often the damage alleged by a plaintiff may be incapable of specific proof.

Patent actions

Damages in patent infringement claims differ with respect to whether the patentee would have manufactured his or her invention or process, or would have granted licences to third parties to exploit it. The distinction is illustrated in *Pneumatic Tyre Co v Puncture Proof Pneumatic Tyre Co* (1899), where there was an infringement of a patent for bicycle tyres. The court held that evidence which related to orders for tyres gained by the defendants should not have been assessed on the basis that the orders would have gone to the plaintiff. The plaintiffs were only entitled to damages on the basis that the orders would have gone to licensees from whom the plaintiffs were entitled to a royalty.

In *Aktiengelleschaft für Autogene Aluminium Schweissung v London Aluminium Co (No 2)* (1923), Sargant J held 'what has to be ascertained is that which the infringer would have to pay if, instead of infringing the patent, he had come to be licensed under the patent'. Simply stating the amount concerned may be hotly disputed because of market forces and inequalities of bargaining power. The issue reached the House of Lords in *General Tire Co v Firestone Tyre Co Ltd* (1975). The basic principles applicable to damages for patent infringement were the same as for economic tort – the sum which puts the injured party in the same position he would have enjoyed had the wrong never occurred. Thus, where an inventor exploited his patent by granting royalty licences, sums could be calculated on the value of the licence. Before a going rate of a royalty could be taken into consideration, the court would examine the comparable circumstances to those in which the patentee and infringer were assumed to strike a bargain. Lump sum agreements entered into with other licensees might not fix a reasonable basis for calculating damages.

It can be appropriate for the court to take the number of infringing articles and multiply that by the sum that would have been paid to make the manufacture of the article lawful (see also *Meters Ltd v Metropolitan Gas Meters* (1911)). The onus falls upon the plaintiff to produce evidence to guide the court, and the judge is required to take into account the licences actually granted and the rates of royalty and apply these so far as possible to calculating the bargain hypothetically made between the patentee and the infringer.

In the case of inventors who manufacture or use a process themselves, the calculation can be even more complicated, often involving a diversion of customers. In *United Horse Shoe & Nail Co v Stewart* (1888), Lord Halsbury stated that the amount of damages 'can rarely be made the subject of exact mathematical calculation'. In *Watson Laidlow & Co v Pott Cassells & Williamson* (1914), the court held that the measure of damage was the amount of profit that the plaintiff could have made had he and not the defendant made the sales of the infringing items. Compensation was awarded for the use or sale of every infringing machine in the market.

In *Catnic Components Hill & Smith* (1983), the plaintiffs were awarded the loss of manufacturing profits on the assumption that most of the sales of the disputed lintels would have been made by them but for the involvement of the defendants. The plaintiffs were not entitled to losses incurred in respect of non-patented lintels which would have been sold in mixed packages – this would be a form of 'parasitic damages'.

In *Gerber Garment Technology v Lectra Systems* (1995), the scope for awards of damages was extended to allow a plaintiff to recover on a wider basis including manufacturing and marketing costs and the costs on each infringing item.

Trade marks and passing off

Damages for trade mark infringement and passing off are similar to one another. Nominal damages may be awarded for infringing the use of a mark (*Blofield v Payne* (1833) – one farthing for use of a razor wrapper) but the principal head of damage is the loss of business arising through diversion of customers (*Manus AKT v RJ Fullwood and Bland Ltd* (1954)).

In *Alexander v Henry* (1895), damages were awarded for fraudulent use of the plaintiff's name mark which destroyed their good will in the thread and cotton market in Mexico. Damages were awarded on the basis of the plaintiff's loss of sales, the quantum of damages being loss of profit and business. Inferences can be drawn that sales by the defendant would have gone to the plaintiff, but this is not the situation in every case (*Leather Cloth Co v Hirschfield* (1865)).

In *Draper v Trist* (1939), it was held that the court will generally assume that damage occurs where a defendant puts a quantity of goods on the market which are calculated to be wrongly taken as the plaintiffs'. There was no need to prove individual transactions. Each case will turn on its facts and the evidence available.

An inquiry into damages will only be directed if a plaintiff can establish an arguable claim to the recovery of a sufficient sum to justify the exercise (*McDonalds Hamburgers Ltd v Burger King UK Ltd* (1987)).

Copyright

In *Moore v Clarke* (1842), it was held that on proof of piracy, damage would be presumed. Damages could be nominal as in *Holmes v Langfier* (1903) where a photographic portrait was published without permission and damage was similarly presumed.

In *Work Model Enterprises Ltd v Ecosystem Ltd and Clix Interiors Ltd* (1996), it was held that for damages to be recoverable the infringement must be their effective cause – to be decided by the common sense of the court. If there was no sufficient nexus between the use of the text and the harm of which the plaintiff complained, the damage was deemed not to occur. The plaintiffs argued that losses would not have occurred but for the copying of their brochure, but the court held that it was the defendant's competition in lawful articles which was the cause of the alleged damage. The court considered it undesirable that the statutory remedies for protection of intellectual property rights be applied to the recovery for damages of other rights. The court distinguished the approach taken with patented articles in *Gerber Garment Technology v Lectra Systems* (1995).

Calculating the damage to a plaintiff can be difficult in financial terms since it is frequently only part of a work which is copied, and each case will turn on its facts. If a defendant has infringed copyright where a plaintiff might have required a licence, the calculation of lost royalties may be ascertained. In *Ash v Dickie* (1936), extracts of a book were reproduced in a newspaper. The sale price of the newspaper was taken as the value of each copy and then a proportion of the total value was recoverable by the plaintiff. In *Stovin Bradford Ltd v Volpoint Properties Ltd* (1971), a fair licensing fee was calculated on the basis of a fair remuneration in terms of what owners would have paid for a licence to use plans for a building. Since the amounts recovered may be small, the law includes the possibility of additional damages as a deterrent to flagrant infringers.

Additional damages were possible under s 17(3) of the 1956 Copyright Act and s 97(2) of the CDPA 1988. In *Williams v Settle* (1960), Sellars LJ held that this section could justify exemplary damages in a case of 'flagrant infringement of the right of the plaintiff'. In *Nicholas Advanced Vehicle Systems v Rees Oliver* (1979), Templeman J, in awarding additional damages, regarded the condition satisfied where the defendants had 'received benefits and inflicted humiliation and loss'. The case involved copyright drawings of Formula One racing cars and the conduct of one party had been deceitful and treacherous.

However, in *Prior v Lansdowne Press Pty Ltd* (1977) (Supreme Court of Australia), additional damages were held not to be awardable where the conduct of the defendant was a matter of mistake and carelessness. In *Cala Homes (South) Ltd and Others v Alfred McAlpine Homes East Ltd* (1996), it was held that statutory additional damages could be awarded whether a plaintiff elected for damages or an account of profits. An award was a separate power of the court.

Confidential information

In *Dowson v Mason Potter* (1986), the Court of Appeal considered damages for breach of confidence. The court took the view that the value of such information could be on the basis of a presumed market value arising between a willing seller and a willing buyer. If an inventive step were involved, as in a patent case, the damages should be the capitalised value on a royalty basis. In *Dowson v Mason Potter*, the court examined the position where the plaintiff would not have parted with the information but would have retained it for manufacturing purposes. In such a case, loss of profits rather than the value of the information was the true measure of damages. Slade J approved the comparison with the approach taken in patent infringement actions.

Fortunately, the remedy of an account of profits, although discretionary, mitigates to some extent the injustice of infringers finding it profitable to usurp the rights of others because of difficulties in assessing the amount of actionable damage.

Question 4

Why is the criminal law increasingly important in the protection of intellectual property rights? Do ample civil powers make criminal sanctions superfluous?

Answer plan

The issues to be considered are:

- Criminal sanctions in IP law
- Civil jurisdiction
- *CBS Songs v Amstrad* (1988)
- Anti-counterfeiting provisions
- Public interest

Answer

Although statute based, the protection of intellectual property rights was originally very much left to the civil law by way of a wide range of civil remedies, the scope of which the courts have willingly extended. Nonetheless, criminal law has been utilised to protect the rights of proprietors, and increasingly in recent years. Criminal sanctions exist in copyright (ss 107–10 of the CDPA 1988); with regard to performers' rights (ss 198–202 of the CDPA 1988); fraudulent reception (s 297 of the CDPA 1988); trade marks (s 21 of the TMA 1994); patents (ss 110–11 of the PA 1977); registered designs (ss 33–35A of the Registered Designs Act 1949); and plant varieties (ss 13 and 27 of the Plant Variety and Seeds Act 1964).

At first sight these protections may seem surprising. The courts have on occasion drawn a comparison between copyright law and criminal law. For instance, 'Thou shalt not steal' in *Macmillan and Co Ltd v K & J Cooper* (1923) *per* Lord Atkinson. However, such views were rejected by the House of Lords in *CBS Songs v Amstrad* (1988). The courts have also shown a reluctance to allow the civil law to cover criminal acts, and case law indicates that the criminal law has at best been an unreliable method of protecting intellectual property rights. Given that the rights themselves can be hard to define, as can precise infringement, the law of theft has proved inappropriate. Mere sale of pirated music was not a larceny at common law (*R v Kidd and Walsh* (1907)). In *Rank Film Distributors Ltd and Others v Video Information Centre (A Firm) and Others* (1982), Lord Frazer of Tullybelton pointed out that the definition of 'property' under the Theft Act 1968 did not appear to include copyright and indeed the Theft Acts exclude intangible property. In *Oxford v Moss* (1979), an undergraduate student dishonestly came by the proof of a question paper for an examination. After reading the contents he returned it. A prosecution could not lie for the taking of the information because no tangible property had been removed.

Thus the law of theft did not apply to many situations such as the borrowing of cinema films by projectionists for copying (*R v Lloyd* (1985)). Similar difficulties could be found in analogous cases. In *Reid v Kennet* (1986), the appellant worked in a video hire shop and purchased video cassettes which he knew to be infringing copyright. He was charged with 11 offences of possessing infringing material by way of trade. The conviction was quashed on the basis that a person purchasing infringing copies was not caught by the offence which involved trade sales. Since possession was not an offence, he could only have been charged as an accomplice to a trade offence.

Conspiracy charges have sometimes been an alternative. In *R v Willets* (1906), it was held that if two or more persons combined together to make printed music for sale at the expense of the copyright owner, this would be held to be a conspiracy to deprive the owner of copyright and punishable as a criminal conspiracy.

The interrelation between civil and criminal sanctions where the law is unclear has never been easy to determine. On occasion, the courts have seen the two as analogous, but at other times have rejected it (*Re Island Records* (1978)). Criminal obligations are only generally enforced by the penalties. If a statutory duty is prescribed but no remedy by way of penalty or otherwise is imposed, it can be assumed that a right of civil action accrues to the person who is affected by the breach. If such a duty can be established, an action will lie for breach. However, in other cases criminal law cannot be enforced by civil process (*Cutler v Wandsworth Stadium Ltd* (1949)).

Certainly a High Court judge enjoys very wide powers in a civil case. It should be noted, however, that the court only enjoys these wide powers where defendants are actually in breach of court orders rather than for the civil wrong involved. In *Phonographic Performance Ltd v Amusement Caterers (Peckham) Ltd* (1963), it was held that for a civil contempt the court's powers could include an order for sequestration and that a fine could be imposed as well as committal of the directors. *Taylor Made Golf v Rata (a firm)* (1996) involved contempt proceedings. These penalties, however, are only imposed for flouting court orders rather than as a remedy for the plaintiff.

In view of the global nature of counterfeiting, efforts have been made on the international level through trade-related aspects of intellectual property in the GATT negotiations and at EC and national level to respond to the problem. The CDPA 1988 reflected the need to counter large-scale piracy and in recent years the courts have been increasingly open to the use of criminal law.

In *CBS Songs v Amstrad plc* (1988), the House of Lords recognised copyright law had not foreseen 'and cannot cope with mass production techniques and inventions which create a vast market for the works of a copyright owner but also provide opportunities for his rights to be infringed'. Forgery and counterfeiting can be on such a scale that sole traders can no longer be expected to effectively restrain it.

Defendants may argue that a party cannot be subject to sanctions under both civil and criminal law. In *Thames Hudson Ltd v Design and Artists Copyright Society Ltd* (1995), the defendants sought a stay on a criminal prosecution where civil remedies had already been utilised. The court held the application vexatious. Parliament had elected to provide that in certain circumstances breach of copyright constituted a crime and that directors who connived at fraud could be restrained by both civil and criminal law.

Barriers between civil and criminal law have been eroded under s 72 of The Supreme Court Act 1981, which removes the privilege against self-incrimination in criminal proceedings. Normally a person must answer any question in civil proceedings, except where to answer would expose that person to a criminal penalty. Under s 72(1), the privilege against self-incrimination is withdrawn in intellectual property proceedings which are defined in s 72(2). The words 'related offence' included in the section are given their natural meaning and will include any offence which is revealed (*Universal City Studios Inc v Hubbard* (1984)).

The criminal sanctions in various statutes provide penalties which act as a deterrent to infringers. For the owners of intellectual property rights, there is the advantage of avoiding direct involvement with proceedings and costs which will be borne by the state. On occasion this may require action on an international level and consideration of EC law. In *R v Bridgeman & Butt* (1995), an attempt was made to quash a prosecution brought for making 'smart' cards for sale to expatriate residents in Spain to allow the decoding of encrypted satellite television broadcasts contrary to s 297A of the CDPA 1988. Section 298 granted qualifying broadcasters a right to protect their broadcasts and provided remedies for infringement of those rights analogous to copyright owners in respect of breach of copyright. The broadcasters were the only persons who could authorise a decoder and the offence was punishable even though it took place abroad.

Sophisticated criminal gangs who have no qualms about flouting the intellectual property rights of an individual can only be effectively controlled by the criminal law. Wider considerations than the rights of individuals affected by counterfeiting and infringement are recognised as being at stake. In *Coca Cola v Gilbey and Others* (1996), it was considered that there was a public interest in stopping the actions of a criminal organisation involved in the widespread counterfeiting of soft drinks. Individuals deliberately flouting the rights of private persons on a large scale for big rewards were unlikely to be deterred by the threat of a civil action. Indeed, the risk to the public involved with a civil trial make an essentially inappropriate response. With counterfeiting (being undertaken) on a large scale, many proprietors may find it impossible to fund a civil action to restrain infringement, given that it may well be impossible to recover costs if the infringers disappear.

New offences in connection with the misuse of registered trade marks provide a good example of the wider anti-counterfeiting provisions. Section 92 of the TMA 1994 makes it a criminal offence to apply a registered trade mark to goods or their packaging without the consent of the proprietor. Section 90 gives powers to the Commissioners of Customs and Excise to make regulations covering notices which the proprietor of registered trade marks may issue to Customs and Excise under s 89 to treat imported items as infringing. Information can also be relayed to trading standards to commence prosecutions. Forfeiture powers are provided for under s 97 to seize infringing articles, in the case of a prosecution for any relevant offence.

Far from making criminal law superfluous, the increasing complexity and expense of the civil process make the existence of criminal law sanctions all the more important in the task of protecting intellectual property rights. Given widespread counterfeiting, their exercise may provide an effective way of suppressing infringers of all descriptions whose activities harm not just the proprietors of intellectual property rights but also the wider public interest of consumers.

Question 5

Anton Piller and Interlocutory Relief

Harker Recordings are record and CD producers who discover that Varney and an organised gang are producing counterfeit CDs and selling them at raves and festivals. Through inquiry agents, Harker Recordings discover that Varney has stored 50 crates of CDs at premises in North London and that papers and documents are going to be stored that month at the home of Varney's girlfriend, Lucy, where Varney often stays whilst the gang base their operation at his home. Advise Harker Recordings as to suitable remedies to ameliorate their position and whether Varney can claim any privileges.

Answer plan

A question which requires a knowledge of Anton Piller orders and proceedings under RSC Order 29.

The issues to be considered are:

- Anton Piller orders
- RSC Order 29
- Practice on serving Anton Piller orders
- Section 107 of the CDPA 1988
- Section 72 of the Supreme Court Act

Answer

The High Court has an inherent jurisdiction to make orders for the preservation of documents and evidence. The remedy appropriate for Harker Recordings is to seek an Anton Piller order against Varney. As Varney and his associates are unlikely to comply with the normal process of discovery in civil proceedings, Harker Recordings should be advised to apply *ex parte*, pursuant to the authority of *Anton Piller KG v Manufacturing Processes Ltd* (1976), to obtain a special form mandatory injunction requiring Varney to allow a search of his premises and to remove the infringing CDs. Harker Recordings should clearly specify the premises where they believe the infringing tapes and CDs to be (*Protector Alarms Ltd v Maxim Alarms Ltd* (1978)). This will require care in drafting because general forms of words such as 'any other premises' will not be permitted unless a good reason can be shown.

The essential prerequisites for obtaining an Anton Piller order were set out by Ormrod LJ in *Anton Piller KG v Manufacturing Processesas* (1974): (i) a strong *prima facie* case; (ii) the damage, whether potential or actual, must be very serious for the plaintiff; and (iii) there must be clear evidence that the defendants have in their possession incriminating documents or objects and that there is a real possibility that they may destroy such materials before any application *inter partes* may be made. The requirement of a strong *prima facie* case was emphasised in *Columbia Picture Industries v Robinson* (1986) where it was stated that a plaintiff must show a strong case of infringement of his or her rights and that the potential damage is serious.

The claim that Harker will bring is infringement in the copyright of recordings by Varney and his associates. Under s 16, Harker Recordings enjoy the rights; they will have a claim, given the unlawful nature of the enterprise in which Varney is engaged.

As a further requirement for obtaining an Anton Piller order, Harker Recordings will have to make a full disclosure of facts, including any weak points in their case. Since the order is made *ex parte,* all relevant known facts should be put forward, however, if a deponent makes a statement in an affidavit, the court should accept it (*R v IRC ex p TC Coombes* (1991)).

Additional safeguards should be included in the order itself. The order must be drawn up so as to extend no further than necessary to obtain the preservation of property or documents which may otherwise be destroyed or removed. The material copied (such as details of Varney's associates) should then be returned to the owner. The solicitor for Harker Recordings should make a detailed record of the material and nothing should be removed which is not listed in the order.

An example of the relevant safeguards can be found in *Booker McConnell v Plascow* (1985). An undertaking in respect of damages by Harker Recordings will be required.

The three aims of the order will be to seize the infringing copies, to obtain information on the distribution and sale of the infringing copies and to obtain the names and addresses of the other conspirators. The order may allow solicitors and employees of Harker Recordings to enter premises on a particular date and photocopy documents and remove the illicit CDs and recordings from the premises. A further requirement would be to restrain Varney from altering, defacing or destroying any articles referred to in the order (see *EMI v Pandit* (1975)). The order must be served by a solicitor, together with copies of the relevant evidence and exhibits, and also include Varney's right to seek advice.

It was suggested in *Universal Thermosensors Ltd v Hibben* (1992), that the specimen order provides for it to be served by an experienced supervising solicitor who is not from the firm representing Harker Recordings. If the premises are likely to be occupied by a woman only, and the supervising solicitor is not a woman, at least one person attending should be female.

Before issuing proceedings the Practice Direction of 28 July 1994 should be consulted by the solicitors for Harker Recordings. If they suspect that Lucy will be on the premises, they should seek to ensure that a female solicitor will be in attendance. The Practice Direction stresses the discretionary nature of the remedy and provides for standard forms for orders and Mareva injunctions.

The order should be directed to Varney and may require him and Lucy to hand over all listed items in their possession and control. The defendants will also be required to disclose where all the listed items are, the name and address of everyone to whom he has offered the CDs and full details of the relevant dates and quantities of listed items. Varney and Lucy will also be prohibited from communicating with third parties, except for the purpose of obtaining legal advice. They will be further forbidden from warning anyone else that proceedings have been or may be initiated against them by Harker Recordings until the return date for the order.

It will be vital for Harker Recordings to obtain further information on the identities of tortfeasors, therefore, the order should also be worded to compel Varney to disclose the details of the names and addresses of his associates. Varney could be required to give all the information by way of affidavit as part of the order and to exhibit documents such as labels, receipts and records which relate to each illicit CD or recording supplied or offered. A suitable precedent might be that in *Rank Film Distributors Ltd v Video Information Centre* (1982).

Any attempt by Varney or Lucy to obstruct entry will be a contempt of court, punishable by committal under Order 49 or a fine. It will also be highly prejudicial evidence at trial against Varney. The scope of an Anton Piller order would allow Varney and Lucy to refuse immediate compliance with the order for no more than two hours if they seek to make an urgent application to the court to have the order discharged or varied. However, they will do so at their peril. If they use such a delay to breach the order, for example, by destroying material, the consequences will be grave. Contempt proceedings may follow if there is any reason to believe there has been an abuse of the court process to conceal incriminating evidence. Similarly, frivolous applications will be dismissed. As Lord Donaldson commented in *WEA Records Ltd v Vision Channel 4 Ltd* (1983), 'The courts are concerned with the administration of justice, not with playing a game of snakes and ladders'.

Varney will not be able to raise the privilege against self-incrimination. In *Rank Film Distributors v Video Information Centre* (1981), the House of Lords held that a defendant such as Varney would be protected even if answering questions might incriminate him of an offence (in this case the offences under s 107 of the CDPA 1988). The privilege was also upheld in *AT & T Istel Ltd v Tully* (1993) but, as the House of Lords noted, it had been abrogated by statutes.

In *Tate Access Floors v Boswell* (1990), the privilege against self-incrimination could be raised at the Anton Piller application if a prosecution for conspiracy to defraud might follow. However, under s 72(1) of the Supreme Court Act 1981, the privilege against incrimination of self and spouse is withdrawn in certain proceedings. Under s 72(2), such proceedings include any proceedings pertaining to an intellectual property right and proceedings for the disclosure of information or passing off, which would include the claims which Harker Recordings allege against Varney and Lucy.

In *Coca Cola v Gilbey and Others* (1996), the Court of Appeal considered an appeal against a refusal by a judge to discharge an Anton Piller order against one of 16 defendants involved in the passing off of counterfeit Coca-Cola and Schweppes lemonade. The court rejected claims that the Anton Piller order breached the privilege against self-incrimination. Under the provisions of s 72, the fact that a person might be exposed to criminal proceedings was not justification. The court also rejected a claim that a real risk of physical violence against the defendant in retaliation for providing information through the court was grounds for discharge of the Anton Piller order. Lightman J said that the rule of law had to be upheld, the proper remedy being police protection and contempt proceedings against any persons caught. The mere fact that joint tortfeasors had a propensity to violence did not free a defendant from the obligation to provide information to protect the interests of the victim of the tort. The court also held that there was a public interest to be found: (1) in the suppression as soon as possible of the fraud on the public; (2) that tortfeasors should not have the excuse of being able to plead danger to themselves to avoid disclosure; (3) that men of violence should not be able to silence those with a knowledge of wrongdoing; and (4) that the evil men of violence behind the organisation should be identified. In the current situation, unless Lucy and Varney can show exceptional grounds there will be no basis to challenge the Anton Piller order.

In the event that the court does not grant an Anton Piller order, Harker Recordings should seek an injunction instead, although they may be refused their costs (*Systematicia Ltd v London Computer Centre Ltd* (1983)).

[illegible] Notes [illegible]

Chapter 2

Copyright and Design Rights

Introduction

Based on statute, copyright should be understood as an essentially negative right, preventing others from copying or reproducing a work which qualifies for protection. The basic starting point for every question is the Copyright Designs and Patents Act 1988, considered in the light of a number of authorities (mostly pre-1988) where identical or similar terms were considered by the courts.

Students should always bear in mind that it is the expression of work in material form which counts, not ideas. Usually a question will give an opportunity to observe or mention that a copyright cannot exist in a pure idea (eg, *Green v New Zealand Broadcasting Corporation* (1989)) or in a banal idea (*Kenrick v Lawrence* (1890)). It must also be recognised that there are a wide range of permitted acts and exceptions, which may leave a copyright owner featured in any question with only a partial monopoly.

The majority of questions set on copyright involve literary works in one form or another (including computer programs which are treated as literary works), followed by those dealing with artistic works or musical works.

As a basic approach to answering problem questions, the following matters should be considered:

- Does copyright subsist in the work? Examples of authorities illustrating the wide range of protected works can be cited.
- Identify the category of the work in question and any authorities which can be used to distinguish such works (eg artistic works which are judged by the effect on the eye).
- Is the work original? That is, does it originate with a particular author as opposed to being copied. Copyright work only extends to original works. (Note, however, that 'original' has a partial definition for design rights under s 213(4), meaning 'not commonplace'.)
- Are there any exceptions which apply to protection? Usually this amounts to deciding whether the work is substantial enough to qualify for protection.

- Remember that more than one copyright may exist in a work.
- Who is the author? This will be with reference to ss 9–11 of the CDPA 1988 and the circumstances in which the work is created.
- Note that the copyright owner may not be the same person as the author. Remember that only the copyright owner or person with rights in the copyright may sue.
- Is there infringement? Identify the rights which have been infringed as either primary infringements, referring to to ss 16 and 17 in particular, and ss 18–21, and secondary infringement under ss 22–27. It is also necessary to be alert to the far-reaching effects of s 17(2) which provides that reproduction may be in any material form.
- How many different reproductions have there been?
- Are there any defences or permitted acts which the defendant may raise?
- Remedies – is the grant of an injunction justified, on the balance of interests? Are the parties in competition?

Most questions set for students involve literary, artistic, dramatic and musical copyright under Part I of the Act, so this chapter will concentrate on this area. Questions involving design rights are not often encountered but the approach is similar.

Checklist

Students should be familiar with the following areas:

- Copyright Designs and Patents Act 1988
  - ss 1–15; works which qualify for protection, authorship, duration of copyright
  - s 16; exclusive rights of the author – primary infringement
  - ss 22–26; secondary infringement
  - ss 28–72; permitted acts
  - s 213; new design right
- Parliamentary and Crown copyright
- Fair dealing

- Moral rights
- Registered Designs Act 1949
- *Associated Newspapers v News Group* (1986)
- *Bauman v Fussell* (1979)
- *Beloff v Pressdram* (1973)
- *C&H Engineering v Klucznic* (1992)
- *Cummins v Bond* (1927)
- *Donoghue v Allied Newspapers* (1938)
- *Exxon v Exxon Insurance Ltd* (1982)
- *Francis Day Hunter v Bron* (1963)
- *Francis Day Hunter v Twentieth Century Fox* (1940)
- *Green v New Zealand Broadcasting Corporation* (1989)
- *Hubbard v Vosper* (1972)
- *Ibcos v Barclays Mercantile High Finance* (1994)
- *Interlego v Tyco Industries* (1979)
- *Kenrick v Lawrence* (1890)
- *King Features Syndicate v Kleeman* (1940)
- *Ladbroke v William Hill* (1964)
- *Pike v Nicholas* (1869)
- *Ravenscroft v Herbert* (1980)
- *Sillitoe v McGraw Hill Books* (1983)
- *University of London Press v University Tutorial Press* (1916)
- *American Cyanamid v Ethicon* (1975)

Question 6

Summarise the rights which the author of a literary work published in the UK enjoys under the Copyright Designs and Patents Act 1988.

Answer plan

A straightforward question where the student's chief difficulty will be in dealing with the large volume of material which is involved in covering it.

The issues to be considered are:

- Part I of the CDPA 1988
- Nature of copyright
- Definition of a literary work
- Definition of an author (s 9)
- Rights of an author (ss 16–28)
- Licences
- Limitations on rights
- Moral rights

Answer

Copyright protection exists for all qualifying literary works produced on or after 1 August 1989. The CDPA 1988 restates and amends the existing statute law on copyright, expressly preserving copyright conferred by the Copyright Act 1956. The law is flexible in its approach, however, if a work did not enjoy protection before 1988, the Act will not assist.

The copyright of a work which an author enjoys is essentially of a negative character, consisting of a right to prevent other persons, individual or legal, from reproducing the work without permission. The law does not prohibit copying *per se*; there is no tort of copying. The law seeks to allow authors to enjoy certain exclusive rights with regard to their works. However, there are a number of important exceptions and qualifications to these rights which restrict the extent of the author's monopoly. It is not always possible to clearly delineate the extent of these restrictions.

An author will only enjoy rights in a literary work which is original (s 1(1)(a)). The term 'original' refers to the source of the work, in the sense of it emanating from a particular author. At its simplest, copyright only arises for an author in those works which he or she creates. It was stated in *British Broadcasting Co v Wireless League Gazette Publishing Co* (1926) that 'The word "original" does not in this connection mean that work must be the expression of original or inventive thought. The originality which is required relates to the expression of thought. However, the Act does not require that the expression must be in an original or novel form, but that the work must not be copied from another work – that is, it should originate from an author'.

Under s 3(1), a literary work is defined as any work, other than a dramatic or musical work, which is written, spoken, sung and accordingly includes: (a) a table or compilation, and (b) a computer program. Section 3(1)(c) was subsequently added by the Copyright (Computer Programs) Regulations 1992, reg 3, to include the phrase 'preparatory design material for a computer program'. A wide range of works will be classified as literary works (one of the aims of the CDPA 1988 being to update copyright law) and a literary work may also enjoy copyright as a dramatic work or musical work.

An author cannot use copyright under the CDPA 1988 to stop the reproduction of the ideas behind a literary work, or prevent another person producing a work dealing with the same subject or material or utilising the same plot (see *Green v New Zealand Broadcasting Corporation* (1989)).

It is a crucial requirement for the author of a literary work to ensure that it is recorded in a material form. Under s 3(2), copyright is held not to subsist in a literary work 'unless and until it is recorded, in writing or otherwise'. If an author has not had his ideas committed into a tangible form, no copyright will arise, however, the recording need not be with the permission of the author.

In order to have the benefit of copyright protection, the author must have created a literary work which is no more than a single work or title (*Exxon v Exxon Insurance* (1982)) – no copyright subsists in titles. Literary works enjoy protection whether published or unpublished (s 153(1)(a)), and copyright will subsist in the work, even if the author never intended to make it available to a wider audience (eg private diaries).

Under s 9, copyright will subsist with the person who creates the work (subject to ss 10 and 11). The CDPA 1988 further provides that the author must be a British citizen or subject, domiciled or resident in the UK (s 154(1)). As residence is not defined in the legislation, it will fall to be determined by the facts (see *Shah v Barnet LBC* (1983)). In the case of an unpublished work, the author must be a British citizen or resident at the time the work is made. In the case of a published work, the relevant time is the date of first publication. The effects of the CDPA 1988 is limited to the UK and UK territories (to which it may be extended by Orders in Council).

Alternatively, the work will qualify for copyright protection when published (s 155). Publication is defined by s 175 to mean: (a) the issue of copies to the public; and (b) including making it available to the public by means of an electronic retrieval system. As a consequence, no account is taken of periods when the work was being conceived or developed.

Section 10 provides for the author to be a joint author where the work is produced by more than one person in collaboration and where it is not possible to distinguish the work of each person. There must have been a joint enterprise and conception for this to apply. An author will not be deprived of sole ownership, simply where mere alterations, amendments or improvements have been suggested by another and incorporated (*Levy v Rutley* (1871); *Wiseman v George Weidenfield and Donaldson* (1985)). A joint work will not arise where there are distinct contributions (such as a work compiled by an editor, including drawing individual pieces from different authors). Each individual author will retain copyrights personally in their own individual work, subject to contractual agreement.

Copyright in a joint work is a tenancy in common (*Powell v Head* (1879)). Providing that at least one of the joint authors satisfies the residency condition, then the work qualifies for protection. However, an individual author may not reproduce and exploit the work or grant licences without the consent of the others, but one joint author may sue for infringement (*Lauri v Renad* (1892)).

Even unknown authors are recognised by the CDPA 1988; copyright expiring 50 years after first publication, performance or broadcast. An unknown author is one whose identity cannot be ascertained by 'reasonable inquiry' (s 9(5)). Copyright lasts for the lifetime of the author, plus 50 years after the end of the calendar year in which the author dies (s 12) or 50 years following the death of the last surviving author (joint authors).

Under s 16, the author of a work enjoys exclusive rights to:

- copy the work;
- issue copies of the work to the public;
- perform, show or play the work in public;
- broadcast the work or include it in a cable program;
- make an adaptation of the work or do any of the above.

Section 16(2) provides that to do any of these acts without the authority of the author is an infringement of copyright. The infringing acts are further defined as the doing of the act in relation to the work either 'as a whole' or 'any substantial part of it', either directly or indirectly (s 16(3)(a) and (b)). Strict liability applies to the acts listed in s 16, even if the copier believes, albeit erroneously, that he or she was entitled to execute a copy. A person who innocently copies an intermediate version, indirectly copying an original, will commit an infringing act (see *Hanfstaengl v Empire Palace; Hanfstaengl v Newnes* (1894)).

Licences can be oral, in writing, or implied. The restrictions set out in s 17 effectively allow an author to grant different rights to different parties. For example, novels may be sold in hardback and paperback, or as adaptations or translations. Any such agreement by an author to transfer copyright in a work must be in writing (s 90(1)).

It must be stated that the law does not pinpoint precise boundaries, and the extent of the author's copyright cannot be exactly determined. To an extent each case will turn on its facts. The permitted acts are a set of qualifications, but for which, and if not excepted, an exclusive monopoly for an author would otherwise result. The permitted acts may even be of assistance to the author because criticism or review are excepted acts.

Finally, the author enjoys a series of moral rights. For the first time in law, the CDPA 1988 provides rights to 'paternity' and 'integrity' and the right not to have works treated in a derogatory manner (ss 77–89). For the author of a literary work, the right of paternity allows the author to be recognised as author of the work in a number of situations where the work is exploited commercially. Under s 9, there is a general right of action for infringement which entitles by s 96, including entitling the copyright owner to remedies including injunctions, damages, an account of profits, and statutory remedies set out in the Act to control infringing copies.

Question 7

Valerie gives a lecture to a business seminar on 'The future of risk analysis in the construction industry'. Her lecture is in two parts. The first part is a detailed address based upon notes written by herself, expounding two theories propounded by Valerie and issued as materials to the delegates. The materials are marked with a copyright symbol. The first part also includes a short role-playing section to enliven the address by extracting a volunteer from the audience to illustrate some difficult concepts. The content of this is flexible. The second part of the talk consists of some personal reminiscences, and also includes some stories which are typical in risk analysis and certain commonly-told stories in the industry.

Valerie is aware that the audience takes notes during both parts of her lecture. However, she is not aware until afterwards of the following.

Barry, a journalist, has taken detailed notes, adding some odd thoughts of his own on Valerie's ideas. He then uses them to compose a critical article repeating key parts of her speech in an article on risk assessment. He thinks the speech largely condemns itself and makes little input. He copies the materials distributed at the seminar.

Cuthbert has taken detailed notes in shorthand, translated them into Japanese and published the speech verbatim in a Japanese business paper.

Carver has made a video of Valerie's talk.

Agnes has made a sound recording of the lecture and is now repeating it to paying audiences, appropriating many of Valerie's ideas.

Answer plan

A relatively straightforward question requiring identification of subsistence of copyright in oral lectures and notes and the use that can be made of them.

The issues to be considered are:

- Identify the protected works
- Is there copyright protection?
- Ownership and author's rights under s 16

- Implied licences and infringement
- Permitted acts – ss 29, 30 and 58 of the CDPA 1988
- Remedies

Answer

Position of Valerie's lecture

Valerie enjoys rights under the Copyright Designs and Patents Act 1988 to protect her lecture. Some parts of it, however, may not enjoy such strong protection as others because of the varied nature of the contents. Section 1(1)(a) of the CDPA 1988 provides that copyright subsists in original literary, dramatic and musical works. Valerie's lecture will qualify as a literary work by virtue of s 3(1) which defines a literary work as any work other than a musical or dramatic one which is 'written, spoken or sung'. Thus, the actual words which Valerie speaks which form the lecture will be protected, as will the notes she distributes which she has marked with a copyright symbol. Conceivably, the role-playing section of the address, depending on the involvement of a member of the audience, might qualify as a dramatic work under s 3(1). The lecture is original in the sense that it originates from Valerie who has composed it from her two theories and a collection of experiences and stock incidents which she has compiled.

Under s 9(3), the author of a literary, dramatic, musical or artistic work is taken to be the person by whom the arrangements necessary for the creation of the work have been undertaken. In the absence of any evidence as to the possibility of ownership vesting in another person, the author of the address and materials will be Valerie, with the possible exception of *ad lib* items during the role play.

Crucial for copyright protection is the proviso in s 3(2) that copyright does not subsist in a literary (or dramatic) work unless or until it is recorded in material form 'in writing or otherwise'. This will cover the written records made by Barry and Cuthbert and the video recording made by Carver and sound recording made by Agnes. All references to the time at which a work is made under the CDPA 1988 are a reference to when the work is first recorded.

Copyright will exist in the written notes which Valerie has made and the materials which she has distributed. Copyright will also exist in the notes to the non-copyright material – which are referred to as the common situations and commonly told stories in the industry – providing that knowledge, skill and taste have been employed in producing them (*Macmillan & Co v Cooper* (1923)). Since they include theories propounded by Valerie, it is certain they will be classed as qualifying original works. Although copyright will not attach simply to a theory or idea (*Green v New Zealand Broadcasting Corporation* (1989)), Valerie will enjoy protection in the form in which her work is expressed.

Assuming this is the first occasion that the lecture has been delivered, the words in the lecture as a whole will qualify as a protected work because they have been recorded in various ways. The question states that the work has been recorded in a number of ways: by Valerie herself in the form of the notes, and also by the records made by Barry, Cuthbert, Carver and Agnes in their particular forms. The recording of a lecture in any material form will attract protection under s 3(3) of the CDPA 1988 which states that it is immaterial whether work is recorded with the permission of the author. These provisions follow from the recommendation of the Whitford Committee, that copyright should vest in a person uttering original spoken words and should be subject to copyright protection when recorded by another (para 609 (iii)). This alters the position which existed under the old law in *Walters v Lane* (1900), that a reporter who recorded the speech of Lord Roseberry gained a separate copyright protection in the record as opposed to the copyright of the speaker in his or her own words. Therefore, the mere fact that Valerie is unaware of the recordings will not deprive her of copyright in her own material.

The weakest part is the element of the role play. This may qualify as a dramatic work but if it is essentially unscripted and *ad lib* it may not attract protection (*Tate v Thomas* (1908); *Green v New Zealand Broadcasting Corporation*)). It is also possible that the lines themselves may be too short to attract protection. Common jargon will not be protected (*Sinanide v La Maison Kosmeo* (1928)) and stock incidents will not qualify as original works.

Since Valarie is a qualifying author, she will enjoy the exclusive rights set out in s 16 of the CDPA 1988 to reproduce, issue, perform, or broadcast or authorise any of these things. Substantial copying will amount to an actionable infringement. Her exclusive rights are to some degree reduced because she has allowed note taking. The inclusion of a copyright symbol on the notes would be an indication that there was an express assertion of copyright rights. Each defendant would be likely to plead that their recording of the lecture was justified since note taking was permitted and no restrictions were imposed.

In *Nicols v Pitman* (1884), the plaintiff, an author and lecturer, gave an address from memory although he had the same lecture in manuscript form. The defendant, the inventor of a system of shorthand notation, took notes verbatim of what was said and then published them in a magazine. The court held that where a lecture is delivered to an audience, whether the lecture has been recorded in writing or not, the audience are at liberty to take the fullest notes for their own personal purposes but they are not permitted to use them afterwards for gain. With this in mind, the position of the four defendants should be considered.

Barry

Although Valerie's lecture is original, her copyright will not be infringed unless a substantial part of her speech is taken and used in the article. Barry has clearly taken a substantial amount. The parts of Valerie's address which are commonplace or from non-copyright sources may be taken and used by Barry provided he introduces sufficient independent skill and labour into the article he writes (see *Warwick Films v Eisinger* (1969)) and has used the address to locate original sources (*Pike v Nicholas* (1869)).

The court will look at the value of the material taken and the use made of it by Barry (*Ladbroke (Football) Ltd v William Hill (Football) Ltd* (1964)) to decide whether he has created an original work of his own rather than an infringing copy. Much will depend on the amount of independent input which he puts into the article. The extra comments referred to are likely to be insufficient to attach originality to the work. In *Caird v Sime* (1887), Lord Halsbury considered the copying of a lecture by a student who published his own version of it. Lord Halsbury held that in the case of 'an unlawful reproduction of a literary work; it does not become less of an injury to the legal right because the reproducer has disfigured his reproduction with ignorant or foolish additions of his own'. The lecturer was entitled to restrain publication.

Barry may raise two possible permitted acts as a journalist. Fair dealing with work is permitted, provided Barry does actually make proper use of the lecture for the purposes of criticism or review. Conceivably, Barry may be able to avail himself of s 30 which permits fair dealing for the purposes of news reporting. Barry must provide a sufficient acknowledgement and use the work fairly. In order to do this he must impart a sufficient degree of comment and criticism on Valerie's lecture (*Sillitoe v McGraw Hill Books* (1983)). Sufficient acknowledgment is defined in s 178 as meaning that the work is identified by both the title and the author.

Under s 58(1), where a record of spoken words is made, in writing or otherwise, for the purposes of: (a) reporting current events, or (b) broadcasting or including in a cable programme service the whole or part of the work, it is not an infringement of any copyright in the words as a literary work to use the record or material taken from it, or to copy the record, or any such material, provided certain conditions are met.

The qualifying conditions under s 58 are very important and will not justify Barry's use of Valerie's speech without express permission from her. Section 58(2) provides that: (i) the record must be a direct record of the spoken words and not taken from a previous record or from a broadcast; (ii) the making of the record was not prohibited by the speaker, and where copyright already subsisted in the work it did not infringe the copyright; and (iii) the record is not of a type prohibited by the speaker.

Applying these provisos, Barry's record will not qualify as parts will have been taken from the notes and no permission was given by Valerie for Barry's use of her lecture. As a consequence, any use by Barry will be an infringement.

Cuthbert

Cuthbert will be in a similar position to the defendant in *Nicol v Pitman* (1884). Whilst there was an implied licence to take notes, there was no permission to use them for commercial purposes. Transformation of the work into Japanese will not suffice to confer a fresh copyright. Although translations of a traditional literary work may confer originality (*Byrne v Statist* (1914)), the provisions of the CDPA 1988 will render Cuthbert's treatment of Valerie's speech an infringement. Section 17(2) provides for reproduction of a work in any material form. Section 22 further provides that an adaptation or translation will be an infringement, so the work being transformed into an article in a Japanese business paper will amount to the creation of an infringing copy.

The publication of the article in Japanese will also be an infringement of Valerie's exclusive right to first rights to issue copies of her work to the public.

Carver

Carver's video of the lecture is a potentially infringing copy, because the licence given by Valerie was limited to the making of written notes. Although a person is entitled to take photographs or make films of subjects, the filming of the talk will amount to the making of an infringing copy under s 17(2). An author retains the right to the making of copies in the form that he or she may specify.

A court is unlikely to infer that the necessary permission was given to video the talk and an injunction may lie. The only permitted act of which Carver might avail himself is under s 29, which permits the making of copies for the purposes of private study and research. However, the court may not consider the secret recording of the lecture as fair dealing.

Agnes

Applying s 17(2), the recording made by Agnes will also be an infringing copy. The subsequent recital of the lecture by Agnes will also amount to an infringement of the copyright under s 18, which prohibits including the work in any lecture, address or sermon. Although Valerie cannot have a monopoly on theories, the personal expression of her theory is retained by herself and repeating verbatim the content of her talk will be an infringement. The commercial gain by Agnes through repeating the lecture and using the material will give rise to actionable damage.

Remedies

Valerie will be entitled to an interlocutory injunction against each of the defendants to prevent reproduction of her lecture. The granting of the injunction is discretionary and consideration will be given to the principles in *American Cyanamid v Ethicon* (1975) to restrain potential harm. The balance of convenience lies with granting the injunctions to Valerie, as she has an established consultancy business to protect. Following the decision in *Series 5 Software Ltd v Philip Clarke and Others* (1996), the court may take into account the relevant strengths of the parties' cases. The defendant's ability to pay damages will also be a factor. In addition to seeking damages, Valerie could consider pursuing an account of profits against Agnes. Under s 97(2), the court may award additional damages considering the flagrancy of the breach. In Agnes' case, this is substantial given the wholesale appropriation of the lecture without Valerie's acknowledgment.

Question 8

'The law of copyright is concerned with protecting quality, not quantity.' Discuss with reference to decided cases.

Answer plan

A question involving an important point of copyright law but on which there is surprisingly lack of clarity and a relatively small amount of authority. The major case is *Ladbroke v William Hill* (1964). However, with a bit of ingenuity it is possible to consider a wide range of material.

Answer

In *Ladbroke v William Hill* (1964), Lord Reid stated, 'the question whether the defendant has copied a substantial part depends much more on the quality than the quantity of what he has taken'. In some cases the issue is clear cut, for example, where an entire work has been appropriated, such as an unauthorised recording of a song or a piece of music, but in others it is uncertain. It is naturally of importance to writers and artists who want to use extracts from the work of qualifying authors but who wish to remain within the law. Fair dealing and quotation for the purposes of criticism and review are among the permitted acts available, but their boundaries are hard to identify with precision. No precise formula has been identified for how much a person can actually take from the work of another before infringement arises, and no boundary can be drawn.

At first sight, it might seem that quality is not a factor, given that the courts have held that literary copyright subsists in diverse items such as lists of football pools (*Ladbroke v William Hill* (1964)), instructions for use of weedkiller (*Elanco v Mandops* (1979), telegraph codes (*Anderson & Co v Lieber Code Company* (1917)), or lists of items stocked by chemists (*Collis v Cater* (1898)). In terms of artistic quality, the courts need not enter into any exploration of worth or merit, and s 4 of the CDPA 1988 provides that works are protected 'regardless of artistic merit'.

Similarly, attempts to apply a percentage basis have been unreliable, indicating that the courts do not take a purely quantitative approach. In *Sillitoe v McGraw Hill Books*, appropriation of 5% of a novel amounted to a substantial appropriation. In *Express Newspapers v Liverpool Daily Post and Echo plc* (1985), Whitford J held that one-700th of a literary work copied by a defendant amounted to a substantial part of it. The classic position was expressed by Petersen J in *University of London Press v London Tutorial Press* (1916): 'what is worth copying is worth protecting'. Certainly, it is not possible to identify a cut-off point. A single page may be sufficient, as in a football almanac, where explaining the 'off-side' rule was an infringement (*Trengrouse v 'Sol' Syndicate* (1901–04)). In *Chapple v Thompson Magazines* (1928–35), four lines from a popular song used in an introduction to part of a serialised story were not a substantial infringement. There were some 80 lines in the original, but the court was clearly unimpressed by the content and considered that copyright should not be used as an instrument of oppression. However, a different view was taken in *Kipling v Genostan* (1917–22), where four lines of Kipling's poem '*If*' were considered of greater value and their use without permission in a vitamin advertisement was an infringement of copyright.

In *Spelling Goldberg Productions Inc v BPC Publishing Ltd* (1981), it was held that a tiny proportion could be substantial if it possesses a key feature by which the whole work is identified or recognised. A similar approach was taken in *EMI v Papathanasiou* (1987), known as the 'Chariots of Fire' case, where it was held that the test is qualitative, not quantitative, although quantity may betray quality.

The truth is that the complexities of copyright protection cannot be reduced to simple expressions of quality and quantity. In deciding whether infringement has occurred, a court may need to examine a wide range of factors. Even if there has been copying, it does not mean a remedy will lie.

Copyright infringement arises under s 16(3)(a) of the CDPA 1988 as doing an act restricted by the copyright in relation to the work as a whole or any substantial part of it. The question of what may be a substantial part of a protected work is one of fact in each case and is relevant to determining what is fair (*King Features Syndicate Inc v O and M Kleeman Ltd* (1941); *Hubbard v Vosper* (1972)). However, defining what is 'substantial' can be more problematic.

In order to determine whether a party has taken a substantial part of a work amounting to copyright infringement, it appears that the court must embark on what is effectively a three-part test. Firstly, it must establish that there has been copying of a qualifying work. It must secondly determine what is substantial with reference to the quality of what has been taken. This involves the third element, an assessment of the value of what has been taken to the original.

The value of what has been copied has been addressed in a number of cases in terms of whether it identifies the earlier work or encapsulates it, and whether the labour and skill of an author has been unfairly appropriated. As a result, the courts will look beyond the volume of material reproduced and assess it in terms of the skill, labour and effort applied by the author. The courts have also made distinctions where material is derived from a stock of common sources, and wider use may be made of some works than others.

The trend of the courts has been to assess quality in terms of the skill and effort which an author has expended in a work. If a defendant has not availed him or herself of earlier sources and information but instead makes use of the plaintiff's work, then copyright will be infringed. The principle has been applied to cases involving technical information, some of which was in the public domain. In *Elanco Products Ltd v Mandops (Agrochemical Specialists) Ltd* (1979), the plaintiffs had invented a herbicide, the patent of which had expired. The herbicide was sold with an accompanying leaflet. Buckley LJ held that the defendants were entitled to make use of information that was in the public domain but not to appropriate the plaintiff's skill and judgment, saving themselves the trouble and cost of assembling their own information.

As a result, it would appear that the author of a work involving commonplace or banal material will be exposed to the danger of having larger quantities of his or her work appropriated than the author of a more specialised work requiring originality (in the sense of novelty or uniqueness) or talent for its execution.

Reproduction in another medium can constitute infringement as in *King Features Syndicate v O & M Kleeman* (1941), where dolls of Popeye the Sailor were an infringement. This is also recognised in s 17(3) of the CDPA 1988, where reproducing a work in another form or transforming a two-dimensional work into a three-dimensional work or *vice versa* will amount to an infringement.

In *Hawkes v Paramount* (1934), a news film of a group of schoolboys playing 28 bars of 'Colonel Bogey' at the opening of a school was held to be a substantial infringement of the musical copyright, even though it was an inadvertent recording. The position is somewhat different with artistic works (1). In *Catnic Components Ltd v Hill & Smith* (1992), it was held that the plaintiff's artistic work is protected, not any information which it is designed to convey. If it is said that a substantial part of it has been reproduced, whether or not the part can properly be described as substantial, it is the visual significance in artistic works which is relevant.

In the case of computer programs, *John Richards v Flanders & Chemtech Ltd* (1993), the court took the view that when considering substantiality the similarities between the two programs should be considered individually, and only then should the question whether the entirety copied was substantial be addressed. This was to be decided with regard to quality not quantity, taking into consideration originality and the distinction between idea and expression in asserting quality. In assessing substantiality, it was also necessary to filter out elements dictated by efficiency, external factors and elements in the public domain.

The avoidance of developing a fixed rule has been dictated by two factors. The first factor is that each case will turn on its facts and on legislation which applies to the wide varieties of work. The second factor is the existence of a wide range of permitted acts, and the fact that copying will not amount to an infringement if the use made of it constitutes a fair dealing for stated purposes, fair dealing itself a term which is probably beyond precise definition (*per* Lord Denning in *Hubbard v Vosper* (1972)). Assessed in terms of fair dealing, the quantity of material taken is but one factor in assessing whether there is actionable infringement, once the preliminary question of whether what has been taken is substantial. In *Hubbard v Vosper,* Lord Dillon suggested that it might be possible in some cases to take the whole of a copyright work and still fall within the concept of fair dealing. In such a situation, however, the issue is the use to which the defendant has put the work after copying part of it which is arguably of far greater importance than quality or quantity. Given that only a small amount needs to be taken to constitute infringement, arguably use of the work is a better test.

Note

1 However, if the same facts were to recur today, the film maker would be protected by s 31 of the CDPA 1988.

Question 9

'Copyright does not protect ideas, only their expression.' Discuss.

Answer plan

A question which requires the student to review authorities which have referred to the dichotomy between ideas and expression (as it is frequently termed).

The issues to be considered are:

- Ideas in copyright
- Material form of expression
- Authorship and suggested ideas
- Industrial cases

Answer

In *Hollinrake v Truswell* (1894), Herschell LC referred to the 'fallacy perpetrated by counsel that copyright could subsist in a idea'. In *Hollinrake v Truswell,* the plaintiff failed in a claim for copyright in a device for measuring the dimension of sleeves in the form of a cardboard measurement chart. Rejecting the claim, the court identified the fallacy as the 'failure to distinguish between literary copyright and the right to patent an invention'. However, it is a fallacy which has survived to the present. Over the last 100 years, the courts have repeatedly stated that copyright protection extends only to the expression of ideas, not to the ideas themselves. Seemingly unchallengeable authority has accumulated on this point, but it has not deterred litigants from attempting to claim copyright in abstract ideas.

The requirement that a work must be put in a tangible form is one of the determining factors. This will be of great importance even if the author is apparently unconscious of what is actually being created, and the control of arrangements whereby the work is produced is left to another. Similarly, it was stated by Lord Denning MR that, 'Ideas, thoughts, fancies in a man's brain are not protected' but once reduced to material form are capable of copyright protection (*Ladbroke (Football) Ltd v William Hill (Football Ltd)* (1962)).

In *Donoghue v Allied Newspapers Ltd* (1938), Farwell J stated, 'A person may have a brilliant idea for a story, or for a picture, or for a play and one which appears to him to be original; but if he communicates that idea to an author or an artist or a playwright, the production which is the result of a communication of the idea to the author or the artist or the playwright is the copyright of the person who has clothed the idea in form' In *Donoghue,* a 'ghost writer' wrote up the experiences of a successful jockey. It was held that copyright was owned by the newspaper employing the journalist who had produced the articles purportedly by the jockey, and not the jockey who simply recounted his experiences but did not commit them to writing. Farwell J stated that, 'If the idea, however original, is nothing more than an idea, and is not put into any form of words or any form of expression such as a picture, then there is no such thing as copyright at all'.

For instance, in *Cummin v Bond* (1927), the author was actually supposed to be a ghost, a deceased Glastonbury monk who purportedly communicated through a medium. The pen was held by the medium who was in a trance and who responded to prompting and questioning from the defendant. The court (refraining from inquiring into the reality of the alleged monk) held that copyright attached to the medium who actually wrote the alleged utterances down.

However, the physical act of committing words or images into a material form is not always the determining factor, and the courts have, in the interests of practical necessity and commercial reality, accepted certain refinements of these principles. A secretary, who takes down a dictation of notes, or a mere copyist is not an author (*Riddick v Thames Board Mills Ltd* (1977); *British Oxygen Co Ltd v Liquid Air Ltd* (1925)), an approach that can be justified on the basis that originality for the purpose of copyright arises from the application of skill, labour and effort in creation, not simply the physical labour of compiling a work.

It is well established that there will be no copyright in a banal idea. In *Kenrick v Lawrence & Co* (1890), the plaintiff sought to claim copyright in the concept of a hand filling in a ballot paper. The plaintiff had paid an artist to execute it for campaigns to induce illiterate people to vote. The court stated, 'mere choice of subject can rarely, if ever, confer upon the author of the drawing an exclusive right to represent the subject'. The court affirmed that there could be no copyright in a banal idea. If an expressed idea was commonplace and simple, nothing short of exact literal reproduction would infringe the copyright in it. Similarly, if there is no other way of expressing a certain subject, there will be no copyright capable of protection. (A point subsequently applied in a computer software case, *Total Information Processing Systems Ltd v Daman Ltd* (1992) although since doubted.)

In *Bagge v Miller* (1917–23), the plaintiff had suggested the idea for a sketch but left it to the defendant to compose it into a dramatic work. The court took the view that 'The mere suggestion of an idea which is embodied by another in a dramatic work written by him does not constitute the originator of the idea an author or a joint author of the dramatic work'.

In *Wiseman v George Weidenfield & Nicholson Ltd and Donaldson* (1985), the plaintiff had been a helpful critic and adviser in assisting the second defendant to turn a novel into a play. He had not written any dialogue and, whatever his degree of artistic involvement, could not be said to be a joint author. The courts have distinguished between the situations where a person has ideas and is then commissioned to produce work, but in each case a work has been made subject to contract or under equity.

In *Green v Broadcasting Corporation of New Zealand* (1989), broadcaster Hughie Green brought an action for copyright infringement based on a television variety show he had conceived and broadcast successfully in the UK called 'Opportunity Knocks'. The New Zealand Broadcasting Corporation produced their own version of the show incorporating the same format, approach and catchphrases. Hughie Green claimed copyright protection in the literary, musical and dramatic format of the show. However, because of the skeletal nature of the scripts, simply providing a formula for the production of a talent show contest, no copyright could be claimed. The scripts themselves only gave guidance, and it could not be determined how the material would ultimately be presented on screen. That would only be apparent to those who watched the programme.

The New Zealand Court of Appeal and the Privy Council took the view that copyright could not protect a general idea. It was stretching the meaning of coincidence to believe that the New Zealand Broadcasting Company could have independently originated a similar show. However, the Court of Appeal quoted with approval the judgment in *Tate v Thomas* (1908) that since copyright created a monopoly, there had to be certainty in the subject matter of that monopoly in order to avoid injustice to the rest of the world.

The seeming clarity of the law in this area has been muddled by remarks taken out of context and by the continuing optimism of some plaintiffs. Admittedly, in *Mirage Productions v Counter Feat* (1991), the idea of aggressive humanoid sporting turtles being the subject of copyright was reluctantly given some endorsement, but this has not been followed and was only an interlocutory decision.

A distinction was made in *Rees v Melville* (1914) between ideas which could not be the subject of copyright and situations and incidents in a dramatic work which could be. The court might, in certain circumstances, have to consider that the mode in which the ideas were worked out and presented might constitute a material portion of the whole play, and the court must have regard to the dramatic value and importance of what, if anything, was taken. This would be so even though no language was directly taken.

Attempts have recurred in the commercial and industrial world to protect, in particular, the design of products. However, the courts' approach has remained consistent unless evidence of the copying of a literary or artistic work already in existence could be shown. The case of *Kleeneze Ltd v DRG (UK) Ltd* (1984) involved an infringement action over the design of a letterbox draught excluder. The court held that the defendants had taken the plaintiff's concept, but none of the skill and labour that went into the design of the product were in issue. In the absence of patent protection, the court held the defendant was entitled to copy. The defendants had simply seen one of the plaintiff's products and produced a variant themselves.

To some extent, the vulnerability of mere ideas under copyright law has been mitigated by the doctrine of confidential information (see *Frazer v Thames Television* (1984)), but the best advice to those blessed with minds which generate new ideas is to ensure they are expressed in material form, preferably in as complex a way as circumstances or argument can suggest.

Question 10

Jenny is an unemployed graphic artist. To earn some money she takes up painting murals at the request of parents who want to decorate the bedrooms of their children. Often the children ask Jenny if she will paint pictures of favourite cartoon characters from television programmes and films, or paint portraits of favourite toys derived from the programmes. Jenny is concerned about the copyright position of doing so.

Jenny also wants to know who is entitled to the copyright of her pictures and whether she can stop other artists copying them. She is also concerned about a portrait she made of a cuddly squirrel being copied by a rival artist, Druitt, to whom she showed some of her sketches. Unfortunately she cannot find the original. Advise her.

Answer plan

A common type of question which requires the application of both the CDPA 1988 and case law, starting with s 4 of the Act and the concept of 'eye appeal', infringement and a specific point on evidence.

The issues to be considered are:

- Section 4 of the CDPA 1988
- 'Eye appeal'
- Section 17 of the CDPA 1988
- Infringement
- *King Features Syndicate v Kleeman* (1941)
- Section 9 of the CDPA 1988
- Remedies

Answer

This question raises issues of copyright protection of artistic works. Original artistic works enjoy copyright protection under s 1(1) of the CDPA 1988. Section 4(1)(a) defines artistic work as including a graphic work, photograph, sculpture or collage, irrespective of artistic quality.

Artistic works are distinguished from other works by their appeal to the eye (*Anacon Corporation v Environmental Research Technology Ltd* (1994) and *Interlego v Tyco Industries* (1988)), and an artistic work will be classified as such despite the inclusion of some non-visual elements (*Interlego v Tyco*). Simply expending effort, skill and judgement in executing a copy will not necessarily confer on Jenny's work the required originality.

Taking the general idea and inspiration from a cartoon or toy will not be an infringement (*Bauman v Fussell* (1978)). However, if Jenny takes more than the idea and actually copies, she could be liable for infringement of copyright in the artistic works associated with the characters.

In the case of the cartoon characters, copyright will subsist in the original drawings as artistic works under s 4, and also in any film or cable broadcasts which she might use. Copying from an image on a television screen could infringe the copyright in the film (s 5), a broadcast (s 6), or a cable broadcast (s 7). In the case of the toys, these will qualify either in terms of either the copyright in the original artistic drawings or as works of artistic craftsmanship under s 4.

Section 17(3) of the CDPA 1988 provides that in relation to an artistic work, copying includes the making of a three-dimensional copy of a two-dimensional work and *vice versa*. Copying in relation to a film, television broadcast or cable programme includes making a photograph of any substantial part of any image forming part of the film, broadcast or cable programme. Jenny's act of painting a cartoon character will amount to a reproduction in a material form. Since it is possible for a work to be both infringing and original (*Warwick Film Productions v Eisinger* (1969)), Jenny would have to ensure that the work involves a sufficient degree of originality to ensure that no inference of copying can be made. It can no longer be excepted, in light of s 17, that a change in medium can be significant to confer originality on her work, as may previously have been the case under such authorities as *Martin v Polypas Manufacturers* (1969). In *MacMillan Publishing Ltd v Thomas Reed Publications Ltd* (1993), an allegation of copying of navigational charts was raised. The allegedly derived charts had an entirely different appearance visually because of the use of a different style. It was held that sufficient original skill and labour had been conferred on the work concerned.

The owners of the copyright in the animated characters will be determined with reference to ss 9 and 11 of the CDPA 1988. Section 9 provides that the owner of a copyright in a work is the person who created it. However, this is abrogated by s 11, which provides that in the case of a work created by an employee for an employer, the original artists who produced the cartoons may well have transferred their own copyright to the film makers or broadcasters concerned, either through agreement or by virtue of their employment. Regard should also be given to s 9(5) which states that the copyright will subsist in the person who makes the arrangements necessary for the cable broadcast.

Tests for copying

In cases of artistic works the courts have looked to what is copied and whether it is a significant part. In *West v Francis* (1822), which arose from the copying of seven prints with minor alterations and the addition of colour, Bayley J held, 'a copy is that which comes so near to the original as to give every person seeing it the idea created by the original'. This remains a valid test. In *Spectravest Inc v Aperknit Ltd* (1988), similarity in artistic works was judged by the impression on the eye. The visual significance is to be judged by the target audience (*Billhofer Maschinenfabrik Gmbh v TH Dixon & Co Ltd* (1990)). In this case, a judge deciding the issue would assume the view and perspective of an ordinary member of the public who watches cartoons.

An analogous case for both the drawings and the toys is *King Features Syndicate v Kleeman* (1941) involving three-dimensional 'Popeye' dolls and brooches which were copied from a two-dimensional cartoon series which had been published in magazines and newspapers. The court examined the drawings and the features of the dolls and noted similarities between the two in the features represented (eg the chin, swollen forearms, baggy trousers etc). There was clear evidence of copying, even if no precise drawing could be identified as the source for the infringing artist.

A similar approach was taken in *Mirage Studios v Counter Feat Clothing Co Ltd* (1991) ('Ninja Turtles'), it was held that it was not necessary to identify the precise drawings alleged to have been infringed. In a case where the plaintiff produces many versions of the copyright work, as will be the case with any coherent cartoon animation, where each drawing differs slightly from another, it will frequently prove impossible to identify a particular drawing copied by the defendant.

In *Billhofer Maschineenfabrik GmbH v TH Dixon & Co Ltd* (1990), it was said, *obiter*, that in considering causal connection in whether an alleged infringement was copied from a copyright work, it was the resemblance in inessentials, the small, redundant, even mistaken elements of a copyright work which carried the greatest weight, because these were the least likely to have arisen as a result of independent design. Copying from Jenny's own recollection, even if unconscious, will not be a defence against infringement proceedings if there is a causal link between a cartoon character and a mural portrait or image which Jenny produces (*Francis Day Hunter v Bron* (1963)).

Only if the cartoon characters are exceedingly simple drawings might there be an argument that they were not protected (*Kenrick v Lawrence* (1890)). In *Politechnika Ipari Szovetkezet v Dallas Print Transfers Ltd* (1982), it was held that in the case of very simple drawings the degree of similarity must be close. However, since copyright has been held to subsist in three simple circles (*Solar Thompson Engineering Co Ltd v Barton* (1977)) or geometric shapes there may be copyright which Jenny would risk infringing. In *Warwick Film Productions v Eisinger* (1969) and *ZYX Music v King* (1995), it was held that a work could be original but parts of it will nonetheless infringe which suggests that it is possible that Jenny will own copyright in some parts of her work and not others. To protect her position Jenny should seek the necessary licence from the copyright owners to reproduce the work, although the risk of being detected in the infringement might be considered slight.

Copyright ownership

Section 9 of the CDPA 1988 states that the first ownership of copyright rests with the author who first creates the work. This will apply to the ownership of the copyright in the works Jenny creates, subject to any agreement to the contrary with the commissioner. However, she would be entitled to make copies of her work under s 65 which are included among the permitted acts. With regard to the copying by Druitt, the same principles that restrict Jenny from copying cartoon characters will restrict him from copying Jenny's artistic work of the squirrel. She could seek an injunction to protect her copyright.

Failure to produce an original picture or design will not be fatal to a claim for infringement of copyright by Jenny. In *Lucas v Williams* (1892), the plaintiff claimed that a photograph was an infringement of an engraving but was unable to produce the original photograph. The court held that the original need not be produced and evidence given by a witness who had seen both would be sufficient.

Question 11

The Bearded Head are a rock band formed by four squatters in Hackney producing what they call the final degeneration of rock-'n'-roll. The act consists of attempting to play tunes and lyrics of their own joint composition with each of the members donning what they call 'combat beards' – large false beards which they wear throughout the performance. Their music and songs are composed in group sessions with each member contributing ideas.

Randy, a member of the band, secretly records one of their performances and then puts the music through a synthesizer. He takes the recording to Mash Studios where he attempts to persuade Micky Mash, the owner, to buy the recording. Randy claims he was the sole composer of the music and that the rest of the Bearded Head died in a gunfight. Micky Mash does not believe the story but takes a copy and tells Randy he will get back to him. Randy leaves in disgust. Later Micky replays the tape and decides to reproduce some copies to distribute to various clubs as an experiment. He orders copies to be made and telephones contacts in various clubs, telling them to expect a supply and new backing music.

Meanwhile, Randy takes a trip to France where he arranges to have 100 copies of the recording turned into CDs, calling it 'Beard Music'. He then returns to England where he gives one to Jerry, a club owner who is organising a 'Battle of the Bands' competition. Jerry wants to use the music during intervals and is so taken by the idea of beards that he requests at least one member of each band to wear a false beard or grow one by the date of the competition.

Meanwhile, the other members of Bearded Head discover what Randy has been doing and vow to take legal action. They discover that Randy is now hawking the remaining CDs at railway stations. Advise the remaining members of Bearded Head as to their legal remedies.

Answer plan

- Musical works – ss 1 and 4 of the CDPA 1988
- Performance rights – s 180 of the CDPA 1988
- Ownership; joint authors – ss 9 and 10 of the CDPA 1988
- Infringement; primary and secondary – ss 16(2), 22–27 of the CDPA 1988
- Importation of infringing copies
- Remedies – Anton Piller orders and injunctions

Answer

The rights of the members of Bearded Head to their music arise from s 1(1) of the CDPA 1988 which states that copyright subsists in original literary and musical works. Under the Copyright Act 1956, a song set to music will enjoy two separate copyrights – a copyright in the words and a separate music copyright (*Redwood Music v B Feldman & Co Ltd* (1979)). The words of Bearded Head's songs will attract literary copyright protection, being defined as any work which consists of words designed 'to be written, spoken or sung'. The musical notes arranged by them will be protected as a musical work, defined as 'a work of music, exclusive of any words or actions intended to be sung'.

Section 3(2) lays down that copyright does not subsist until the music has been recorded in material form. This could have been achieved either by notes that the members of Bearded Head make at their composing sessions, or alternatively by the secret recording made by Randy at a performance. In addition, the individual members of Bearded Head will also have rights in their performances by virtue of s 180 of the CDPA 1988.

Ownership of the copyrights is determined by reference to ss 9 and 10 of the CDPA 1988. The definition of an author is given in s 9, which provides that copyright will subsist with the person who creates the work. In this case ownership of the literary and musical copyrights will rest with all members of Bearded Head, as each has contributed in creating the work. They will be considered as joint authors under s 10 which provides that a work of joint authorship will arise where the separate input of the authors are indistinguishable from each other. Each of them will hold the copyright, including Randy. A member of the group who merely suggests the idea of a work, leaving it to the others to develop it, will have no remedy (*Wiseman v George Widenfield & Nicolson* (1985)). The members of Bearded Head will each hold the copyright as tenants in common (see *Powell v Head* (1879)). As a result, the works cannot be reproduced or dealt with other than with the consent of all the owners, and one owner is not entitled to grant licences to others to reproduce the work. As a consequence, Randy will be liable to infringement proceedings if he has carried out a restricted act in relation to the s 16 rights which each of the Bearded Head's members share. In addition, any of the members of Bearded Head may sue individually for infringement (*Lauri v Renad* (1892)). Parts of the work which have not been recorded in writing or note form may also be protected on the basis of confidential information.

The key to determining whether there have been infringing acts will be to consider the use which Randy has made of his recording, to which he has made alterations through the musical synthesizer. His initial recording of the work may be classed as an infringing act contrary to s 16(2) if he has copied a substantial part of the music and literary work. The courts can infer copying through similarities between the copyright work and the alleged infringement, and in the case of musical works the court assesses the effect on the ear. In *Stephenson v Chappell & Co Ltd* (1935), the use of identical notes constituting the melody in two songs was *prima facie* evidence of infringement. If the similarities are explicable by the fact that the phrases complained of were commonplace in music, there would be no infringement. In assessing whether infringement has occurred, the court will attach greatest weight to the resemblance in inessentials, the small redundant features such as the bad notes and even mistaken elements. This is because they are least likely to have been the result of an independent design and may lead the court to conclude that everything in the alleged infringement was copied. When the court has identified copying, it must then decide whether what was taken was a substantial part, which depends upon whether it was sufficiently important (*Billhofer Maschinefabrik Gmbh v TH Dixon & Co Ltd* (1990)).

This can readily be assumed by the fact that four complete compositions are recorded. In *Hawkes v Paramount Films* (1934), some 28 bars of the tune 'Colonel Bogey' were captured on a newsreel film. The extract was held to be a substantial part of the music. This was regardless of the film maker's intention, who was covering the opening of a school. Generally, if only a small part of a musical work is reproduced but it is sufficient to identify the earlier work, there will be an actionable infringement.

The making of further copies by Micky will amount to primary infringement of the Bearded Head's copyright through indirect copying of Randy's infringing copy. Under s 16(3)(b), indirect copying is as much an infringement as direct copying, provided there is a causal link with the original work.

The issue of copies by Randy will amount to a breach of s 18 of the CDPA 1988, which deals with the right to issue copies to the public. Under s 175(1), publication is defined as the issuing of copies of literary, dramatic, musical or artistic works to the public. The performance of the songs by Bearded Head will not amount to the publication of their work under s 175(4)(a)(i); because a literary, dramatic or musical work is not published merely because it has been performed in public. The initial offer of a single copy to Micky may not amount to publication, as mere offer or exposure to sale is not a publication (*Infabrics Ltd v Jaytex Shirts Co Ltd* (1982)) and limitation of class of persons to whom the work is offered may not amount to publication (*OSCAR Trade Mark* (1980)). In *Francis Day Hunter v Feldman & Co* (1914), an issue of only six infringing books was held to be publication, particularly where there is an intention to produce more for future demand, but the point will not be beyond argument. Alternatively, the second distribution of tapes by Randy using the copies manufactured in France could amount to publication contrary to the rights in s 18. A further alternative is that Micky Mash is responsible for breach of Bearded Head's first publication rights by the copying and distribution of copies to the various club owners. The determination of this issue will be important in terms of primary liability for Micky if Randy's initial disposal is classed as the first placing of an infringing work on the market. Subsequent sales or disposals do not infringe the right (s 18(2)(a)), although secondary infringement remains a possibility.

Authorisation of the production of infringing copies is a further act for which liability may attach to both Randy and Micky under s 16(2). Authorisation has been given a wide meaning and a person can be vicariously liable for any act of infringement. Establishing whether there has been a primary infringement by Micky will be important as liability will not attach for authorising a secondary infringement.

The playing of the tapes as backing music by Micky's club contacts or in Jerry's club will be breach of the restricted act under s 19(1) of performing in public a literary, dramatic or musical work. Under s 19(2), performance includes any mode of acoustic presentation by way of sound recording.

Position of secondary infringement

Sections 22–26 of the CDPA 1988 will catch a wide variety of secondary infringements. A person who knows or has reason to believe that a copy is infringing will be guilty of secondary infringement if, in the course of business, he possesses it, sells it, lets it for hire, offers or advertises it for sale or hire, exhibits or distributes it, or if he distributes it otherwise in the course of business to such an extent as to prejudice the copyright owner. Both Micky and Jerry may be in a difficult position as it has been held in *RCA Corporation v Custom Cleared Sales Party Ltd* (1978) that the defendant may be assumed to have the ordinary understanding expected of persons in his line of business. As music piracy is far from unheard of in the music industry this may place a considerable burden upon them.

Randy and anyone assisting him with knowledge will be liable for secondary infringement for importation of infringing copies. Under s 22, an infringing copy amounts to an item which, if it had been made in the UK, would be an infringing copy.

Further liability will attach to Micky Mash on the same principle where he makes further copies, knowing or suspecting that the copy he has received from Randy is an infringing copy. Liability could attach for actual possession of the copy, dealing with it (distribution to clubs) and providing the apparatus and means for making infringing copies.

If Jerry is unaware that the copy is infringing, he will not be liable for secondary infringement in terms of permitting the use of premises or of providing apparatus for an infringing performance. However, as soon as Jerry becomes aware that the copy of the Bearded Head's recordings is infringing, he will have the necessary knowledge. The courts have allowed a period of grace to rectify the breach.

The idea of a band with beards is unlikely to warrant any protection as bare ideas are not protected (*Green v New Zealand Broadcasting Corporation* (1989)). As a stage effect, it is probably too banal and also fails by being unrecorded (*Tate v Fulbrook* (1908)).

The remedies available to members of Bearded Head, whether individually or jointly, would be an interlocutory injunction to restrain the copying, distribution and performance of their work and an order to prevent any future importation. They might also seek an Anton Piller order to recover copies of the infringing recordings and details of those who have received them. Anton Piller orders have been held appropriate in cases where recordings of performances have been made without permission (*Re Island Records* (1978)).

The copies being sold at railway stations may be seized in accordance with s 100 of the CDPA 1988, which provides for peaceful seizure of infringing items in public places.

Question 12

Kirsty is the editor of Strange Days magazine which covers stories of mysterious, curious and unusual events. Kirsty wants to include a feature 'Strange Days from the 'Forties', a review of unusual and strange events of 50 or more years ago.

She wants to include the following:

- A photograph found deposited in an archive purportedly showing a flying saucer landing on the Isle of Mull in 1947. The photographer's name is given as 'Dr L Puller'. Dr Puller cannot be traced.
- Photographs of 'Private Sponger', a British soldier in World War II who deserted to join the British Frei Corp, a Nazi battalion of traitorous British soldiers who fought for the Germans on the Russian Front. Kirsty finds photographs of Sponger in a government archive which reveal that his past was disguised and that after the war Sponger became employed in the expanding postwar supermarket trade. Eventually Sponger became a senior manager. He appears in a promotional film made by the supermarket chain, Freshports plc, in advertisements on cable television.
- A model of a ship which vanished without a trace in the English Channel in 1949. The owners of the model are the insurance firm who paid out the claim. They refuse permission to photograph the model, but a Strange Days photographer manages to photograph it surreptitiously.

Answer plan

A difficult question which requires detailed consideration of the provisions of the CDPA 1988 and the schedules. It includes the sole remaining example of perpetual copyright that is given to unpublished works of unknown authorship.

The issues to be considered are:

- Section 4 of the CDPA 1988
- Section 12 of the CDPA 1988
- Schedule 1 CDPA 1988

- Section 30(2) of the CDPA 1988
- Section 163(3) of the CDPA 1988 – Crown copyright

Answer

The photograph by 'Dr Puller'

The CDPA 1988 defines a photograph as a recording in light or other radiation on any medium on which an image is produced (s 4(2)).

It would be advisable for Kirsty to make inquiries as to how the photograph came to be deposited with the archive. If Dr Puller cannot be identified or traced, a case could be made that ownership of the physical material of the photograph lies with the archive, but this does not entitle them to the copyright.

The position of a photograph taken since 1 August 1989 is that the person who takes the photograph will be the owner of the copyright. The term of protection given to photographs taken on or after 1 August 1989 is 50 years from the end of the year in which the author dies, and in the case of joint works the term of copyright is 50 years from the end of the year in which the last surviving author died. However, the photograph by Dr Puller was taken prior to the commencement of the CDPA 1988.

The Copyright Act 1956, which came into force on 1 June 1957, granted copyright protection in a photograph for 50 years from the end of the first publication and also gave perpetual copyright for unpublished photographs. Since Dr Puller's photograph was taken before 1957, it would be covered by s 18 of the Copyright Act 1911 which gave a term of protection of 50 years from the date of first publication. Under s 21 of the 1911 Act, the copyright owner in a photograph was the owner of the negative. Published meant issuing reproductions of the photograph and, arguably, inclusion of the photograph in the archive would not amount to publication.

Schedule 1, para 12 of the CDPA 1988 (which applies by virtue of s 170) provides that copyright for a published photographs and photographs taken before 1 June 1957 subsists until the date it would have expired under the 1956 Act. Para 12(3) states that copyright in anonymous or pseudonymous works (other than photographs) will subsist if published until the end of the period of 50 years from the end of the calendar year in which the new copyright provisions come into force (1 August 2039) or if made available to the public within the meaning of s 12(2). Under s 12(2), a work of unknown authorship has a copyright lasting 50 years from when it was first made available to the public. However, if it remains unpublished, copyright will be preserved. If the photograph by `Dr Puller' is classed as unpublished, it will enjoy perpetual copyright. The inclusion of the photograph in an archive does not in itself amount to making it available to the public. Classified as an artistic work under s 4(1)(a), a photograph could be made public by exhibition in public, inclusion in a film or being included in a broadcast or cable programme service. Even if Kirsty takes the approach of 'publish and be damned', s 12 provides that the photograph will still remain in copyright because, in assessing the period, no account is taken of an infringing act.

Copyright can be assigned to another person, but only if the photographer agrees. An assignment of copyright should be in writing but a verbal contractual agreement can be equally binding. The owner in respect of pre-CDPA 1988 photographs was the person who owned the material on which the photographs was processed. Thus, the person who owned a roll of film would obtain the copyright in the photograph. The position since 1 August 1989 will be that the person who takes the photograph will be the owner.

Section 104(5) covers situations where the author is either dead or his or her identity cannot be ascertained by reasonable inquiry. The work is presumed to be original. It will be a infringing act by Kirsty to take a substantial amount of the independent work which went into creating the copyright of the photograph. In *Bauman v Fussell* (1978), it was held that the capture of a strange or unusual event could be part of the skill and ability of the photographer.

Kirsty will not be able to claim that reproduction of the photograph was a permitted act. As editor of an investigative magazine, it might have been possible for Kirsty to take advantage of the fair dealing, review or news reporting provisions under s 30. Unfortunately, photographs are an excepted from the fair dealing provisions of s 30.

As a result of these statutory provisions, an unpublished photograph of unknown authorship remains in perpetual copyright, but the chances of an infringement action will become increasingly unlikely as time goes on.

If the work is an infringement, it will be no defence to show that a defendant has added new and substantial elements of his or her own as it is possible for a work to be both original and infringing.

The government archive photographs

Since the photograph is described as an official photograph, copyright will vest in the Crown. Photographs taken before 1988 were owned by the person who owned the film and it is a logical inference that the film was taken by a Crown employee or servant. However, there might be a question as to whether the Crown owns the film if it ultimately turns out to be a commissioned work.

However, there was a problem with works commissioned by the Crown. There is no definition in the 1956 Act of what is meant by 'under the direction or control of Her Majesty or a Government Department' and it is not clear whether this included a commissioned works body that existed under Crown licence but did not make works under direction from the Crown (*British Broadcasting Co v Wireless League Gazette Publishing* (1926)).

Section 163(1) of the CDPA 1988 provides that the Crown is the first owner of any copyright in a work created by a servant or officer of the Crown acting in the course of his or her duties. This is wider than the general right of an employer under s 11(2), because it extends to cover office holders. Crown copyright is unaffected. Crown copyright lasts for 125 years from the calendar year in which the work was made (s 163(3)(a)), unless published within 75 years from being made, whereupon the copyright period will be 50 years (s 163(3)(b)).

Alternatively, a public interest claim might be raised under s 171(3) but this might be hard to sustain and permission should be sought.

The promotional film

The advertisement was in a film taken by the supermarket. The clip of Sponger in the film is also broadcast as part of a cable service. The film may qualify for protection under s 5 and the cable broadcast – if it fulfils qualifying conditions – will be protected by virtue of s 7. Section 17(4) makes it clear that copying in relation to a film, television broadcast or cable programme, including making a photograph of the whole or any substantial part of any image forming part of the film, broadcast or cable programme, will be an infringement. If Kirsty arranges to take a photograph, it will be an infringement and anyone else involved with the process could be subjected to proceedings for secondary infringement. However, Kirsty could claim that reproduction would constitute a permitted act under s 30(2), which allows for reproduction for the purpose of reporting current events, providing there was sufficient acknowledgement.

The model of the ship

A still photograph of the model ship is likely to be an infringement. The model of a ship could be protected as a sculpture or a work of artistic craftsmanship (s 4 of the CDPA 1988). The question does not specify when the model was made but continuity of the law is maintained by Schedule 1, para 3 of the CDPA 1988. If it was a commissioned work, the insurance company is likely to own the copyright (Schedule 1, para 11 of the CDPA 1988) providing that the law in force at the time the work was created will determine ownership. Under s 17(3) of the CDPA 1988, it is an infringement to make a three-dimensional copy of a two-dimensional work and *vice versa*. If publication goes ahead without licence, it could be restrained by injunction.

Question 13

In the 1940s and 1950s, Arthur Slapper was a popular musical entertainer known for playing a ukulele. In 1992, shortly before his death, he sold the rights to some of the performances to his wife Betty and songs to Silver Ease Ltd which specialises in producing nostalgic recordings for an aging audience. The most popular of his songs were numbers called, 'When I'm singing classics' and 'No hanging round the bar'.

In 1995, Silver Ease Ltd is bought out by Markham who grants a licence to Wickedvibe Musicals who propose to put on a musical about a serial killer in the 1940s. The musical contains a scene set in the condemned cell where an Arthur Slapper impersonator performs a song called, 'When I'm hanging felons', a parody of the original Arthur Slapper, and 'No hanging round the bar'.

Betty is disgusted at the parody and wants to restrain it. She is further offended by Markham Ltd suggesting that the lyrics were not written by Arthur.

She also wants to hold a memorial service for Arthur at the local chapel, to play several of the songs and to have a longer recital with invited guests and friends at a private fan club, including recordings that Betty made of her husband. Advise Betty as to her position.

Answer plan

A question which requires an understanding of how copyright constitutes a form of intangible property which can be assigned or licensed and may be distinct from the actual physical expression of the work which the author has created.

The issues to be considered are:

- Literary and musical works – s 1(1) of the CDPA 1988
- Assignment – s 90 of the CDPA 1988
- *Re Dickens* (1935)
- Parody conferring originality
- Performance rights
- Permitted acts
- Meaning of public

Answer

The crucial factor will be whether there has been a complete assignment of Arthur's rights via the will to Betty, or whether they have devolved to Wickedvibe Ltd.

Under s 1(1)(a) of the CDPA 1988, copyright subsists in qualifying original literary, dramatic, musical and artistic works and in sound recordings. The works of Arthur Slapper would qualify as literary works (the musical scores and the lyrics) and as musical works (the melody). The work must be original in the sense that it was produced by Arthur as being opposed to being copied. The CDPA 1988 expressly preserves existing copyrights. Under s 12, the copyright will last for 50 years from the end of 1992 when Arthur died. Although Betty may possess the physical expression of Arthur Slapper's songs in the form of the original scores, once the subject of the copyright has been expressed in material form, it does not thereafter depend upon the physical expression for its validity (*Re Dickens* (1935)). Accordingly, although Betty holds the manuscripts, she will not have had the copyright transferred to her.

As the author of the work, Arthur Slapper had the sole right to transfer the assignment or reproduce the work of any substantial part thereof in any material form and to perform the work or any substantial part of it. The details and scope of the purported licence or assignment should be scrutinised closely as the assignee or licensee will only have rights in respect of their own portion. Copyright under s 90(1) of the CDPA 1988 is classed as personal or movable property, the equivalent of a chose in action. Transfer can be achieved by assignment, operation of law or testamentary disposition. A licence granted by a copyright owner will be binding on successors in title, with the exception of a *bona fide* purchaser without notice for valuable consideration (s 90(4)).

The CDPA 1988 does not make any express provision for bequeathment of some rights but not others, as is expressly stated to be possible with assignments. Where the copyright owner dies leaving a will, the copyright passes automatically to the executors. When the administration of the estate is completed the title to the copyright will pass to the beneficiary. The works, although made before the CDPA 1988, will enjoy copyright subject to Schedule 1, paras 5–9. If, however, there has only been a partial assignment of certain rights that have devolved to Markham, it is possible that some rights may have been assigned and not others. Betty would have rights in the copyright material she inherited which would subsist for 50 years after the death of her husband and could be transferred to her heirs. Section 90 of the CDPA 1988 provides that copyright is property which may be assigned or inherited. To be valid, assignment has to be in writing (s 90(1)).

In *Metzler & Co v J Curwen & Sons Ltd* (1928–35), the composer of incidental music assigned it to a company. After the death of the composer, his widow purported to transfer the rights in a composition to the defendant. In any event, there may not be an actionable infringement. If Markham has licensed Wickedvibe musicals to use the work, there will be no infringement of her copyright. The use of the song by Wickedvibe, if authorised, could not be restrained by Betty. If there has been complete assignment, Betty will have no title and will thus have no right to restrain the dealing with the work.

If the rights ultimately vest with Betty, it is likely that she will be able to sue for infringement. A parody will not be a defence. Although in *Joy Music Ltd v Sunday Pictorial Newspapers* (1960) it was held that a parodying work could confer a new copyright because of the effort, labour and skill applied to the creation of the parody, this approach has not been followed in subsequent decisions (*Schweppes Ltd v Wellingtons Ltd* (1984)).

In *Redwood Music Ltd v Chappell & Co Ltd* (1982), it was held that the plaintiff can hold copyright in a work even if it is established that part of the work infringes the copyright of another. In *ZYX Music GmbH v King* (1995), a plaintiff was held to be entitled to prevent others infringing. The effect of the assignment to Markham would be to vest in Markham the right to prevent any other person performing the song or any substantial part of it in public. Markham's rights are contained in s 16 of the CDPA 1988 and anything done without licence will amount to infringement.

Performance

Arthur Slapper will have enjoyed performance rights under s 180(2). These will include his performances before 1 August 1989 by operation of s 180(3) (although any acts done before that date or subject to any agreement do not become infringement). The term performance includes a dramatic or musical performance or a reading or recitation. Performers' rights are also recognised in part but they will not assist here.

It is not possible to assign performance rights but they can be transmitted by express provision in a will. The recording that Betty has will operate as an exception. The rights are independent of any copyright relating to the song itself (s 180(3)), which may potentially cause problems for Betty if all rights in the song and words have been assigned to Markham. Performing rights conferred by the CDPA 1988 continue to subsist in relation to a performance until the end of a period of 50 years from the end of the calendar year in which the performance took place (s 191).

However, as the parody put on by Wickedvibe is independent of any performance, Betty will not be able to claim. To be a qualifying performance, it has to be by a qualifying individual in a qualifying country (s 181).

Moral rights

A claim might lie for breach of moral rights which may be transferred under a will or to personal representatives. Rights would include false attribution (s 77) and the right to object to derogatory treatment (s 80). Schedule 1, paras 22–23 of the CDPA 1988 would operate. Schedule 1, para 22 puts moral rights into effect as Arthur died after the commencement date of the CDPA 1988 (1 August 1989). Alternatively, s 43 of the Copyright Act 1956 gave an author the right to be acknowledged.

Performance at the funeral and fan club event

Section 19 of the CDPA 1988 states that the performance of the work in public is an act restricted by the copyright in a literary, dramatic or musical work. Section 19(2)(a) provides that performance in relation to a work includes delivery in the form of lectures, addresses, speeches and sermons and under s 19(2)(b) in general, includes any mode of visual or acoustic presentation. However, in Part III of the CDPA 1988 there is provision for a permitted act which would enable the recordings to be played at the funeral and by the fan club. Under s 67, it is not an infringement of the copyright in a sound recording to play the recording for the purposes of a club or society, other organisation which is not established or conducted for profit and where the main objects are charitable or are otherwise concerned with the advancement of religion, education or social welfare and any proceeds for admission charges are applied solely for the purpose of the organisation. An analogous provision is made under Schedule 2, para 15 with respect to recording rights.

In *Harms (Incorporated) Ltd v Martans Club (Ltd)* (1926), the court considered a performance in a club as a performance to the public. The court held that in determining such a question the court could examine the constitution and rules of the club, the invited guests, the class of members and the probability of injury to the copyright owner.

Section 59 allows a reasonable amount of a work to be read or recited in public. The section does not define a reasonable amount. Given the nature of the proceedings, whether Betty owns copyright or not, it is unlikely that the court would restrain either event.

Question 14

Discuss the concept of fair dealing with a copyright work in terms of the permitted acts of study, criticism and news reporting under Part III of the CDPA 1988.

Answer plan

Questions dealing with specific permitted acts are not common because of their range and diversity. Where questions touch on permitted acts, it is usually with relation to fair dealing under ss 29 and 30 of the CDPA 1988. The term fair dealing was recognised long before the 1988 Act and the authorities discuss it in the broadest of terms, giving a student much scope in an answer.

The issues to be considered are:

- s 29 of the CDPA 1988
- Fair dealing
- Acknowledgement
- News reporting – s 30 of the CDPA 1988

Answer

Copyright is only a partial monopoly. There is no tort of copying and the law has always upheld a number of important exceptions whereby a person may reproduce parts of the work of another without risking infringement. Some 50 sections of the CDPA 1988 provide a system of general rights and specific rights to copy otherwise protected works, but only two refer to fair dealing, a concept known prior to the CDPA 1988.

Under s 29 of the CDPA 1988 it is a fair dealing with a work to copy for the purposes of private research and study. This is not unlimited and is restricted under s 29(3) where the copying goes outside the permitted acts allowed to librarians, and in any case where copying is for more than one person at 'substantially the same time for substantially the same purpose'. Fair dealing under s 30 of the CDPA 1988 encompasses the copying of a work for the purposes of criticism, review and reporting of current events.

The Act does not define fair dealing and surprisingly few authorities have examined the point, given the huge volume of literary, artistic, musical and dramatic works which exist worldwide. Fair dealing is very important because the courts have often held that taking a relatively small amount of a work is sufficient to be an infringement of copyright. In *Hubbard v Vosper* (1972), Lord Denning stated that fair dealing was in itself incapable of an all-embracing definition; each case would turn on its facts.

In *Beloff v Pressdram* (1973), Ungoed Thomas stated that fair dealing was not of itself a justification of infringement of copyright. He further stated that 'Fair dealing is a question of fact and impression to which factors that are relevant include the extent of the quotation, its proportion to comment, whether the work is published or unpublished and the extent to which the work has been circulated'. In his view, leaked material could not amount to a fair dealing. What is fair is a question of fact and degree. The court will look at a number of factors including the quantity and significance of the matter taken, whether the activity is in competition with the plaintiff, whether the work is published or unpublished and whether the defendant acted maliciously (*British Oxygen v Liquid Air* (1925); *Hubbard v Vosper* (1972)).

In particular, he considered that fair dealing went to the 'root' of publication and applied to the circumstances in which a work was reproduced. Conversely, where there is an overriding public interest in the information being copied to enable it to be made available, copyright protection will not apply and the dealing may be deemed fair. This was the situation in *Hubbard v Vosper* (1972) where there was a public interest in making known the activities of a cult promoting quack remedies.

If the defendant is using the information to compete with the plaintiff, the court is less likely to find that the use has been fair. The court will consider intention – whether the work is actually used for criticism. It was suggested by Brightman J in *Ravenscroft v Herbert* (1980) that the law would allow a greater use of a historical work than of a novel 'so that knowledge may be built upon knowledge'. In practice, the intention behind use of material should arguably be one of the most crucial factors, since if a pirated work is brought out commercially, the result could be a corresponding loss of sales and royalties for an author. Looking at intention and commercial consequences may be a more just criteria than the amount of a work which is actually being reproduced. It does not depend on a single criterion 'whether large chunks of the copyright material have been used as opposed to small chunks', *per* Walton J in *Associated Newspapers Group plc v News Group Newspapers Ltd* (1986). In *Hubbard v Vosper* (1972), Lord Dillon went so far as to suggest that fair dealing might on occasion involve quoting the whole of a work without infringing copyright. Simply reproducing work in a different form will not be a fair dealing (*ITP Ltd v Time Out* (1984)).

The courts will scrutinise the claims made by defendants closely. In *Sillitoe v McGraw Hill Books* (1983), the defendants published extracts of the plaintiff's books for sale to students of English literature. Their claimed defence of fair dealing failed as the copying was for their own commercial purposes, not for those of the students who might legitimately raise fair dealing.

In *Johnstone v Bernard Jones Publications Ltd* (1938), it was held that if the work is set out and criticised that will be sufficient, providing the amount of criticism is sufficient. Any form of criticism is covered and it need not be hostile, although this can sometimes tie up with free speech issues. There is a public interest in free speech on matters of public controversy, which can be grounds for allowing otherwise infringing acts (*Kennard v Lewis* (1983), where the defendant produced a hostile parody of a CND leaflet). However, the claim of free speech will not automatically be a justification (*Associated Newspapers v News Group plc* (1986)).

However, a fair dealing defence can now only be made out where there has been a sufficient acknowledgement under s 178, the fairness being derived from the fact that the party copying is not seeking to assert authorship or rights over the work.

A work is not reviewed where it is merely reproduced without comment, where it is merely explained or where it is reproduced in a different form or employing different language.

Originally, it was held that there could be fair criticism even if the work was not attributed to its author (*Johnstone v Bernard Jones Publications Ltd* (1938)). Whether an acknowledgement was sufficient was considered in *Sillitoe v McGraw Hill Books* (1983). Davies J considered that the defendants, who had included the name and title of the works by the various plaintiffs, had not given sufficient acknowledgement. Using a dictionary definition, Davies J considered that acknowledgement included the 'act of recognising the position or claims of a person'. There was nothing in the use of the copyright texts by the defendants as study notes which suggested that it was a copyright work and they had treated it as a non-copyright text. However, in *Express Newspapers plc v News (UK) Ltd* (1990), it was held that it is the author, not the copyright owner, who requires the acknowledgement.

The phrase 'for use for criticism or review' does not mean that the copyright work is actually the one which is subject to the criticism or review. Fair dealing can be raised as a permitted act in all categories of copyright work with the exception of photographs (see s 30(2)).

Section 30 of the CDPA 1988 provides for copying as a permitted act for the purposes of news reporting of current affairs. In *British Broadcasting Corporation v British Satellite Broadcasting* (1992), it was held that the defendant was entitled to use short excerpts from the BBC's broadcasts of the World Cup to show highlights on a sports programme, on the basis that this amounted to 'fair dealing ... for the purpose of reporting current events'. The court held that reporting of current events was not confined to news programmes but could be used in other programmes featuring news. The court held that having regard to the quality and quantity of the extracts taken and their use in genuine news reports allowed the defendant to raise the statutory defence. A sufficient acknowledgement will be necessary in the case of a literary, artistic, musical, or dramatic work but no acknowledgement is required in connection with the reporting of current events by means of a sound recording, film, broadcast or cable programme (s 30(3)).

Copying from old sources may be permitted under the ambit of current affairs, as historical events can easily be a source of contemporary news (*Associated Newspapers Group plc v News Group Newspapers Ltd* (1986)).

Closely related to this is s 31 which covers incidental inclusion. It covers all kinds of works and could mean that what were formerly classed as infringements would not be so today on the same facts. In *Hawkes v Paramount Films* (1934), some 28 bars of 'Colonel Bogey' played by a boys' band at the opening of a school were captured on a film which had as its prime purpose the recording of the opening ceremony. By virtue of s 31, this would no longer infringe and extraneous copyright works which are inadvertently included will not be actionable infringements. There will be an exception – the deliberate inclusion, in the case of a musical work or a literary work, of material such as background music or words spoken or sung with music. Under s 31(3), a deliberate inclusion prevents a finding of accidental inclusion.

Although the scope of fair dealing in the permitted acts is a broad one, the statutory exceptions may be criticised for a lack of clarity and definition in the expressions used. Since it is left to the courts to interpret fair dealing, there is an accompanying risk of anomalous decisions and a corresponding lack of certainty as to the amount of text which may be legitimately taken. As few decisions go beyond the interlocutory stage, the lack of clear statutory definition (with the exceptions of photocopying) can potentially leave many authors uncertain of their position and unable to ascertain whether the use that has been made of a work has been fair, or alternatively whether the use by others of their own work may amount to an infringement. With such a lack of clarity, the cost of litigation may well deter many authors from enforcing their rights under s 16 of the CDPA 1988.

Question 15

Hal Corporation produces computer software for use by unemployed graduates, providing information on welfare benefits and pensions derived from official sources.

Arthur is a software writer for Hal who is 'head-hunted' by another firm, Grolier Computers Ltd. Hal are concerned that Arthur may use copies of the programs he had written or obtained during his employment with them. Meanwhile, the Scam Action Group make copies of the program and distribute it to the public. They also put on a piece of radical street theatre which highlights elements of the program and they perform it to an audience in the street.

Advise Hal as to their rights in copyright.

Answer plan

A complex question covering a lot of material. In answering this question, it is necessary to examine reported decisions relating to computer software and the specific regulations which apply.

The issues to be considered are:

- Original literary works – s 1(1) of the CDPA 1988
- Section 3(1) of the CDPA 1988
- *Ibcos Computers v Barclay Mercantile High Finance* (1994)
- *John Richardson Computers v Flanders* (1993)
- Copyright (Computer Programs) Regulations 1992
- Infringement
- Sections 50(A) and 50(B) of the CDPA 1988
- Sections 17, 18, and 19 of the CDPA 1988

Answer

Copyright protection extends to original literary works under s 1(1) of the Copyright Designs and Patents Act 1988. Under s 3(1)(a), tables and compilations are protected, and s 3(1)(b) protects computer programs.

In order to be original, the work must be the product of a substantial degree of skill or effort employed in creating it by the author (*University of London Press Ltd v University Tutorial Press Ltd* (1916); *Ladbrooke (Football) Ltd v William Hill (Football) Ltd* (1964)).

In this case, the software sold by Hal will satisfy the requirement of originality in that although it uses information derived from other sources (including matters which may be the subject of Crown or Parliamentary copyright (ss 163 and 165), it has applied the information in the broader structure of the program. The screen display would be classed as a product of the program, not the program itself (*John Richardson Computers Ltd v Flanders* (1993)).

The law on computer programs

The earliest cases on computer programs treated them as equivalent to literary works (*Thrustcode Ltd v WW Computing Ltd*

(1983)). This approach was put into statutory form by the Copyright (Computer Software) Act 1985 and is now covered by s 3(1)(b) of the CDPA 1988. Also protected are preparatory designs for a computer program under s 3(1)(c).

In addition, the Copyright (Computer Programs) Regulations 1992, which came into effect on 1 January 1993, amended the CDPA 1988 and apply to computer programs whenever created. The regulations were based upon European Community Directive 91/250/EEC. Regulation 4 inserts a new s 50 into the CDPA 1988. The effect of these provisions will be to attach copyright protection to the computer program.

Ownership of copyright

Section 11 of the CDPA 1988 provides that the author of a work is the first owner in any copyright unless an author is an employee who creates the work in the course of employment. Authorship is determined by reference to ss 9 and 10 of the CDPA 1988, s 9 stating that the author is the person who creates the work while s 10 provides that where two or more authors collaborate in the creation of a work, and the contribution of each is not distinct, then the work will be of joint authorship. If Arthur was an employee, Hal would be entitled to the copyright in any program produced. Each case will turn on its facts and the court may look at a number of factors. However, if Arthur was an independent subcontractor, the answer could be different. Hal Corporation might rely on the *obiter* view of the Court of Appeal in *Massine v de Basil* (1936–45). 'But even if the author could rightly be regarded as an independent contractor the court was of the opinion that it ought to be implied as a term of the agreement that any work done by the plaintiff would be done on the basis that the (company) who had paid for the work should be entitled to such rights as might arise from that payment, and that (it) should not be deprived of the benefit of it merely on the ground that a person whom (it) paid was an independent contractor.'

Making copies

Under s 50(A)(1) of the CDPA 1988, a lawful user of a computer program is entitled to make back-up copies if necessary in the course of lawful use of the program. Grolier may be lawful users if they are using the software within the terms of any licence under which they have acquired it, but this does not go as far as issuing the product under their own name. Under s 50(B), Grolier will also be entitled to carry out decompilation. Decompilation is permitted where it is necessary for a lawful user to do so to create an independent program which can be operated with the decompiled program or another. However, the information is not allowed to be used for any other purpose and an express restriction is imposed by s 50(B)(3)(d).

Infringement of software

It will not be sufficient to show that there has been copying of functional parts of the program. It is arguable that if there is only one way of expressing the information then there will be no infringement (*Kenrick v Lawrence* (1890) cited in *John Richardson Computers Ltd v Flanders & Chemtech Ltd* (1993), where Ferris J adopted the approach of the US courts).

However, this approach was criticised in *Ibcos Computers Ltd v Barclays Mercantile Highland Finance* (1994). Jacob J considered claims by a plaintiff that copyright subsisted in: (1) individual programs and sub-routines; (2) the general structure of the software; and (3) certain general design features of the software as defined in expert reports adduced by the plaintiff. He held that the approach to be taken was whether copyright subsisted in the relevant works and then assess whether they had been copied by making substantial comparisons of the two works in issue. The court also took the view that the construction of a program and the way in which the individual programs were brought together was important, stating that 'UK copyright cannot prevent the copying of a mere general idea, but can protect the copyright in detailed ideas'. In considering earlier authorities such as *Whelan Associated Inc v Jaslow Dental Laboratory Inc* (1987), it was held that copyright may be infringed by the copying of the overall structure of a program rather than upon a line for line basis.

In deciding whether a substantial part of the software has been copied, the court will apply *Ladbroke (Football) Ltd v William Hill (Football) Ltd* (1964), which stated that copying will be determined with regard to the quality of any parts copied rather than the quantity.

Proving copying

In *MS Associates v Power* (1985), the court identified two issues for infringement of copyright of computer programs:

- the plaintiff had to prove that the defendant had access to the program; and
- that there were similarities between substantial parts of the works involved.

In *Ibcos*, Jacob J indicated that the courts will often need to rely on expert evidence of comparisons. The fact that the two screen displays are similar is not proof of copying in itself. Even to copy the screen display will not be an infringement of the underlying program as a literary work. The display on the screen of a computer program is protected as an artistic work in *John Richardson v Flanders & Chemtech Ltd* (1993) and *Atari v Philips* (1994).

The copyright in a computer program itself is protected, not the results obtained from it. Anyone is free to write a program on the same subject matter, but copyright will protect the skill, labour and effort in Hal's program.

Subject to any defence that may be raised, Grolier Ltd are likely to be liable for infringement if they have appropriated a substantial part of the skill and labour used by Hal Corporation as a result of Arthur using the software. It does not affect the issue that the material is publicly available. Indeed, it was stated in the judgment of Whitford J in *ITP Ltd and BBC Ltd v Time Out* (1984), 'Anyone reading a copyright work based upon publicly available information is of course free to go away and, starting with the public source and from that source, to produce his own work which may correspond very closely with the work of the earlier author. What he is not entitled to do is take a short cut'.

From the facts it appears that Grolier Ltd have infringed the copyright in Hal's program under s 16 by making infringing copies and under s 17(2) for issuing a written outline. Depending on the facts there may also be infringement in the copyright computer software by virtue of s 21(3)(a) or (b) or s 21(4) by translating one computer program into another.

Scam Action Group

The Scam Action Group infringe Hal's copyright by making copies of the software (s 16(2)). By copying and reproducing the information in leaflets, Scam also infringe copyright under ss 17(2), 18(1) and 16(3). The street theatre would also be caught by s 18 which makes it an infringement to perform the work in public. By giving out copies of Hal's product, it might be argued that Scam are authorising further infringement. However, in *CBS Inc v Ames Records Ltd* (1982), Whitford J stated that, 'Any ordinary person would, I think, assume that an authorisation can only come from someone having or purporting to have authority and that an act is not authorised by somebody who merely enables or possibly assists or even encourages another to do that act but does not purport to have any authority which he can grant to justify the act'.

Remedies

A number of remedies are potentially available to Hal. An interlocutory injunction could lie to prevent further infringement by the making and sale of Grolier's product. An interlocutory injunction may also be sought against the Scam Action Group. Remedies for delivery up of infringing copies should also be sought.

Question 16

Jeremy is a former member of the 'Law, Order and Discipline Campaign' led by Harold, a well-known Member of Parliament. Harold has designed all the campaign materials including stickers and posters with catchy slogans such as 'Burglars – string 'em up', 'More Rope' and 'Jail cannabis smokers Now!'. Harold has also written for the press and television and cable programmes denouncing crime and calling for the return of various ghoulish punishments. Naturally Harold has spoken in Parliament and has also contributed to Home Office circulars and reports.

Jeremy resigned from the campaign after he discovered that Harold was pocketing the profits from sales. Jeremy also discovered from letters which arrived at the campaign office that Harold was a shareholder in Grout Corporation, a US security company, which is planning to open privatised jails in the UK, and which naturally has a vested interest in as many people being jailed as possible. Grout Corporation was giving encouragement to Harold to press for an expansion of the prison building system on which they can capitalise. Realising what was going on, Jeremy made copies of the documents and his own copious notes.

In his resignation letter Jeremy tells Harold that he intends to expose the truth about his dealings. Jeremy plans to write a book, a satirical novel, and some pamphlets reproducing the campaign's literature and internal letters with his notes. A TV producer also contacts Jeremy and asks him to co-write a television script for an investigative programme. However, just as he begins to edit his material, Jeremy is shaken to receive a letter from Harold's solicitors which contains the following paragraph: 'Our client owns all copyright in all speeches and documents emanating from his campaign against crime, made both in and out of Parliament. This includes all confidential correspondence you may have improperly seen. To prevent you from publishing or broadcasting any of this copyright material whatsoever, we are applying for an injunction and commencing an action for damages against you'.

Jeremy has since been served with an interlocutory injunction obtained *ex parte* and a statement of claim for damages. There is a return date of three days for a hearing to consider whether the injunction should remain in force.

Answer plan

The following issues are to be considered:

- Literary works
- Section 1, 9 and 30 of the CDPA 1988
- Titles
- *Hubbard v Vosper* (1972)
- Fair dealing
- Public interest

Answer

Although the question states that Jeremy has been the subject of proceedings issued against him, Harold's claims to enjoy copyright protection in the campaign materials of the Law Order and Discipline Campaign and in his public writings and utterances are not as firmly grounded as Harold himself might wish. Certainly, he may be entitled to some, but not all, and Jeremy may raise a number of permitted acts or defences which allow him to lawfully use extracts from material produced by Harold.

Firstly, Jeremy should dispute the copyright entitlement to the material. Whilst Harold may be able to claim copyright in some of his writings (such as his articles for newspapers) as literary works under s 1(1) of the CDPA 1988, his solicitors have pressed his claims for copyright protection too far. Harold is unlikely to hold the copyright in the television and cable broadcasts because of s 9(5). Parliamentary copyright and Crown copyright will apply to government publications, so Harold will not be able to sue in his own right (1).

Slogans

It is doubtful whether the slogans on the campaign materials qualify as literary works because they are so short. Firstly, could they qualify as a literary work under s 1 of the CDPA 1988? In *Dicks v Yates* (1881), it was held that titles could not be protected by copyright, reversing the decision that the title 'Trial and Triumph' in *Weldon v Dicks* (1878) was protected as a copyright work, although an action in passing off might be sustained in some cases.

In *University of London Press v University Tutorial Press* (1916), Petersen J held that a literary work was one which afforded either information, instruction or pleasure, although the court stated, 'The word "literary" seems to be used in a sense somewhat similar to the use of the word "literature" in political electioneering literature'. Arguably, Harold's slogans might classify as literature (in the sense that they convey the policies of the campaign) but they may not be substantial enough to obtain protection. In *Exxon v Exxon Insurance* (1982), the court held that copyright could not subsist in a single word, even if labour, skill and energy had been expended to produce it.

The nearest authority is *Francis Day Hunter v Twentieth Century Fox* (1940), a case arising originally from the use of a song lyric – The Man Who Broke the Bank at Monte Carlo – as the title of the defendant's film, where their Lordships could find no ground in copyright 'to prevent the use by respondents of these few obvious words, which are too insubstantial to constitute infringement, especially when used in so different a connection'. In *Sinanide v La Maison Kosmeo* (1928), a banal advertisement was denied copyright protection.

In *Chappell & Co Ltd v DC Thompson & Co* (1935), it was not an infringement to reproduce four lines of a popular song as the chapter heading in a novel because it was not a substantial part and the court could see no loss to the plaintiff. There may be an artistic copyright, as artistic works under s 4(1), but this will depend on the use to which Jeremy puts them.

Letters

Private letters are protected by copyright. A letter, though merely a business one, is a literary work (*British Oxygen Co Ltd v Ltd v Liquid Air Ltd* (1925); *Tett Bross Ltd v Drake and Gorham Ltd* (1934)), belonging to the writer rather than the receiver of the letter. This could be a defence available to Jeremy against any claims brought by Harold for copyright in Grout's letters, since Harold would not be their author for the purposes of s 9 of the CDPA 1988. Grout Corporation would have to be joined to the proceedings. Merely receiving letter does not confer a licence on the recipient to reproduce it (*Macmillan & Co v Dent* (1907)). The question states that the letters were internal correspondence. If they were not of a confidential nature Jeremy could communicate their contents but not publish them (*Macmillan & Co v Dent* (1907)).

Permitted acts

Jeremy is likely to be able to claim permitted acts of criticism, review and news reporting as well as the defence of fair dealing. In *Hubbard v Vosper* (1972), the Court of Appeal held that a claim for copyright in a letter as a literary work would not be upheld in every instance. It is likely that its use by Jeremy will fall within fair dealing. Fair dealing is a question of fact; it covers not only criticism of the literary style of an author but also the doctrines or view expounded. Fair dealing could extend not only to published works but also to unpublished ones where they had been widely circulated. In *Hubbard v Vosper*, the defendant published confidential letters but it was in the interest of the public for the material to be reproduced in a book by the defendant. Lord Denning stated, 'We never restrain a defendant in a libel action who says he is going to justify. So in a copyright action, we ought not to restrain a defendant who has a reasonable defence of fair dealing'. Lord Denning gave the example of a report produced for shareholders; it could be reproduced by a newspaper for the purposes of reporting, which is analogous to the reports from the Grout Corporation.

Dillon LJ further stated that the fact that a defendant reproduced every single word of a work criticised or reviewed does not in itself preclude a defendant from relying on the defence under s 6(2) of the Copyright Act 1956. Thus, Jeremy could quote the various slogans even in the unlikely event of them constituting literary works and might also quote the letter and circulars.

In *Frazer v Evans* (1969), the court refused an injunction to restrain the publication of extracts from a report in a newspaper. The court held that it would not restrain publication, even if defamatory, where the defendants stated they would claim justification and fair comment, or where an article reproduced a short extract for which the defendants claimed fair dealing. The refusal to suppress free speech was an argument considered in *Kennard v Lewis* (1983). Kennard sought an injunction to protect his copyright in materials he had produced in support of the Campaign for Nuclear Disarmament (CND). Lewis had brought out a leaflet attacking the Campaign for Nuclear Disarmament, which was obviously based on the material produced by the plaintiffs. The court refused the injunction, holding that because of the heightened political controversy then surrounding the merits of unilateral nuclear disarmament it was wrong to curtail free discussion and debate on the issue. The interests of free speech will not succeed simply on being asserted – the court will examine the conduct of the parties. In *Associated Newspapers Group plc v News Group Newspapers Ltd* (1986), an interim injunction was granted to prevent *The Sun* newspaper from copying extracts from private correspondence between the Duke and Duchess of Windsor which was being printed on a daily basis by the *Daily Mail*, which enjoyed a limited right to produce them. *The Sun* had reproduced the letters not for the purposes of criticism or review, but simply to attract readers. An important issue in many cases has been whether an alleged fair dealing is in commercial competition with the plaintiff (eg *Johnstone v Bernard Jones Publications Ltd* (1938) and *Moorhouse v University of New South Wales* (1976)). Here whilst Jeremy might be expected to obtain royalties from his book and payment by the television company, he would not be in direct commercial competition with Harold and his campaign, which is political rather than commercial in nature.

The courts have also considered public policy and the wider public interest in addition to free speech when determining whether injunctive relief is granted. If the court considers that Harold is deceiving the public, this may be a ground to refuse an injunction. In *Slingsby v Bradford Patent Truck and Trolley Co* (1905), a plaintiff was denied copyright protection in a brochure where he falsely claimed ownership in certain patents.

A public interest defence might be raised by Jeremy as a further ground to resist the injunction. Originally in *Beloff v Pressdram* (1973), it was clear that this could only be raised where serious threats to the country or the public were concerned, but the defence was extended in *Lion Laboratories v Evans* (1984). In order to obtain an injunction, the plaintiff had to show more than just an arguable case that the defendant had infringed or was about to infringe copyright. Each case was to be considered on the basis of fairness, justice and common sense in relation to all the facts and law relevant to the case. The public interest defence has been further acknowledged by s 171(3).

These permitted acts will also be applicable to the artistic copyright (if any).

In the application for the injunction, the court will consider the tests in *American Cyanamid v Ethicon* (1975). As in *Hubbard v Vosper*, the court may take the view that a party that comes to court for an equitable remedy such as an injunction must come with clean hands. In the circumstances, Jeremy should be advised to strongly resist the injunction as he has a good case against it and is likely to succeed in the improbable event that the matter proceeds to trial.

Note

1 Section 45(2) of the CDPA 1988 provides that copyright is not infringed by anything done for the purposes of reporting parliamentary or judicial proceedings provided that the work copied is not itself a published report.

Question 17

Brian is the author of a book 'Winter Of Discontent: The Last Days Of Richard III', a guide to historical sites associated with Richard III. After publication Brian discovers that Rhona is putting on a Richard III coach tour. Richard III enthusiasts are driven around the sites featured in the book, guided by Rhona. Brian is appalled by reports he hears of the tour. Apparently, at certain points on the tour, Rhona dresses up in 15th century costume, affects a limp and a hunchback and speaks in a metallic voice reminiscent of a Dalek. Although Brian does not know the precise details of the content of the talk that Rhona gives on the tour, he feels that his copyright is being infringed and the whole subject is being vulgarised. He also discovers that the owners of one of the sites on the tour, Moldebury Castle, have photocopied three pages from his book with the help of a local printing firm, Trewcopy Printers, and are distributing it to tourists. Brian approaches his solicitor, who has no knowledge of copyright. The solicitor approaches you for an opinion. Advise Brian on the merits of a claim.

Answer plan

A question which involves an examination in the case of Rhona of the potentially wide range of acts which might constitute infringement of Brian's copyright in his book against the permitted acts which allow for limited copying. The question also raises issues of both primary and secondary infringement.

The issues to be considered are:

- Parts I, II and III of the CDPA 1988
- Literary works
- Infringement
- Proof of copying
- Fair dealing
- Secondary infringement and knowledge
- Permitted acts – s 59 of the CDPA 1988
- Remedies

Answer

Brian is unlikely to succeed in suing Rhona for copyright infringement unless he can prove marked similarities between his book and the content of her tour, indicating copying or that what is being copied is substantial. However, he will have a case against Moldebury Castle and liability may well attach to Trewcopy.

As a qualifying author of a book, Brian will enjoy the copyright in an original literary work under s 1(1)(a) of the CDPA 1988 which subsists in original literary works. Under the Act, a literary work consists of words which are written spoken or sung. Any illustrations may be protected as artistic works under s 4 of the CDPA 1988.

Brian's claim for infringement against Rhona will be based upon s 19 of the CDPA 1988 which makes it an infringement to perform a substantial part of a copyright work in public. Clearly, a guided tour could amount to the performance of a work if Rhona quotes or recites material directly from Brian's book or from memory. It is an infringing act to make an unauthorised adaptation under s 21 and it is specifically an infringement to turn a dramatic work into a non-dramatic work and *vice versa* under s 21(3)(a)(ii) of the CDPA 1988. There is no need for an adaptation to be recorded in material form to constitute a primary infringement of the original work (s 21(2)). Even an unconscious recollection may amount to an infringement (*Francis Day Hunter v Bron* (1963)). Under s 16(1), Brian could argue that there is an infringement if his book is turned into a dramatic work without his licence or that there has been an unauthorised adaptation of his work. Copyright in a book can be infringed where an undue amount of material is used, even if the language is different or the order of material is different or scrambled (*Chatterton v Cave* (1878); *Elanco Products Ltd v Mandops (Agrochemical Specialists) Ltd* (1980)).

If Rhona has independently created her work with no reference to Brian's book, there will be no causal connection and thus no actionable infringement (*Billhofer Maschinenfabrik GmbH v TH Dixon & Co Ltd* (1990)). Brian cannot prevent Rhona from producing a work relating to Richard III as copyright does not confer a monopoly in subjects. There is no copyright in a general idea which underlies the basis of a literary work (ie sites and localities relating to Richard III) *Green v New Zealand Broadcasting Company* (1989).

Nor can there be a monopoly in historical incidents. In *Harman Pictures NV v Osborne* (1967), the works were a book and a screenplay for a cinema film both concerning the charge of the Light Brigade. The court took the view that the essential issue was whether a work was original in that skill and labour were applied. An author was held to infringe where 'instead of searching into common sources and obtaining your subject matter from thence, you avail yourself of the labour of your predecessor, adopt his arrangements and questions or adopt them with a colourable variation, it is an illegitimate use'.

In *Ravenscroft v Herbert* (1980), the court considered infringement of a non-fiction work by reproduction as a fictional work. The court will consider the volume of material taken in terms of quality rather than quantity. It will look at how much of a qualifying work is matter which is the subject of copyright protection and what is not, and the *animus furandi* of the defendant – the intention of the defendant to take for the purpose of saving time and labour – and whether the works are in competition.

In deciding whether there has been copying, the court will compare the two works (*Francis Day Hunter v Bron*). The burden of proof will initially be upon Brian to show similarities between his book and the words spoken by Rhona on her tour. If similarities can be shown, the onus then falls upon the defendant to explain or account for the similarities. If an author cannot provide a plausible explanation, then the court will infer that there has been infringement (*Corelli v Gray* (1913)).

The key question is thus likely to be whether Rhona has made use of Brian's book other than as an inspiration. In *Pike v Nicholas* (1869), the defendant was led by the plaintiff's book to certain historical sources which he copied (although denying it strongly in court). However, merely using common sources to propound the same theory as the plaintiff (the alleged descent of the English nation from the ancient Britons) was not an infringement and a certain similarity could be expected because of the use of common sources.

In *Moffat and Paige Ltd v George Gill and Sons Ltd* (1901), the use of non-copyright sources to produce rival texts on Shakespeare's *As You Like It* was considered. It was held that authors may use all common sources of information and that it was a legitimate use of a copyright work to take it as a guide to the common sources. A copyright text could also be legitimately used to test the completeness of a work, having regard to the common sources of knowledge. Crucial was whether the second author had simply adopted the work of another as opposed to consulting the earlier sources.

Accordingly, if Rhona has used Brian's guide as a source of information to conduct her own research and she has employed effort and skill in examining the original sources, she will be covered. If she has bestowed no research of her own or used sufficient effort in composing the content of her talks to the audience but relied on a substantial amount of Brian's work, she will have infringed copyright. However, it may be necessary to examine the text even if she has copied an unoriginal source from Brian's book; the court may not make a finding of infringement against her, following the approach in *Warwick Film Productions v Eisinger* (1969).

The vulgarisation of Richard III of which Brian complains might well be evidence against a conclusion of copying in showing a material difference between Brian's book and her talk, since it will be evidence of independent labour and effort having been applied in the creation of the work, conferring originality upon it.

If there are unique parts to Brian's book which Rhona quotes, she may be able to claim fair dealing as an act permitted by s 30. This will be possible provided she gives sufficient acknowledgment as required under ss 30 and 178 as to the title of the book and to its author, and the quotation is for the legitimate purposes of criticism or review. By undertaking sufficient criticism or review, Rhona will effectively be employing sufficient labour, effort, and skill to confer originality of her own. Alternatively, Rhona might claim the benefit of the permitted act exception under s 59 of the CDPA 1988, allowing the reading or recitation in public of a reasonable amount of copyright text without infringing.

Owners of Moldebury Castle

The owners of Moldebury Castle are likely to have infringed Brian's literary copyright by reproducing two pages from the book. There may also be an arguable infringement of the typeface and typographical composition, protected under s 1(1)(c) as defined by s 8. Copying will be a primary infringement, contrary to the exclusive rights enjoyed by Brian under s 16(1) in terms of copying a substantial part under s 16(3). Copyright protects quality not quantity and a court will consider the value of the part appropriated and its relation to the work as a whole. Even a small amount of text being reproduced is capable of being a substantial part if it is of value in terms of the whole. This will be a question of fact and degree.

Alternatively, as Moldebury Castle simply reproduce without any acknowledgment of Brian's authorship or without any attempt at criticism or review, they will be liable for authorising reproduction contrary to s 16(2). Reproduction by photocopier will amount to making an infringing copy in its most blatant form (*Moorhouse v University of New South Wales* (1976)). The issue of copies to visitors of Moldebury Castle will be an infringement of exclusive rights of issuing copies to the public (s 18).

Trewcopy Printers

Trewcopy may be subject to proceedings for secondary infringement under ss 22–26 of the CDPA 1988 and may be joined as defendants to the action. They will be liable for possessing or dealing an infringing copy or further or alternatively by providing the means for making an infringing copy. Since, an essential element of a claim is knowledge, it will be necessary to show that Trewcopy knew or should have known on reasonable grounds that reproduction of the pages from Brian's book was unlawful. In *R v Kyslant* (1934), it was held that having knowledge could include 'shutting one's eyes to the obvious'. Indeed, it would only be necessary for Brian's solicitor to write to Trewcopy to impart the necessary degree of knowledge upon them. The directors of Trewcopy may find themselves individually liable in the action. In *Besson (AP) Ltd v Fulleon Ltd* (1986), it was held that the director of a small company can be rendered personally liable for secondary infringement by the actual ordering or physical performance of the copying.

The appropriate remedy for Brian will be to apply for an interlocutory injunction to restrain the photocopying by Moldebury Castle and Trewcopy. Actual damages could be hard to quantify. The court will apply the principles enunciated in *American Cyanamid v Ethicon* (1975). If Moldebury Castle and Trewcopy are simply restrained from photocopying extracts from Brian's book, they will be able to continue the legitimate sides of their business so the balance of convenience lies with granting the injunction.

Question 18

Discuss the protection of design rights in UK law before and since the enactment of ss 51 and 52 of the Copyright Designs and Patents Act 1988.

Answer plan

A question which requires a knowledge of the background to ss 51 and 52 of the Registered Designs Act 1949.

The issues to be considered are:

- Sections 51 and 52 of the CDPA 1988
- Copyright in technical drawings
- Section 213 of the CDPA 1988

Answer

Sections 51 and 52 of the CDPA 1988 affect the position of design documents and models and, together with the creation of an unregistered design right, have made a substantial change to design protection in the UK.

Originally, the Registered Designs Act 1949 provided protection for designs which have 'eye appeal'. These are designs which fall within the definition of s 1(3) of the RDA 1949 as being 'features of shape, configuration, pattern or ornament applied to an article by any industrial process, being features which in the finished article appeal to and are judged solely by the eye'. The eye is that of the person to whom the design is directed, frequently the potential purchaser, and 'the appeal is that created by the distinctiveness or shape, pattern or ornament calculated to influence the customer's choice' (*Interlego v Tyco Industries Inc* (1988)).

The design right thus created is a property right owned by the person who is its author, the person who created the work (s 2(1)), the creator being the author (s 2(3)). Under the Registered Design Act 1949, the period of protection was originally 15 years, since extended in the case of new designs to a maximum of 25 years under s 269(2) of the CDPA 1988. In order to enjoy industrial design right protection, it is a requirement that the design must be new (akin to novelty under patent law, to which the area is sometimes compared).

The registered proprietor of the design has the exclusive right to make, deal in, and import for commercial purposes articles for which the design is registered. Infringement is analogous to copyright in the question of whether there has been a substantial infringement. However, under the previous law, s 10 of the Copyright Act 1956 provided that a design lost copyright protection if it was either registered under the RDA 1949 or was multiplied by an industrial process more than 50 times.

A problem with registered design protection soon emerged, however. Delays in the registration procedure meant that designers were unable to restrain pirate copying, particularly in the Far East. Countering this problem led to the Design Copyright Act 1968 which conferred unregistered marketed designs with a protection lasting 15 years. The Design Copyright Act 1968 amended s 10 of the Copyright Act 1956 so that copyright was not lost in a work involving a registerable design, but merely limited to 15 years after industrial application and marketing of a 'corresponding design'.

Contemporaneously, it was recognised that functional designs – lacking eye appeal – could be protected from copying through copyright if the design subsisted in the form of design drawings or other original artistic works. Where a design was not registerable, copyright in design drawings or plans could be used to prevent unauthorised reproduction of the article concerned (*Dorling v Honnor Marine* (1965)). This was because reproduction of an artistic work was defined to include the conversion into three-dimensional form of the artistic work, a two-dimensional work and *vice versa* (s 48(1) of the Copyright Act 1956). In order to infringe the defendant's copyright, the three-dimensional object had to be recognisable by a non-expert as a reproduction of a two-dimensional artistic work in which copyright was claimed (s 9(8) of the Copyright Act 1956). For example, in *Antocks Lairn v Bloohn* (1972), the defendants infringed copyright in the designs for chairs by making three-dimensional chairs with slight variations. The overall effect was so similar, however, that a claim for infringement of copyright in the drawings was upheld.

The effect was that copyright protection lasted for the whole of the author's life plus 50 years. It did, however, depend on the creation and existence of an original artistic work during the design process. Thus technical drawings were protected irrespective of artistic merit. The protection conferred was substantial. For example, even washers for nuts and bolts could enjoy a full copyright protection for the life of the author plus 50 years (*British Northrop Ltd v Texteam Blackburn Ltd* (1974)). The decisions in *Dorling v Honnor Marine* (1965) (*per* Cross J) where parts for building a boat were an infringement of plans and photographs and *Amp Inc v Utilix* (1972) confirmed that drawings for designs which were unregistrable under s 1(3) of the RDA 1949 enjoyed full copyright protection. The floodgates of copyright litigation were opened and copyright, which the courts have always maintained is not a complete monopoly, could be seen to be threatening to produce a monopoly in ordinary industrial shapes.

In *Hoover v Hulme* (1982), Whitford J decided that industrial application and marketing also limited copyright in a non-registerable design to 15 years. This was subsequently overruled by the Court of Appeal in *British Leyland v Armstrong Patents* (1986). A temptation obviously lay to unscrupulous plaintiffs who could prove infringement in copyright, to obtain orders for delivering up infringing copies, with a view to securing as great a market share as possible and closing down commercial rivals. The position was criticised by the House of Lords in *British Leyland Motor Corp v Armstrong Patents Co* (1986). The Berne Convention on copyright protection left it open to Member States who were signatories to protect industrial designs in the method they best saw fit, so Parliament used the opportunity of the passage of the 1988 Act to restrict the scope for copyright protection.

Section 51 of the CDPA 1988 provides that it is not an infringement of any copyright in a design document or a model recording or embodying a design for anything other than an artistic work or a typeface to either make an article to the design, or to copy an article made to the design. The section removes copyright protection from the design of an article's shape or configuration, except where the article is: (i) an artistic work in its own right, enjoying copyright under the Berne Convention, or (ii) a typeface.

Under the transitional provisions, Schedule 1, para 19 suspends for 10 years after commencement the operation of s 51 in relation to designs recorded in a design document or embodied in an article prior to commencement. During the last five of those 10 years, licences will be available as of right to carry out the acts under s 51. Thus, some copyright protection is preserved.

A design document under s 51(3) is merely a record of a design and can be in two or three dimensions – not necessarily a drawing. Models, sculptures and computer programs could be the original design document. Copyright protection lost by virtue of s 51 is mitigated by the creation of the unregistered design right under s 213, a new development which goes further than copyright in that no 'work' is actually required, although the design must be recorded in a design document under s 263. To copy such a design is not an infringement of copyright but it may be an infringement of an unregistered design right under ss 226 and 227. Once infringement of copyright does not apply design rights under s 236 may operate.

A design must fall within s 213(2) of the CDPA 1988, which defines the term 'design' as encompassing the 'design of any aspect of the shape or configuration (whether external or internal) of the whole article or part of it'. Again, a design must have 'eye appeal'. Certain similarities may be found with copyright in that the design under s 213 must be an original one, in the sense that it originates with the designer rather than being a copy. The further qualifications are that the design must be recorded in a design document after 1 August 1989 and must qualify for protection under the provisions of s 213(5) of the CDPA 1988.

Section 52 of the CDPA 1988 succeeds s 10 of the Copyright Act 1956, providing that where an artistic work has been exploited by or with permission of the copyright owner, by making an article through an industrial process, protection is limited to 25 years (s 52(1) and (2)) from the end of the calendar year in which the articles are first marketed. Under s 52, the item can be marketed in the UK or elsewhere. Films are specifically excluded under s 52(6)(a). Sections 51 and 52 cover 'articles' but the term is left undefined. In *Re Concrete Ltd* (1940), it was held that a building could not be an article (*per* Morton J). Where the article designed is itself an artistic work, copyright in a design document or model is retained. It may be necessary to rely on copyright in a preparatory design document rather than in a finished work because the originality may reside, and hence copyright subsist, at the earliest design stage. Industrial application may, however, shorten the copyright protection for an artistic work under s 52 to 25 years.

Under Regulation 2 of the Copyright (Industrial Process and Excluded Articles) (No 2) Order 1989, an industrial process is one which involves the production of more than 50 articles which do not form part of a set. This follows the approach in the Copyright (Industrial Designs) Rules 1957 which also defined an industrial process as one involving the mass production of more than 50 items. Copyright protection is thus restrained for things not included within the definition of 'article' such as sculptures (other than casts or models to by multiplied by an industrial process) (reg 3(1)(a)); wall plaques, medals and medallions (reg 3(1)(b)) and a wide range of printed literary and artistic material including post cards, calendars, maps and similar items (reg 3(1)(b)).

Question 19

Godfrey manufacturers parts for agricultural machinery. He sees a tractor made by Montague Ltd including a decorative horn based on a statue of the Goddess Demeter. He also copies a horn and various internal parts from a model he has seen. He also sees various industrial parts for the machinery and makes sketches or parts of the designs. He passes some to Conrad, who runs a spare part business and who makes copies of the parts for sale. On discovering what is happening Montague Ltd, the manufacturers, threaten to bring proceedings against Godfrey and Conrad. Advise them as to their position.

Answer plan

Montague Ltd are likely to be the owners of the design rights or copyright of each of the items which Godfrey has copied or part-copied. Their ownership is likely to have arisen by virtue of a contract of employment or a commission whereby the original designer drew up the initial designs. Much will depend upon the date that the designs were created.

The issues to be considered are:

- Section 4 of the CDPA 1988
- Section 51 and 52 of the CDPA 1988
- Design right – s 213 of the CDPA 1988
- Primary infringement
- Secondary infringement
- Defences
- Passing off

Answer

The horn for the tractor

The extent of copying by Godfrey will be the first question to determine in the case of the statue/horn. If Godfrey has copied a substantial part, it may potentially be an infringement of copyright in the design, unless he can take advantage of the permitted acts provided by ss 51 and 52 in Part III of the CDPA 1988, specific to the copying of industrial articles.

Section 4 confers protection on sculptures and works of artistic craftsmanship. If the case proceeds, the court will first have to determine whether the statute is an artistic work or a work of artistic craftsmanship. Of crucial importance will be the intention of the designer at the time the horn was created (*Hensher v Restawhile Upholstery* (1976)). Under ss 51 and 52 of the CDPA 1988, the making of an article to a design (or copying an article to the design) does not infringe copyright in a design document or model embodying a design, where that design document or model is for anything other than an artistic work. Under s 51(3), a design is defined as the design of any aspect of the shape or configuration (whether internal or external) of the whole or part of an article, other than surface decoration. Section 51 only applies where it has already been established that a substantial part of a design document or model has been reproduced. It is not an infringement to make a drawing from the article, even if the drawing is identical to the underlying design document.

On one analysis, it is possible that it will be a sculpture under s 4(1) of the CDPA 1988 and qualify as an artistic work. Against this it is likely to be argued that the statue is an article produced by an industrial process. (Subsection 1 uses the phrase 'other than as an artistic work'.) If protected as an artistic work, copyright infringement is likely to arise if he goes ahead with copying a substantial part of the model. As a result, Godfrey will be able to take the functional shape of the horn but not the surface decoration, and drawing the decoration will be an infringement. Under s 236, if copyright subsists in a work which consists of or includes a design, it does not affect the infringement.

Section 52 of the CDPA 1988 may come into play because of the industrial application. If (as seems likely) more than 50 articles have been made, the copyright period may be shortened to 25 years from the end of the year in which the industrially produced articles were first marketed, whether in the UK or elsewhere. The date on which this took place will therefore be an important factor in determining any liability. However, the effect of ss 51 and 52 do not erode all Montague Ltd's potential rights, and protection may arise from the unregistered design right under s 213 of the CDPA 1988.

Design right

To qualify for protection, Montague Ltd's design must fulfil the requirements of s 213(2) of the CDPA 1988. The design must have been recorded in a design document dated after 1 August 1989 and be original, not be subject to exclusion, and qualify for protection under s 213(5). It is possible that the work may be protected by an original design right under s 213 of the CDPA 1988, although if the designs were made before the qualifying date, Montague Ltd will not be allowed to bring them within the scope of unregistered design protection (s 213(7)).

If the designs for the parts qualify for protection and the design right has not expired, Montague Ltd will be able to take advantage of the statutory presumption in favour of the plaintiff under s 228(4). Where an article was made to a design in which the design right subsists or has subsisted, the court will act on the presumption that the article was made at a time when the right subsisted unless the contrary can be proved. This will be difficult for Godfrey and Conrad to rebut. To fulfil the requirement of originality, two requirements must be met (*C&H Engineering v Klucznic* (1992)). The two aspects of originality are that the design must not be commonplace in the field of design in question (s 213(4)) and it must originate with the designer, and not have been copied. (Originality seems to impose a requirement equivalent to novelty.) In *C & H Engineering v Klucznic* (1992), the requirement to establish copying before infringement can be proved is similar to copyright but the test of infringement is different. The court must decide whether the alleged infringing article is made exactly or substantially to the design. The court will view similarity in terms of what attracts the eye – the eyes of the person to whom the design is addressed. The test for infringement requires the alleged infringing article or articles to be compared with the design. Thereafter an overall similarity must be found. Section 226 of the CDPA 1988 requires a plaintiff establish copying or copying a substantial part.

Under s 226(1) of the CDPA 1988, Montague Ltd have the exclusive right of reproducing the design by making articles to that design. As owners of the design, Montague Ltd have an exclusive right to reproduce it for commercial purposes by making articles or design documents. Commercial purposes are defined by s 263(3) as things done with respect to the article to be sold or hired in the course of business. Here Godfrey's purpose with regard to the parts he makes is purely commercial and copying will therefore amount to primary infringement as it is done without licence. Equally, Montague Ltd will have an exclusive right to reproduce the design document recording the design for the purpose of enabling articles to be made.

To avoid potential liability under s 213(3) CDPA 1988, the design right is subject to four exclusions. First, the design does not subsist in a principle of construction (s 213(i)(a)). Secondly, s 213(b)(i) provides the 'must fit' exception where the article has features which enable it to be connected to, placed in, around or against another article so that either may perform its function. Thirdly, s 213(3)(b)(ii) excepts features which are dependent upon the appearance of another article of which the article in question is intended by the designer to form an integral part. Fourthly, s 213(3)(c) excludes surface decoration. If Godfrey is engaged in making spare parts for repairs, his work is likely to fall into these exceptions. A number of potential defences exist to an action based upon the unregistered design right.

Copying by Godfrey could amount to primary infringement of the designs. As Godfrey has made drawings for the purpose of making articles, the reproduction by way of the drawings will be an infringement of the rights, as will passing on copies to Conrad who intends to make spares himself.

Conrad will be liable for secondary infringement as regards the articles in his possession under s 228 since he has infringing items in his possession for commercial purposes. Unless any of the defences apply, Godfrey and Conrad should be advised to settle the proceedings with Montague Ltd or enter a licensing agreement. Since knowledge is an element of secondary infringement, Conrad might be able to claim a defence if he had no reason to believe the articles were infringing.

If the copying by Godfrey falls within the last five years of the unregistered design right which Montague Ltd may enjoy, he may be able to claim a licence as of right. Under s 239, Godfrey can take out a licence on terms to be agreed with Montague Ltd or, if no licensing agreement is reached, subject to terms imposed by the Comptroller.

If an action is successfully brought by Montague Ltd, damages or an account of profits may be claimed. A provision also exists for additional damages under s 229(3), drafted in the same language as s 97(3) of the CDPA 1988 for damages for copyright.

Passing off

It is also possible that an action may lie in passing off, if Montague Ltd can prove that the 'get up' is used in the parts. In *Drayton Controls v Honeywell Control Systems* (1992), it was accepted that the appearance of a valve, including the material and colouration, could all be relevant, applying *Reckitt & Coleman v Borden Inc* (1990). It is possible for shapes and colours to be protected by way of passing off (*William Edge & Sons Ltd v William Niccolls & Sons Ltd* (1911)). However, an action in passing off is often unpredictable and it will be necessary to show that Montague Ltd have good will in the appearance of goods. Unless their 'get up' is extremely distinctive and well-known a claim is unlikely to succeed.

Question 20

Glyn and Max are lecturers at the Welsh studies department of Ruthven University, North Wales. They jointly bring out a new version of *The Mabinogion*, a collection of 11 medieval Welsh stories dating from the 14th century in Welsh and English. They add very little information themselves.

The new dual language version of *The Mabinogion* is published and sells very well. However, Glyn and Max are disturbed by the interest shown by Merton Media Corporation, a multinational broadcasting corporation which Glyn and Max believe to be flooding Wales with programmes of dubious cultural merit. Glyn and Max have rebuffed approaches from Merton Media Ltd but seek advice as to their position, particularly in relation to the following suggestions that Merton Media have put forward in connection with their translation of *The Mabinogion*.

- Use of four-line extracts from their translation in a series of advertisements for Merton Media Corporation in Welsh newspapers.
- An adaptation of stories from their translation in a children's programme put out on Merton Media Corporation's children's channel.
- Broadcasting readings from their translation in coverage of the local Eisteddfod's cultural celebration to be filmed on a live broadcast by Merton Media Corporation.

Advise Glyn and Max as to their position. They are also concerned that Ruthven University, who are receiving sponsorship from Merton Media Corporation, may try to claim the benefit of their work.

Answer plan

A question that covers a range of material including the use of non-copyright sources, translations, adaptations and permitted acts.

The issues to be considered are:

- Section 1(1) of the CDPA 1988
- Section 3(1) of the CDPA 1988

- Section 21 of the CDPA 1988
- Section 31 of the CDPA 1988
- Sections 59(1) and 59(2) of the CDPA 1988
- *Stephenson, Jordan and Harrison Ltd v Macdonald and Evans* (1952)
- *Byrne v Statist* (1914)

Answer

Although *The Mabinogion* is not a copyright work, Glyn and Max will have obtained a copyright in their dual language version as an original literary work by virtue of the effort and skill they have applied in producing a translation. Their translation will be a protected original literary work (*Byrne v Statist* (1914)), although they will not be able to claim a copyright in the original sources or subject matter (*Pike v Nicholas* (1869)). Even if their version contains no new facts or notions, it will undoubtedly be subject to copyright (*Jarrold v Houlston* (1857)).

Whether Max and Glyn may claim copyright in their work as a compilation in terms of the arrangement of material is less clear. It is not possible to pinpoint 'the precise amount of the knowledge, labour, judgment or literary skill or taste which the author of any book or other compilation must bestow upon its composition in order to acquire copyright in it ...', *per* Lord Atkinson in *Macmillan & Co Ltd v K & J Cooper* (1923). It is unlikely that they will be able claim rights in their version of *The Mabinogion* as a compilation under s 3(1) of the CDPA 1988 simply in the terms of the arrangement of the material. This is because they did not select the arrangement of the stories, unless they have undertaken radical amendments and alterations in the selection of material (or that it is protectable as such as a dual translation). However, as skill, labour and effort have been expended, copyright in the work will vest with them and it will *prima facie* be an infringement to take a substantial amount of material without their joint permission.

Glyn and Max will hold the copyright as joint authors under s 10 if their work has been a joint effort and creation, and their individual efforts are indistinguishable. The copyright will be owned between them as tenants in common.

Use of four line extracts from their translation in a series of advertisements for Merton Media Corporation in Welsh newspapers

It will be for the court to decide whether four lines could be a substantial amount of the work. In *Chappell v Thompson* (1928–35), four lines from a popular song used in the heading of a chapter of a story were held not to infringe the copyright in the song, the court taking the view that the lines were not of any particular worth. However, in *Kipling v Genatosan Ltd* (1923–28), four lines from the poem *'If'* were held to be an infringement of the famous poem. Arguably the lines were of greater value.

The court will take account of a variety of factors, the most important being whether the amount taken is substantial. Section 16(2) of the CDPA 1988 requires a substantial part to be taken for there to be an infringement. Advertising purposes do not fall into the definition of fair dealing and it will therefore depend on whether the court considers a substantial amount has been taken. This in turn will depend in part on how many extracts are taken.

Adaptation

Under older authorities, to make an abridgement or adaptation of a work was not considered an infringement (*Bell v Walker & Debrett* (1785)). However, the position is now subject to s 21 of the CDPA 1988 which provides that making an adaptation of a work is a restricted act. Under s 21(3), an adaptation is taken to include: (i) a translation; (ii) a version of a literary work which is converted into a dramatic one or *vice versa*; or (iii) a version of a work in which the story or action is conveyed wholly or mainly by pictures in a form suitable for reproduction in a book, newspaper, magazine or other periodical. Acts restricted by ss 17–20 of the CDPA 1988 in relation to an adaptation are also restricted acts in relation to the copyright of a literary, dramatic or musical work.

The CDPA 1988 therefore contains a range of provisions which may be interpreted broadly on Glyn and Max's behalf to prevent an adaptation of their version of *The Mabinogion* by Merton Media Corporation. However, they will be powerless to stop Merton Media Corporation going to the original source and making whatever use they wish of it.

Inclusion in Eisteddfod Broadcasting

It is unlikely that Max and Glyn will be in any position to restrain the broadcasting of their work at the Eisteddfod.

Merton Media Corporation might be able to claim the benefit of the fair dealing permitted act exception under s 30 for the purposes of news reporting. Alternatively, Merton Media Corporation might claim the benefit of s 31 of the CDPA 1988, the permitted act defence of incidental inclusion. Formerly, the law could impose liability for infringement where a party accidentally recorded part of a copyright work in the course of making another work. In *Hawkes v Paramount Films* (1934), 28 bars of the tune 'Colonel Bogey' were sufficient to justify an injunction for infringement when they were recorded in the course of a newsreel film recording the opening of a school, an event accompanied by a boys' band playing the tune. The position would now be different by virtue of s 31(1), which provides that the incidental inclusion of a copyright work is not an infringement.

Merton Media Corporation might also take advantage of the combined effects of s 59(1) and (2) of the CDPA 1988. Section 59(1) provides that the reading or recitation in public of a reasonable amount of a work does not infringe copyright. Section 59(2) provides that copyright in a work is not infringed by the making of a sound recording or the broadcasting or inclusion in a cable service of a work which by virtue of s 59(1) does not infringe copyright, providing that the broadcast 'consists mainly of material in relation to which it is not necessary to rely on the subsection'. Therefore, if the bulk of the material broadcast is not copyright, or permission has been granted, the inclusion of an extract of Glyn and Max's work will be not be an actionable infringement.

Ownership

The ownership of the translation will be determined with reference to the contracts of employment that Glyn and Max have with Ruthven University. Under s 11(2) of the CDPA 1988, where a literary, dramatic, musical or artistic work is made by an employee in the course of employment, his employer is the first owner of any copyright in the work subject to any agreement to the contrary. However, not every case results in the employer being able to claim copyright in a work produced by an employee. Clauses of their contracts may therefore be determinative but, if Glyn and Max have done the work in their spare time and not as part of their duties, then it is unlikely that Ruthven University will be able to sustain a claim. Even if Ruthven University can claim some copyright, they may not be entitled to all. In *Stephenson, Jordan and Harrison Ltd v Macdonald and Evans* (1952), the defendant produced a book containing notes made whilst in the course of employment and the text of three lectures given by the employee during his period of employment. The Court of Appeal held that the employer could claim copyright in the part of the book containing the notes but not in that containing the text of the lectures, since giving lectures was not part of his duties. If the work was made entirely in their own spare time, the court may find that their translation was not made in the course of employment (*Byrne v Statist Co* (1914)).

Chapter 3

Registered Trade Marks

Introduction

Trade mark questions are popular with students because the law involves a relatively straightforward application of the Trade Marks Act 1994. The old registration system – the Part A and Part B registers – are not considered here; effectively trade mark law began afresh on 31 October 1994 when the 1994 Act came into operation. This made radical changes to existing UK trade mark law, putting into effect the provisions of Council Directive 89/104 for the harmonisation of trade mark law throughout the UK.

As yet there has not developed a substantial body of case law for interpreting the 1994 Act, but the courts and the Trade Marks Registry have indicated that they will continue to look to the pre-1994 authorities for determining points of law. As a consequence, students should examine works such as *Kerly on Trade Marks and Trade Names*, (Sweet & Maxwell, 1986) and then search out the references and authorities found therein.

Questions can involve what may be registered as a trade mark and they should be answered in relation to the excluded categories and the provisions of the statute. These are relatively straightforward. More tricky are questions included here which have a procedural slant. Here one has to advise a party on opposition or revocation proceedings involving a mark held by another, and these will throw up all kinds of issues involving practice or procedure, and presumptions in law. Authorities should be read closely to determine whether the judgment is specific to the facts of the case and is not seeking to establish a broad principle. Care should thus be taken in selecting authorities to quote in such questions (the courts themselves having indicated on occasion that in an area where so much turns on the facts of a particular case that it is inadvisable to treat authorities as being of wide application).

More preferable are questions involving similarity between marks, either in essay questions or in questions involving infringement of marks. On simple similarity tests the questions are relatively small; decisions of the Trade Marks Registry are worth consulting in their approach to similarity, as well as those of the higher courts. However, as will be seen, questions which ask about the registration of particular marks can require reference to more obscure authorities which have been decided under the 1938 Act or earlier trade mark legislation. A question on Community Trade Marks is also included in recognition of the growing European influence. Note that many aspects of passing off are relevant to registered trade marks and an understanding of each is vital to successfully answering both.

Checklist

Students should be familiar with the following areas:

- Trade Marks Act 1994
- *The Pianotist* (1906)
- *Wagamama v City Centre Restaurant* (1995)
- *Re Bali Trade Mark* (1969)
- *Smith Hayden's Application* (1946)
- *Re Jellineck* (1946)

Question 21

Outline the major changes achieved by the Trade Marks Act 1994.

Answer plan

A straightforward question requiring direct reference to the TMA 1994.

Answer

The Trade Marks Act 1994 makes radical changes to UK trade mark law and improves the rights of the proprietor of a registered trade mark or his licensee. The Act brings UK trade mark law into line with that of the rest of the European Community, implementing Directive 89/104. The TMA 1994 contains a presumption in favour of registration, and the Registrar no longer enjoys a wide discretion when considering whether to grant or refuse an application, subject to the grounds of refusal in ss 3 and 5. Unlike the TMA 1938, there are no positive requirements that a mark must fulfill other than being capable of graphic representation and of distinguishing goods and services of one undertaking from those of another.

This represents a great extension of what may be registered as a trade mark, s 1(1) specifying any sign which is capable of being represented graphically and capable of distinguishing the goods and services of one undertaking from those of another. The intention was stated in the White Paper: 'No type of sign is automatically excluded from registration ... Depending on the circumstances, therefore, the Trade Marks Office, the national courts or in the last resort the court of justice, will be responsible for determining whether solid colours shades, sign, smell and taste may be trade marks within a box of 8 cm by 8 cm in the application'.

The old system of Part A and B registered under the Trade Marks Act 1938 is abolished. The TMA 1994 allows for the registration of both signs of inherent distinctiveness, such as invented names, and marks which have achieved factual distinctiveness in the market. Geographical names will be more easy to register under the new Act. Under the TMA 1938, it was not possible to register a geographical name, no matter how distinctive, the most infamous case being the refusal by the House of Lords to allow York to be registered for trailers in *Re York Trademark* (1984). It is now possible to register such marks provided there is evidence of distinctiveness.

Restrictions on shapes have now been overturned. Registerability now extends to packaging and three-dimensional signs. Trade mark protection in *Re James* (1886) held that the mark had to be separate from the item marked. In *Re Coca Cola* (1986), the House of Lords refused registration to the distinctive shape of the Coca Cola product. Not every shape will be registerable. However, exceptions listed under s 3(2) include packaging which derives its shape from the goods fashioned, functional shapes and the shapes of packaging giving value to goods.

Colours have long been protected by trade marks and this continues, providing the mark is distinctive. Theoretically, smells and sounds may be registerable, although how this can be achieved by graphic representation is as yet unclear.

New rights to exploit a trade mark have been introduced with the implementation of the TMA 1994. Under s 23, any two or more persons (legal or human) can apply for joint registration of a mark, whereas joint applications were previously limited to partnerships or where both were associated with the products covered.

Section 28(6) of the TMA 1938 prevented trafficking in the mark or character merchandising, where the mark was exploited for commercial gain other than to indicate a connection in the course of trade. The TMA 1994 frees a proprietor to license a trade mark for all the goods and services for which the mark is registered, for a restricted number or for the use in a particular manner or locality. The TMA 1938 avoided use of the word 'license' but instead talked about 'registered users'. Section 28(2) of the TMA 1994 states that a licence is not effective unless in writing and signed by the grantor. Section 25 of the TMA 1994 requires all registerable transactions such as assignments, licences and granting of security interests to be registered for security for the first time under s 24. Collective marks were a requirement of Article a7 *bis* of the Paris Convention and the Community Trade Mark Regulation.

Certification marks are regulated by s 50 and Schedule 2 of the TMA 1994. Certification marks were known under UK law, eg the WOOLMARK. A certification mark for quality indicates that goods and services are certified by the proprietor of the mark in respect of origin, material, mode of manufacture of goods or performance of services, quality, accuracy or other characteristics. The TMA 1994 extends the forms which a certification mark may take, to include shapes, packaging and sensory marks and also services. Existing certification marks are preserved. Section 49 of the TMA 1994 also introduces the collective mark, which differs from certification marks in distinguishing the goods and services of members of an association to which the proprietor of the mark belongs from those of other undertakings. Such marks are registerable under a similar system to that for certification marks, with the exceptions that the absolute grounds of refusal under s 3(1) (geographical names) does not apply.

The mark is protected from unauthorised use which is defined by s 103(2) as including use otherwise than by means of a graphic. Thus, for the first time, oral use of a mark is included, eg catching the trader orally representing a mark as applying to goods or services.

Exclusive rights: infringement

The TMA 1994 extends the proprietor's exclusive rights in two important respects. Under the TMA 1938, the registered proprietor of a trade mark was restricted to preventing the use of a mark in relation to actual goods or services for which the particular mark was registered. An exclusive licensee may also bring proceedings subject to ss 28–31.

Under the TMA 1938, trade mark protection was only possible where goods were of the same description. Where a mark was applied to different category of goods, there was frequently no remedy. The TMA 1994 contains significant changes. Under s 5(3), the Registrar may consider whether an application for registration will have a detrimental effect on the reputation or distinctive character of a well-known mark, even if the proposed registration is for dissimilar goods.

Under s 10(3), a registered proprietor is now able to prevent the unauthorised use of his trade mark in relation to goods or services which are not similar to the proprietor's goods or services, provided the trade mark has a 'reputation' in the UK, and that the unauthorised mark would take unfair advantage of or would be detrimental to the distinct character of the repute of the registered trade mark. The extension in s 10(3)(b) would prevent, for instance, an imitation of a mark used for a soft drink being used on weedkiller, and could protect brand names being extended or expanded into widely different products by deterring other traders from poaching existing good will. The extension under s 10(3) arguably signifies the introduction of the concept of unfair competition into UK law.

However, to date, English courts have been slow to incorporate interpretations from European Community law when considering infringement. In *Wagamama Ltd v City Centre Restaurants plc* (1995), the court rejected the idea that the words in s 10(3), including a likelihood of association, added anything to the concept of infringement in UK law. Laddie J took the view that sometimes Parliament repeated itself or added superfluous words. The view was taken that the TMA 1994 gave domestic effect to the Directive, and that this represented a fresh start and a court was therefore able to distinguish previous rules and approaches to statutory construction. Laddie J took the view that likelihood of association was no more than part of the test of likelihood of confusion.

The TMA 1994 gives a statutory basis for orders which the courts may grant including erasure, removal or obliteration of the mark (s 15(1)(a)), or destruction of the goods where it is not practical to erase the mark. The court can further order the delivery up of the goods to the proprietor.

Section 41(1)(c) of the TMA 1994 permits the registration of a series of trade marks which resemble each other as to their material particulars. There are no longer provisions for express imitations or the right to license. The TMA 1938 was essentially concerned with the public interest and protection from deceptive or misleading trade marks and strictly controlled licensing. The TMA 1994 no longer takes this approach and takes a liberal stance to licensing. The major responsibility now lies with the proprietor of a mark to ensure that the use of the mark by a licensee is not likely to deceive, risking revocation under s 46. Substantive examination by the Registrar no longer occurs, the Registrar limiting his activities to recording details. A licensee may bring proceedings in his own name.

Criminal offenses are introduced by the TMA 1994 following from s 300 of the CDPA 1988 which inserted s 58A into the TMA 1938. Section 92 of the TMA 1994 makes it a criminal offence to apply a sign identical to, or likely to be mistaken for, a registered trade mark to goods, or selling or hiring goods with such a sign or having such goods in possession with a view to sale or hire.

Section 21 of the TMA 1994 introduces into the law for the first time protection against the making of threats other than for the application of a mark to goods or their packaging, the importation of goods and the supply of services.

The White Paper took the view that a proprietor would regulate uncontrolled use of his trade mark from self-interest.

Restrictions contained in the TMA 1938 on assignment have been swept away and s 24 of the TMA 1994 provides that a registered trade mark is transmissible by assignment, testamentary disposition or operation of law in the same way as other personal or moveable property.

Section 24(6) of the TMA 1994 provides that nothing in the Act shall be construed as affecting the assignment or other transmission of an unregistered mark as part of the good will of the business.

Section 56 of the TMA 1994 (implementing Article 6 *bis* of the Paris Convention) provides for the protection of a trade mark that is 'well-known' in the UK, whether or not the trade mark is used in the UK. However, this protection is restricted to preventing registration of a conflicting mark in the case of the same or similar goods and services, where the use is likely to cause confusion.

Section 42 of the TMA 1994 provides that marks shall be registered for an initial period of 10 years instead of seven as under the TMA 1938, with renewal periods of 10 years rather than 14 years, in keeping with the Community system and the Madrid Protocol.

Question 22

Monty and Vera Patriot manufacture a range of moisturising creams and lotions. They wish to register four trade marks under the Trade Marks Act 1994 as follows:

- 'Pure Cream'.
- 'PUAR CREEM' Trade Mark.
- A Sovereign Trade Mark with a Union Jack on it. On the register there is already a similar mark registered by Sovereign Trampoline manufacturers.
- A trade mark consisting of a Belgian flag and Brussel sprout. Monty says that it is a joke aimed at his Belgian friends in the trade but he does use it on business paper occasionally. Advise Monty and Vera as to bars to the registration of the marks.

Answer plan

'Pure Cream' and 'PUAR CREEM' are best dealt with together.

The issues to be considered are:

- Section 1(1) of the TMA 1994
- Sections 3–5 of the TMA 1994
- Lack of distinctiveness
- Bad faith – s 3(6); s 32 of the TMA 1994

Answer

The question involves the issue of registerability of the trade marks applied for by Monty and Vera and the mechanisms of appeal whereby they may challenge a decision of the Trade Mark Registrar. Under the Trades Mark Act 1994, Monty and Vera are entitled to make a joint application as prospective co-owners and under s 22, and they would hold the mark as personal property. Although the Act has a presumption in favour of registration, not all marks may be permitted.

Pure Cream and 'PUAR CREEM'

In order to be a trade mark, the proposed registration must fall within s 1 of the TMA 1994, being any sign capable of being represented graphically which is capable of distinguishing goods or services of one undertaking from those of other undertakings.

Section 1 further states that a trade mark may consist of words, (including personal names), designs, letters, numerals or the shape of goods or their packaging. Both Pure Cream and PUAR CREEM would fall within this definition of words but may not suffice to identify the source and distinguish Monty and Vera's goods from those of other businesses. The concept of a mark being capable of distinguishing was known under the 1938 Register requiring a mark to be capable of distinguishing, arguably a similar test to the TMA 1994 with the addition that marks distinctive in fact will be registerable.

In *Colorcoat Trade Mark* (1990), it was held that the privilege of a monopoly should not be conferred in circumstances where honest men might have to look for a defence. It is right to consider what other traders may wish to do where a mark lacks factual distinctiveness. The requirement of a trade mark is that it must be used to denote the source or origin of the goods or services concerned (*Bismag Ltd v Amblins Chemists Ltd* (1940) which concerned the use of two signs). The mark must be used in the course of trade.

In *Canadian Shredded Wheat Co Ltd v Kellogg Co of Canada Ltd* (1938), Lord Russell stated, 'A word or words, to be really distinctive of a person's goods, must generally speaking be incapable of application to the goods of anyone else'. In *British Sugar plc v James Robertson Ltd* (1996), Jacob J stated that s 1(1) contains a two-part test: it must be a sign and it must be capable of distinguishing. Monty's words are clearly signs but may not be capable of distinguishing. In deciding whether the mark could be capable of distinguishing – the 'Scheme is that if a man tenders for registration a sign of this sort without any evidence of distinctiveness, he cannot have it registered unless he proves it is of distinctive character' (*per* Jacobs, J). This requires the court to consider the mark on its own and whether it is the sort of word 'Which cannot do the job of distinguishing without first educating the public that it is a trade mark'.

Equally applicable are the absolute grounds for refusal of registration contained in s 3(1). Signs which do not fulfill the requirements of s 1(1) and s 3(1)(b) preclude the registration of trade marks which are devoid of distinctive character. A trade mark which is wholly devoid of distinctive character is likely to be descriptive. In the circumstances it seems there is no chance of registering 'Pure Cream'.

It may be that PUAR CREEM may be registerable under the TMA 1994. Invented words have a greater capacity to distinguish since they do not fall foul of the 'devoid of distinctive character' provision of s 3(1)(b). Words that are misspelt are not thereby invented words (*Salt* (1984)). Applying the approach of Jacob J in *British Sugar plc*, above, PUAR is potentially acceptable as a sign consisting of a word mark and could arguably be of a distinctive character as it looks more like a trade mark, being a combination of two misspelt words. In *Williams Ltd's Application* (1917), the work 'chocaroons' combining chocolate and macaroons was refused as it covered a new product, being the applicable name for a product rather than a trade mark. A similar approach was taken in the matter of *SF and O Hallgarton's Application* (1946) for the registration of a trade mark 'Whiskeur' combining liqueur and whisky.

However, the courts have taken a cautious approach with invented words to ensure that they are not an attempt to circumvent the long-standing restrictions on the character or quality of goods. In *TORQ-SET* (1959), Lloyd-Jacob J rejected the proposed name for registration and held that the court or the Registrar is not in any way bound by strict grammatical usage, but that the test relates to the conditions in industry and commerce. If Monty and Vera can establish that the name is distinctive, it will not fall foul of the usage test.

The best known example is *ORWOOLA* (1909) where the mark being a misspelling of 'all wool' was held not to be a distinctive mark adopted to distinguish. The words could be descriptive and, if not made of wool, were thus deceptive and unfit to be a trade mark. A mere meaningless suffix does not make a word registerable. One possibility might be for Monty and Vera to turn it into a slogan.

Sovereign trade mark

The proposed Sovereign trade mark, provided it satisfies the requirements of ss 1 and 3(1) of the TMA 1994, is still likely to fall foul of s 4(1). A trade mark that consists of or contains a representation of the national flag of the United Kingdom (commonly known as the Union Jack) may not be registered if it appears to the Registrar that the use of the trade mark would be misleading or grossly offensive. The burden of proof is on Monty and Vera under s 100 as to use or any particular description of use of a trade mark or of a sign identical to it.

Section 5 grounds are also raised with the existence of a similar trade mark on the register. Sovereign Trampolines have an earlier mark which may be similar, but the goods to which the mark would be applied are not similar. To provide grounds for a refusal of registration, Sovereign Trampolines would have to show that their mark is identical or similar to the proposed registration, and that Monty and Vera's mark would take advantage of or be detrimental to the distinctive character or the repute of Sovereign's mark (s 5(3)). The test of similarity for marks, laid down in *Smith Hayden* (1945), was whether the marks used in the normal manner would be likely to cause confusion.

In *Egg Product Ltd's Application* (1922), it is not the relative rights of the parties, but the interest of the public not to be confused or offended which take precedence. The TMA 1938 used the phrase 'goods of the same description' rather than 'similar goods' used in the TMA 1994, but there seems to be no reason why earlier authorities should not assist. The test for goods of the same description was considered in *Re Jellinek's Application* (1945) with regard being given to the nature and composition of the goods, the respective uses of the articles, and trade channels through which the goods are bought and sold. Here it is remote in the extreme that there could be confusion between purchasers and unusually unobservant persons will be disregarded. This is the only area of vulnerability, although use of the mark by Vera and Monty would again have to be considered.

Belgian sprout mark

The proposed Belgian sprout mark is likely to fail on a number of grounds. Whilst it is possible for a quasi-national emblem to become a trade mark (*Welsh Lady Trade Mark* (1964)), a mark which is applied for in bad faith or with no honest intention to use may not be registered. The provisions as to national flags and emblems equally apply to anything which from a heraldic point of view imitates any such flag, or other emblem, sign or hallmark.

Application may also be refused under s 3(3) of the TMA 1994 where a mark is contrary to public policy or morality. The immorality must be in the mark itself. In *Arthur Fairest Ltd's Application* (1945), a trade mark was rejected on the basis that registration might lead some persons to believe that illegal gambling was in some way authorised by trade mark status. In *Hallelujah Trade Mark* (1976), 'hallelujah' was refused registration for women's clothing. A significant observation of the Registrar was that to be contrary to morality, the use of the mark would '... have to offend the generally accepted mores of the time', and the use of the Registrar's discretion would be warranted if registration would be reasonably likely to offend persons in the community, yet be substantial in number.

In *The Rawhide Case* (1962), Cross J held that the Registrar must act judicially within the TMA 1938. Although the Registrar, in excising his discretion, is not limited to any particular type of consideration, 'he must exercise it on reasonable grounds that are capable of being clearly stated ... A vague feeling of distaste for the applicant or his methods of business cannot justify a refusal to register a mark which satisfies the conditions laid down in the Act'.

The admissions made by Monty infer a lack of *bona fide* intention to use the mark in a trade mark sense and thus call into question his *bona fides* as an applicant. The Registrar has the power to refuse under s 3(6) of the TMA 1994. Section 32(3) requires an application for registration of a trade mark to contain a statement that mark is being used by the applicant, or with his consent, in relation to the goods or services, or that the applicant has a *bona fide* intention that the mark be so used.

Question 23

Rashmi is the successful owner of a chain of Indian food and pickle shops. She registers a trade mark in the name of 'RITASPICE' combining her anglicised nickname and the logo of an eye for the dot in the letter 'i'. One week a family friend, Gita, who is also in the food retail business contacts her complaining of a drop in trade. In a moment of kindness, Rashmi gave Gita a crate of her jarred pickles. Each jar carried her registered trade mark, RITASPICE, Rashmi telling Gita 'try selling these, let me know how you get on in two weeks'.

Rashmi did not have a chance to check Gita's progress but a few weeks later is concerned when a customer comes in and starts telling Rashmi about how impressed he is with Rashmi's new shop. On making further inquiries Rashmi is shocked to learn that Gita has renamed her business 'Gitaspices' and as well as selling Rashmi's stock is marking her goods with a Gitaspice mark. Subsequently, suppliers and delivery workers comment on the similarity when delivering goods.

Rashmi's attempts to dissuade Gita from using the name have failed. Gita has told Rashmi she has 'valid defences in law' and that she is entitled to use the mark regardless and will carry on doing so. Due to a cooling in relations, Rashmi seeks advice on her position.

Answer plan

The issues to be considered are:

- Proprietary Rights – s 9 of the TMA 1994
- Infringement – s 10 of the TMA 1994

- Use in the course of trade – s 103(1) of the TMA 1994
- Similarity
- Confusion of the public
- Remedies

Answer

As the proprietor of a registered trade mark under the Trade Marks Act 1994, Rashmi enjoys a number of important rights. Under s 9 of the TMA 1994, Rashmi enjoys exclusive rights in a trade mark which here consists of a personal nickname combined with the word 'spices'. Personal names can be registered in combination with visual devices (s 1) and, since it has already been registered, it will be deemed to have fulfilled the requirements of distinctiveness and will be considered validly registered (s 72). Section 9(3) of the TMA 1994 states that the rights of the proprietor take effect from the date of registration.

Rashmi will hold her mark as personal property under s 22 of the TMA 1994 and under s 9 is entitled to bring proceedings to protect the mark. The Act sets out the grounds of infringement in s 10(1)–(3). Infringement occurs through using a mark without consent which is identical on the same goods for which the mark was registered (s 10(1)), using an identical or similar mark for goods which are identical or similar where there is a likelihood or confusion of the public (s 10(2)), or using an identical or similar sign on goods which are dissimilar but where the trade mark enjoys a reputation, and use of the mark of will be detrimental to its repuation (s 10(3)). In this case, the use by Gita of a similar mark on identical or similar goods to the mark owned by Rashmi would fall under s 10(2). The onus will be on Rashmi to prove an infringement under s 10(2).

Following the approach in *Origins Natural Resources Inc v Origin Clothing Ltd* (1994), the court will consider that the mark is used in a normal and fair manner and the marks will be compared on a mark for mark basis or a 'sign for sign' basis (*per* Jacob J in *British Sugar plc v James Robertson Ltd* (1996)). To constitute infringement of Rashmi's mark, Rashmi must prove that Gita is using the mark in a trade mark sense, which should pose no difficulties in this case (*British Sugar Ltd v James Robertson Ltd* (1996)).

This approach set out in the *Origins* case was adopted by the court in *Wagamama Ltd v City Centre Restaurants* (1995). In *Wagamama* the plaintiffs were the proprietors of a registered trade mark 'Wagamama', the name used for a Japanese noodle bar and which they alleged was infringed by another restaurant which called itself Rajamama. The court considered both the look and the sound of the name in deciding that there was infringement under s 10(2) of the TMA 1994, applying earlier authority under the TMA 1938, and that customers might be deceived. With Rashmi's mark there could be argument that the first syllable is of the greater importance in determining similarity and that the marks can be thus distinguished. However, the marks are both being applied to similar businesses and the court will not consider the visual aspects alone but will also consider the sound and significance of the names and the general impression (*de Cordova v Vick Chemical Co* (1951)).

In determining similarity, the court may follow the test in *Pianotist* (1906). The approach is to consider the following: (1) the two marks must be taken and judged by both look and sound; (2) the goods to which the mark is applied; and (3) any special circumstances relating to the use of the mark in the trade setting. The court will make allowances for imperfect recollection.

Once similarity has been determined, the court will consider the possibility of confusion (*The European v The Economist* (1996)), and any evidence that this has occurred in practice. The evidence of confusion on the part of the customer will be relevant and admissible, although persons who are liable to confusion do not always make the best witnesses. Whilst it seems that a case for infringement may be made out as above, it appears that there are potential defences which Gita may attempt to raise.

As a defence Gita could try to argue the existence of a licence to use the mark and that the use of the trade mark is with Rashmi's consent. No particular form of words or writing is necessary to create a licence, and on balance it seems likely that a claim of licence could be upheld for disposal of the pickles. Consent is always a defence to a claim of trade mark infringement (*Mouson v Boehm* (1884)) but here there must be serious doubt as to whether the words used by Rashmi could amount to anything more than a limited licence. Arguably, the use of the mark was limited to the sale of the jars of pickles but no further. If there is insufficient basis for a claim of licence, Gita might alternatively seek to raise a defence that her use of the mark has been as a result of a representation or inducement by Rashmi to use the mark and the fact she did not act immediately. The telephone call might be construed as an encouragement to use the mark. This could also cover the acts of putting the pickles into circulation but no further. In *Burgoyne v Godfree* (1905), wine rejected by the plaintiffs in casks bearing their name was sold to the defendants who sold it as a result of a *bona fide* mistake. It was held that the plaintiffs had induced the belief in the defendants that they were entitled to do so.

The weakness in these defence arguments being extended to cover any other trading activity is that Gita has made a subtle alteration to the mark and cannot point to any basis to justify this coming from Rashmi to change the mark. The situation can be distinguished from that in *Habib v Habib* (1982) where the plaintiffs actually set the defendants up in business under the same name. The words used by Rashmi are arguably not sufficient to imply a licence or consent, and her failure to verify the position immediately would not amount to acquiesence.

Alternatively, Gita might argue that she is entitled to trade under her name, as permitted by s 11 of the TMA 1994. Section 11 provides that a registered trade mark is not infringed by the use by a person of his own name or address. The defence was explained in *Mercury Communications Ltd v Mercury Interactive (UK)* (1995) as allowing a trader to be able to trade under the name for which he is known without looking over his shoulder. However, Gita is not simply using her name but a combination of the word 'spice'. Section 11 only protects the *bona fide* use of names and not variations of them such as Gitaspice.

Providing the court decides that there is similarity between the marks and that confusion is likely to arise, an action for infringement will succeed. Alternatively, Rashmi will be able to pursue an action under the law of passing off, the right to do so being expressly preserved by s 2(2) of the TMA 1994.

For a passing off action to succeed, a reputation must be shown, together with the other elements necessary for the action (*Erven Warnink BV v Townsend (1979); Reckitt & Coleman v Boardman*

(1990)). In this case, given the strong similarity between the two marks, there appears to be a danger that customers may well believe that there is a link between Rashmi's business and Gita's beyond the donation of the jars. In *Ewing v Buttercup Margarine Company* (1917), Warrington LJ identified different varieties of damage that could arise through the use of a name leading customers to believe that the defendant's business is a branch of or associated with the plaintiff's business: 'The quality of the goods I sell; the kind of business I do; the credit or otherwise I might enjoy – all those things may immensely injure the other man who is wrongly assumed to be associated with me'. Another aspect of damage could be the constant confusion caused with suppliers making mistakes as to the identity of the business (*Chelsea Man v Chelsea Girl* (1987)). An action for damages may also be sought. Nominal damages will be recoverable for trade mark infringement but actual calculation of damages may be problematic.

Faced with such an actionable infringement of her mark, Rashmi should be advised to seek an interlocutory injunction to prevent any further use of the mark by Gita. As the owner of the registered mark there will be no need to prove any reputation. Applying the tests set out in *American Cyanamid v Ethicon* (1975), the balance of convenience will lie with protecting Rashmi's registered mark and preserving the *status quo*. Rashmi has an established business and has already registered and used the mark. With regard to use of the mark, Gita is in the position of a newcomer who has little investment to date in the mark. Gita's reaction over the telephone will be admissible by way of affidavit, and the court must accept the truth of a statement in an affidavit unless rebutted (*R v IRC ex p TC Coombes* (1991)). The form of the injunction will be to prevent Gita from using the trade mark or a colourable imitation of the mark and applying the mark to any goods she sells. There may also be orders for delivery up or the expunging of the mark from any of Gita's goods under ss 15 and 16 of the TMA 1994.

Question 24

In 1966, Damiens Ltd produced a 'Revelation7' trade mark for weedkillers. Since 1990, they have made little use of the trade mark other than to have a large relief sculpture 'Revelation7' on the front of their company HQ, and they have kept a small stock of Revelation fertilisers on their price lists.

Roland uses the Revelations7 trade mark in his plant food and processed manure business. In 1997, Damiens' solicitors write to Roland seeking to restrain his use of the mark. Roland seeks to register the Revelations7 trade mark. He has previously used the mark on his own products since 1995. Damiens Ltd were aware of this use by Roland but did nothing to prevent it.

On learning of Roland's application to register, Damiens Ltd seek to oppose registration and also issue infringement proceedings. Damiens are worried that their non-use of the mark will be held against them.

Advise Damiens Ltd on their position.

Answer plan

A complex question involving analysis of relevant case law on honest co-current use and abandonment, and a background understanding of the nature of trade mark proceedings and practice.

The issues to be covered are:

- Section 7, 11, 32 and 38 of the Trade Marks Act 1994
- Relative grounds for refusal of registration
- Opposition proceedings
- Honest concurrent use
- *Road Tech Computer Systems v Unison Software Ltd* (1996)

Answer

This question covers the rights of Damiens Ltd regarding their Revelation7 trade mark and whether they can prevent Roland from registering the same mark. Damiens trade mark would have been registered under the TMA 1938 and their rights are expressly preserved and transformed into registering rights under the TMA 1994. Schedule 3(2)(1) of the transitional provisions of the TMA 1994 effectively registers them under the 1994 system. Schedule 3, para 4 provides that ss 9–12 of the TMA 1994 apply in relation to an infringement of an existing registered trade mark after the commencement of the TMA 1994 (ie 31 October 1994).

It is possible to make a back-dated application for registration to the Registrar, which Roland may seek to do as a defence tactic, on the basis that infringement proceedings cannot be brought for a mark which is validly registered. If Roland succeeds, he will be able to take advantage of s 11 of the TMA 1994 which provides that a registered trade mark is not infringed by the use of another registered mark in relation to goods and services for which the latter is registered.

Roland must have a *bona fide* intention to use the mark (s 32(2)). This means that Roland must be intending to make genuine commercial use of the mark. The registering of a mark without an intention to use it renders the mark vulnerable to attack and revocation (*Huggars Trade Mark* (1979)). This could be a danger which Damiens Ltd might encounter in proceedings as way of a defence by Roland.

The question will thus depend upon whether the application for registration will be sustained, in the light of the opposition which Damiens may raise. Any person may raise opposition proceedings to the application under the TMA 1994 (with regard to the TMA 1938, a person had to be aggrieved – considered in *Daiquiri Rum Trade Mark* (1969)). Section 38(2) of the TMA 1994 provides for any person to be able to file formal opposition proceedings. Damiens' notice of opposition must be in writing and state the ground on which the opposition is based. This must be done within three months of the application under the rules made pursuant to s 69 of the TMA 1994.

Damiens may seek to raise s 5 grounds, which provide that a trade mark shall not be registered if it is identical or similar to a trade mark registered for identical or similar goods or services and there exists a likelihood of confusion on the part of the public. Here the mark is not identical because of the extra 's' so the application falls to be considered in light of s 5(2). The Registrar must consider s 7 on concurrent existing use and the problems that the mark may cause in terms of confusion in the market place. Section 7(1) provides that where there is an earlier conflicting trade mark or earlier right, but the applicant can show an honest concurrent use, the Registrar must consider such use in deciding whether to maintain an objection on relative grounds. The scheme of the TMA 1994 and previous authority allow for two identical marks to be registered. It is possible to have two identical marks on the register simultaneously in (*In Re Powell, In Re Pratt* (1878)) where the parties have used the mark independently and each party's claim is *bona fide*. Section 7(2) of the TMA 1994 provides that the Registrar will not refuse an application by reason of an earlier trade mark unless objection in that ground is raised by an earlier registered proprietor. Section 7(2) was the subject of a significant interpretation in *Road Tech Computer Systems Ltd v Unison Software (UK) Ltd* (1996). Robert Walker J held that in the absence of any words conferring a discretion on the Registrar, the true effect of s 7(2) and the word 'shall' was that a refusal became mandatory in the face of opposition such as Damiens would raise here as the proprietor of an earlier mark. Such a construction was also consistent with Article 4.5 of the Council Directive. Therefore, opposition is necessary from Damiens Ltd because of the presumption in favour of registration. Where an applicant such as Roland claims an honest concurrent use of the mark, s 7(2) provides that the Registrar has no power to refuse where satisfied that there has been an honest concurrent use, but refusal is mandatory where the mark is opposed. Section 5(3) provides that a mark shall not be registered where an earlier trade mark has a reputation in the case of dissimilar goods or services.

Section 7(3) of the TMA 1994 provides that an honest concurrent use means such use in the UK by the applicant as would have amounted to such a use under the TMA 1938. The Registrar must consider such use has taken place in deciding whether to maintain an objection on relative grounds. An honest concurrent use was considered in *Re Pirie* (1933). Relevant factors to be considered include:

- the possibility of confusion;
- whether the choice of the word was honestly made;
- the length of the time of use;

- whether there is proof or instance of confusion; and
- the size of the trade and the inconvenience of the parties.

The court will look at the evidence of use by Roland. In determining *bona fide* use, the court will consider whether 'there was really only some fictitious or colourable use and not a real or genuine use' (*Electrolux v Electrix* (1954) *per* Lord Morris) on the part of Roland. The view was taken that a *bona fide* use involves a real commercial use on a substantial scale. The court may also consider Roland's state of knowledge and Roland may not be able to rely on Damiens' delay in issuing infringement proceedings as an argument that he was either permitted to use the mark or that Damien had abandoned the Revelation7 Trade Mark. Applying the approach in *Electrolux Ltd v Electrix* (1954), on the one hand, if Roland knew of the mark, then he might be treated as having adopted the Revelations7 at his peril and he was not entitled to assume that Damiens Ltd had given consent simply because Damiens Ltd had not enforced its right. The other alternative is that Roland did not know of the existing mark and failed to conduct a search of the registry for conflicting registrations. As a consequence of this omission, Roland might be viewed as having adopted the Revelations7 trade mark without the reasonable belief that he was entitled to do so.

A further aspect of the requirement that applications must be made in good faith is that they should not be for an ulterior purpose such as litigation. This may allow Damiens to enter a further challenge to Roland. The existence of any goods which Roland wishes to apply the mark could be important. In *Andrew v Kuehrich* (1913), it was held that an application could be refused where it was made in circumstances where it was likely to deceive. Vaughan Williams LJ held that a trader must have or intend to have goods in connection with which he means to identify himself by use of a particular trade mark which he proposes. However, it is not a legitimate application if the object of the application is to obtain registration to assist in litigation but for which he would not have any goods to which the mark could be applied.

Roland argues that the sporadic use that Damiens have made of the mark since 1966 may amount to abandonment of the mark. Roland also claims that the delay in issuing proceedings amounts to acquiesence. In *Mouson & Co v Boehm* (1884), mere non-use of a mark, though coupled with non-registration, did not amount to abandonment. The business had continued, the moulds for imprinting the mark had been retained and the marked soap was retained on price lists. In this case, Damiens Ltd have retained the mark on goods and have not made any express intention to abandon the mark.

As to Damiens' initial non-action in seeking to restrain the trade mark, it was observed in *Crossley v Lightowler* (1878) that mere suspension of the exercise of a right without evidence of an intention to abandon it is not sufficient to lose the right. In *Electrolux v Electrix* (1954), the view was expressed that the user of a mark which was already the subject of an existing registration was not entitled to assume that consent was given simply because rights had not been enforced. Similarly, in *Shaw v Applegate* (1977), it was held that acquiesence would depend on whether, in the facts of a particular case, the situation has become such that it would be dishonest or unconscionable for the plaintiff or the person having the right sought to be enforced to continue to enforce it (*per* Buckley LJ). So on balance, it seems unlikely that Damiens will be deemed to have either abandoned their mark or consented to Roland using it.

The use of the Revelation7 trade mark as a statue will not amount to use as a trade mark and will not assist them. In *British Sugar Ltd v James Robertson Ltd* (1996), use of a trade mark in a trade sense means in the course of trade – arguably the use of the image is largely decorative if it has not been regularly applied to goods. However, the use of the statute may generate rights in passing off, or alternatively in copyright should Roland seek to register it. In *Re Karostep* (1977), an image used was protected under copyright and the Registrar was able to refuse its registration as a trade mark. The grounds of relative refusal available to the Registrar include the extent to which a mark may interfere with 'other earlier rights' of another trade mark proprietor under s 5(2). Following *Road Tech Computer Systems Ltd v Unison Software (UK) Ltd* (1996), this will also lead to the application by Roland being refused.

It should be remembered that the court enjoy broad powers at the early stages of litigation summary judgment under RSC Order 14A to determine any issues of law such as these, and enjoys a wide discretion to stay proceedings as appropriate pending a decision by the Registrar, or to allow the infringement proceedings to continue but suspend any order until the determination of the registration. The wide discretion of the court is considered in *James & Sons v Wafer Razor* (1995). A stay will only generally be granted where it would serve the interests of justice. In this case, it seems that it would not be in the interests of justice to stay the claim and it seems likely that the Revelation7 trade mark held by Damiens is valid and they may restrain Roland from using a similar one.

Question 25

Regal Scents seek to register a 'Queen Regal' trade mark for their perfume. Eagle Products already own a registered trade mark in the name 'Queen Eagle' based upon perfumes used in the Czarist Royal Court before 1917. Eagle Products wish to oppose the application. Advise Eagle Products on opposition procedures and the likelihood of success.

How would your answer differ if Eagle Products produced glassware?

Answer plan

A question raising issues of similarity between marks and also of trade mark practice.

The issues to be considered are:

- The Trade Marks Act 1994
- Discretion of Registrar – s 5 of the TMA 1994
- Similarity
- *Smith Hayden & Co's Ltd Application* (1946)

Answer

Under Part III of the Trade Marks Act 1994, it is the duty of the trade marks Registrar to maintain the trade marks register established by the Act. The function of the Registrar is to scrutinise the applications for trade marks from would-be proprietors to ensure that the scheme of the TMA 1994 is adhered to and that the owners of existing marks are not prejudiced. In this question, Regal

Scents seek to register a 'Queen Eagle' Trade Mark for toiletries. The registration of trade marks is governed by the TMA 1994, implementing Council Directive 89/104 into UK law.

The mark Regal Scents seeks to register is a word mark consisting of two words to be applied to perfumes. The first issue is whether the Queen Regal mark can distinguish it in the market place. Under the Directive and the Act, there is a presumption in favour of the registration of any sign which fulfills the criteria of s 1(1). It must be capable of being represented graphically and be capable of distinguishing the goods or services of one undertaking from those of another. Failure to meet s 1(1) criteria is an absolute ground for refusal of registration under s 3 – what may be subject to registration is also subject to scrutiny by the Registrar for trade marks. In order to be able to distinguish, there must be 'some quality in the trade mark which earmarks the goods so marked as distinct from those of other products of such goods' (see *Yorkshire Copper Works Application* (1954)).

In *Blue Paraffin Trade Mark* (1977), the applicant had been selling paraffin dyed blue. The application was opposed by other traders who had been selling blue dyed paraffin under the name 'Token Blue'; another company had been selling a pink paraffin. It was held that the words Blue Paraffin contained at least some inherent aptitude to distinguish and did distinguish the goods in fact. Under the test of the TMA 1938, a mark was registerable, provided it had some inherent aptitude to distinguish and that it was to some extent adapted to distinguish the goods of the applicant from others.

On the facts stated, there appears to be no basis for refusing registration absolutely, since the sign does not appear to lack distinctive character, nor does it consist exclusively of signs or indications which may serve in trade as a designation of kind, quality, intended purpose or the other characteristics under s 3(1)(c). No other ground in 3(2) appears to apply and there seems no reason to believe that the mark is contrary to public policy or morality or that it is of such a nature so as to deceive the public under s 3(3). Similarly, opposition on grounds of illegality (s 3(4)) and bad faith (s 3(6)) do not apply.

Eagle Products will be entitled to give notice of opposition under s 38(2) of the TMA 1994. The Registrar is likely to conduct a search of the register and publicise the application. On publication, Eagle Products should give notice to oppose the application within three months.

A possible ground for challenge might be generated by the specially protected emblems provisions of s 4, depending on the nature of the mark proposed by Regal Scents. Sections s 4(1)(c) and (d) preclude marks which have a representation of Her Majesty or any member of the royal family or any colourable imitation thereof and under 4(1)(d) words, letters or devices likely to lead persons to think that the applicant either has or has recently had royal patronage or authorisation. It seems unlikely that the mark will offend against the relative grounds of exclusion set out in s 4 which prohibits the use of the royal arms or images of members of the royal family.

More likely to succeed will be an assertion of prior rights by Eagle Products with reference to the relative ground of refusal for registration under s 5(2) of the TMA 1994. Section 5(2)(b) provides that a mark shall not be registered if it is similar to an earlier trade mark and is to be registered for goods or services similar to those for which the earlier trade mark is protected and there exists a likelihood of confusion on the part of the public, which includes the likelihood of association with the earlier trade mark. Eagle Products Ltd will be the proprietor of an earlier trade mark under s 6(1).

The established test for an opposition based upon similarity and confusion was laid down in *Smith Hayden & Co Ltd's Application* (1946) as adapted by Lord Upjohn in *Bali Trade Mark* (1969). Applying the test to the facts of this question, the *Smith Hayden* test would be used as follows:

> Having regard to the use of the mark Queen Eagle in a normal and fair manner in connection with any goods covered by the registrations of that mark, is the tribunal satisfied that there will be no reasonable likelihood of deception among a number of persons if the applicants use their mark Queen Regal normally and fairly in respect of any goods covered by the proposed registration?

If the answer to the question is yes, the registration could proceed. If (as is likely) the answer is no, then the application will be refused. In determining the issue, the Registrar or court will judge both the look and the sound of the two names, the goods to which they are to be applied, the nature of the customer and all the surrounding circumstances. This test, it should be noted, requires the court to envisage future use of the mark.

Phonetically and visually Queen Eagle and Queen Regal are similar and it would appear quite likely that there could be a risk of confusion. The marks will be considered as a whole on a sign for sign basis (*British Sugar Plc v James Robertson & Sons Ltd* (1996)). The ideas and images conveyed by the mark will be those arising from the use of the word Queen. Furthermore, the fact that both marks would have the same first syllable is likely to weigh heavily with the Registrar or court, if it is considered more likely to lead to confusion (*London Lubricants* (1925) and *Buler* (1966)). The overall impression and the effect of the mark as a whole is paramount (*Bailey* (1935)).

The claim by Regal Scents that the goods to which they intend to apply the mark are different from those of Queen Eagle Products, although one of fact, is unlikely to be upheld, since both are stated to be toiletries, although of a different character. The Registrar is likely to follow the test laid down in *Jellinek's Application* (1946) to determine whether the goods are similar. Under *Re Jellinek* (1946), the tribunal must consider: (1) the nature and composition of the goods; (2) the respective uses to which the goods are put; and (3) the trade channels through which they might be sold.

In *British Sugar Plc v James Robertson & Sons Ltd* (1996), relevant factors in determining similarity of goods for the purposes of s 10 (infringement of a mark) were a comparison of the use, users and physical nature of a plaintiff's and defendant's goods, the way in which they were sold and the extent to which they were competitive. Arguments that the customers might not be the same because of the price differences will fall into the category of 'surrounding circumstances'. Such claims are not likely to carry much weight, given that there might subsequently be variations in the prices of the goods and the possibility that the Regal Scents might in future choose to place their goods higher up the market, and given that the 'life of a trade mark registration is potentially very long indeed'(*Rose Garden Trade Mark* (1995)).

Prior use of the mark by Regal Scents may be relevant in terms of raising relative grounds in the case of honest concurrent use issues. The onus of proof will be on Regal Scents as applicant to show that the trade mark is not likely to cause confusion (*Buler Trade Mark* (1966)).

Registration by Eagle Products for glassware

Eagle Products would be entitled to oppose the registration, but would be seeking to raise grounds of objection to registration within the terms of s 5(3) of the TMA 1994. Section 5(3) provides that a trade mark shall not be registered where: (i) it is identical or similar to an earlier mark; (ii) it is proposed to register it for goods or services which are not similar to those for which the earlier mark is protected; and (iii) the earlier mark has a reputation in the UK (or in the case of a Community trade mark in the European Community) and the use of the later mark without due cause would take unfair advantage of, or be detrimental to the distinctive character or reputation of the earlier mark. There is no need to show a likelihood of confusion, as with s 5(2).

In such a case, the onus would be on Eagle Products to prove that they had such a reputation attached to the mark and that attaching the similar Regal Scents mark to toiletries could harm it. There is no need to prove confusion, but it will be necessary to show that the reputation associated with Queen Eagle would suffer by way of dilution, as in passing off cases such as *Tattinger v Albev* (1993) which involved protecting the name and reputation of Champagne. A number of factors could affect this and although cases are known from Benelux countries, one should hesitate, following *Wagamama Ltd v City Centre Restaurants* (1995), before assuming a court will follow European interpretations.

Alternatively, Eagle Products could seek to oppose the mark on the basis that the mark proposed by Regal Scents might offend against s 5(4)(a). This provides that a mark shall not be registered where its use may be liable to be prevented in the UK by a rule of law, 'in particular, the law of passing off'. If a claim for passing off can be made out, the decision in *Road Tech Computer Systems Ltd v Unison Software (UK) Ltd* (1996) (an application for summary judgment under RSC Order 14) will apply; providing the registration is valid, opposition proceedings by Eagle Products will be mandatory for refusing the application.

Question 26

Discuss the concept of similarity in trade marks. Is it the same test as confusion?

Answer plan

A question which requires a student to cite cases on similarity and draw from a wide range of cases of misperception. When dealing with confusion, the student must remember that often cases will turn on their facts, and statements by judges in cases on confusion may only be of specific application and not intended to establish general propositions of law.

The issues to be considered are:

- Sections 5 and 10 of the Trade Mark Act 1994
- *The Pianotist* (1906)
- *Smith Hayden & Co Ltd's Application* (1946)
- Perception of marks in use
- Possibility of misperception

Answer

The purpose of a trade mark is to distinguish goods of one undertaking from another in the market place. The capacity to distinguish is undermined by the existence of marks which resemble each other. Determining similarity of marks is a duty of the trade marks Registrar and the courts.

Issues of similarity between marks fall to be considered in applications for trade mark registration under s 5 of the Trade Mark Act 1994 and infringement under s 10.

Section 5 of the TMA 1994 gives the Registrar grounds to refuse registration of a mark which is identical or similar to a mark for identical goods (s 5(1)); where a mark is identical or similar for similar goods and there is a likelihood of confusion (s 5(2)); and where a sign which is identical or similar is applied to goods which are dissimilar but the mark has a reputation. The similarity is with marks either already registered or where there is an existing earlier mark.

Section 10 of the TMA 1994 recognises three types of infringement involving any use of a trade mark, each of which will require consideration of similarity issues, with the use by an alleged infringer of an identical sign on identical goods or services (s 10(1)), the use of an identical or similar sign of similar goods and services (s 10(2)), and the use of an identical or similar sign on non-similar goods or services, where the mark would take unfair advantage of, or be detrimental to its distinctive character or repute (s 10(3)). Similar considerations and legal tests are arguably common to both sections. Similarity issues may also be raised in proceeding invalidity, cases involving the use of the royal arms and prosecutions for unauthorised use.

It has long been recognised that each case will turn on its facts and the degree of resemblance necessary to generate deception or confusion cannot be defined in advance. In *Seixo v Provezende* (1866), Lord Cranworth stated, 'It is hardly necessary to say that in order to entitle a party to relief it is by no means necessary that there should be absolute identity. What degree of resemblance is necessary, from the nature of things, is a matter incapable of definition, *a priori*'. There are a number of factors in common with passing off.

The rules for comparison of two signs can be summarised as follows:

- the two signs must be taken and judged by their look and sound;
- the goods to which the marks are applied and the nature and kind of customer;
- the circumstances of the trade concerned (*Kidax (Shirts) Ltd Application* (1959)).

In the case of words or names, the classic test is from *The Pianotist* (1906) in which Parker J, considering the similarities between Pianola and Neola, stated, 'you must take the two words. You must consider the nature and kind of customer who would be likely to buy these goods. In fact, you must consider all the surrounding circumstances; and you must further consider what is likely to happen if each of those trade marks is used in a normal way as a trade mark for the goods of the respective owners of the mark'. If after such consideration, the judge takes the view that there is a likelihood of confusion, registration may be denied or infringement may be found as appropriate.

In *Smith-Hayden & Co Ltd's Application* (1946), the following test was laid down 'having regard to the user of the mark applied for: is the tribunal satisfied that the mark, if used in a normal or fair manner in connection with any goods covered by the registration proposed, will not reasonably be likely to cause deception and confusion amongst a substantial number of persons'. This approach was subsequently applied in *Bali Trade Mark* (1969) and in cases since.

In considering infringement under the TMA 1938, the court compared the registered mark with that used by an alleged infringer to determine whether the mark was 'confusingly similar'. It was explained by Laddie J in *Wagamama Ltd v City Centre Restaurants* (1995), that the court would determine whether, as a result of similarities, an alleged infringer's mark would be thought to be derived from or connected with the registered mark. Similarity was determined in light of the above tests and whether the 'idea' of or principal impact conveyed by the marks was so similar that confusion was likely, with regard to how the marks looked and sounded. This was a practical test, where infringement could be found even if the infringer took steps to prevent confusion in fact occurring.

From decisions made under the TMA 1994, it is clear that both the trade marks registry and the courts will continue to apply the existing case law which grew up under earlier statutes, most notably the TMA 1938. (See, for example, the approach taken by the trade mark registry in *Rose Garden Trade Mark* (1995).) The court and the Registrar determine similarity on a 'mark for mark' basis (*Origins Natural Resources Inc v Origin Clothing Ltd* (1995)) or more accurately, as Jacob J stated in *James Robertson plc v British Sugar Ltd* (1996), correcting himself, on 'a sign for sign' basis.

Regarding similarity tests under the TMA 1994, in *Origins Natural Resources Inc v Origin Clothing Ltd* (1995), Jacob J stated that s 10 presupposes that the plaintiff's mark is in use or will come into use. It requires the court to assume that the mark of the plaintiff is used in a normal and fair manner in relation to the goods for which it is registered, and then to assess the likelihood of confusion in relation to the way the defendant uses his mark, discounting external added matter or circumstances.

In *Wagamama Ltd v City Centre Restaurants Plc* (1995), Laddie J stated, 'When considering infringement it is also necessary to bear in mind the possible imperfect recollection on the part of members of the target market'. It is recognised that marks will rarely been seen side by side (*Reckitt & Colman Products v Boardman And Co* (1990)).

The court or Registrar must consider the totality of the impression given orally and visually as to whether it is likely to cause mistake or confusion. The 'ascertainment of an essential feature is not to be by ocular test alone' (*de Cordova v Vick Chemical Co* (1951)). The effect of the mark on the ear will be considered if it is a word. In *Portakabin v Portablast* (1990), the first five letters of the two marks looked and sounded alike – the additional material did not diminish the similarity. The marks are to be compared as they would be perceived when actually used (*Re Ovax* (1946)). The possibility that marks may become blurred or altered by being stamped or printed or by wear and tear may also be considered (*Re Lyndon* (1886)).

In *Lancer Trade Mark* (1987) it was held that there was no risk of confusion between the Lancer and Lancia marks on cars because of the way the vehicles were marketed. The court will also address the target audience, with distinctions being drawn between goods and services of a specialist nature, and those sold in the general market or to the general public (*GE* (1973)). In each case, the persons associated with goods in the course of trade, whether as retailers or as ultimate purchasers, must be considered (*General Electric Co v General Electric Co Ltd* (1972)).

Consideration will be given to allowing for the possibility of mispronounciation on the part of the public and shop assistants (*Bali Trade Mark* (1969)). Some authorities have suggested that similarity between the first syllables of two words is of most significance, but the mark will be considered as a whole to identify the overall effect of the ideas or images conveyed by the sign.

The considerations of similarity and confusion to an extent overlap as a matter of necessity, but are separate. *The European v The Economist Ltd* (1996) concerned the use of the word European in the titles of two publications where similarity and likelihood of confusion were dealt with separately in turn. Ratee J held the approach was to ask: (1) Is the sign similar? (2) does it result in likelihood of confusion? This illustrates that the two concepts involve different tests and considerations. The test is one of law and the decision is for the judge alone. However, Rattee J added that a '... *prima facie* view that the relevant signs are not similar should be reconsidered if there is some other cogent evidence of the existence or likelihood of confusion between the two on the part of members of the public'.

In *Neutrogena Corporation and Anr v Golden Ltd and Anr* (1996), the correct legal test on the issue of deception or confusion was whether on the balance of probabilities a substantial number of members of the public would be misled into purchasing the defendants' products in the belief that they were those of the plaintiff.

Customers may be considered to be 'ordinary purchasers purchasing with caution' (*Seixo v Provezende* (1866)) but it has never been assumed that a particularly intelligent examination of the mark will be made (*Wotherspoon v Currie* (1872)). The ultimate purchasers of goods are not presumed to be idiotic or unusually unobservant. See Jessel MR in *Singer v Wilson* (1876); *Morning Star v Express Newspapers Ltd* (1979): 'only a moron in a hurry' could confuse the two particular titles.

In essence, the importance of a trade mark is to be capable of distinguishing; thus if a mark is similar to others, this initial requirement of registration will not be fufilled.

Question 27

Magika Clear Rum is a brand of white rum which has been marketed and manufactured in the Caribbean for many years. Since 1976, the Hot Rum Bar in London has sold cocktails called 'Magis' which are made with white rum which are popular with the bar's Latin American and Cuban exile customers. Magika Rum Ltd has supplied rum on a regular basis to the Hot Rum Bar and has supported its happy night promotions where the bar's special cocktails are made up and sold at discount prices. On occasions, the Hot Rum Bar mixed Magis with white rums other than the Magika Rum Ltd brand. In 1996, the Hot Rum Bar is put up for sale. Magika Rum Ltd put in a bid to buy the bar but the Bar is bought by Alistair. Aggrieved by their failure to purchase, Magika Rum Ltd notify Alistair that he cannot use the Magi trade mark or their brand of rum at the Hot Rum Bar. He keeps 'Magis' on the menu and makes variants with other brands of rum. He also makes his own 'Clear Rum' cocktails.

Subsequently, a letter sent to Alistair informs him that he must stop using 'Clear' because it is part of their trade mark and Magika Rum Ltd are applying to have it registered as a trade mark.

Answer plan

A question involving some complicated points on use, practice and procedure and on the discretion of the court when considering to grant an interlocutory injunction.

The issues to be considered are:

- The Trade Marks Act 1994
- Infringement – s 10 of the TMA 1994
- Revocation – s 47 of the TMA 1994
- Use of a trade mark other than by graphical representation – s 103 of the TMA 1994
- Discretion with injunctive relief in isolated instances

Answer

In this question, Magika Rum Ltd sought to sue Alistair for trade mark infringement in relation to activities in the Hot Rum Bar and the marketing of Magic Clear Rum.

Magika Clear Rum Ltd have a registered mark in 'Magika Clear', registered under the Trade Marks Act 1938. Rights follow through the transitional provisions of the TMA 1994.

Under s 9 of the TMA 1994, a proprietor of a registered trade mark has exclusive rights in the trade mark. The acts constituting the infringement of Magika's trade mark are set out in s 10. In deciding whether a s 10 infringement has taken place, the court has to decide whether the sign registered as a trademark is used in the course of trade, and then to consider whether that use falls within one of the defining subsections. To be infringing, it must be being used in a trade mark sense. The use of the name Magi appearing on the price list will *prima facie* be an infringement.

Alistair should be advised to enter a defence to any claim and commence opposition proceedings under s 38(2) of the TMA 1994 Alternatively, if the mark has been registered, Alistair should seek to revoke the registration held by Magika Rum Ltd on the basis of s 46(1)(c), where in consequence of acts or inactivity of the proprietor, it has become the common name in trade.

In *Second Sight Ltd v Novel UK Ltd and Novel Inc* (1995), a clear distinction is drawn between challenges to an initial registration, and therefore its validity, and challenge to continued registration. Validity of the original registration and the substance or continuance in force of a registration at a date of any alleged infringement is essential to the existence of the cause of action.

'Magi' trade mark

At the time it was registered, Magi would have been distinctive for the product concerned. Section 47(1) of the TMA 1994 further provides that a mark shall not be declared invalid if, in consequence of the use which has been made of it, it has after registration acquired a distinctive character in relation to the goods or services for which it is registered.

Where a mark has a generic use, it may fail for want of distinctiveness (*Costa Brava Wine Co v Vine Products* (1969) involving the word sherry) as in passing off cases.

A further defence which Alistair might use is under s 11(3), which deals with limitations of a effect of a registered trade mark. A registered trade mark is not infringed by the use in the course of trade of an earlier right which applies only in that locality. Here the earlier right applies only in that locality. It might be argued here that the earlier right was the waiver or licence given by Magika to use the mark.

There is an argument under s 46(c) of the TMA 1994 that, in consequence of the acts or inactivity of the proprietor, it has become the common name in the trade for a product or service for which it is register. This may lead to behaviour of Magika being scrutinised for their activity or lack of it. Registration may be lost under s 46(1)(c) where generic use has come about 'in consequence of acts or inactivity of the proprietor'. Much will depend on how Magika have actually used their mark elsewhere.

An analogous case under the old legislation is *Daiquiri Rum Trade Mark* (1969), where the mark was removed from the register upon proof that the name was used in trade for a cocktail and had lost its distinctiveness.

Alternatively, Alistair can seek revocation of the mark. Section 47(5) of the TMA 1994 provides that where court action is pending, such an application must be made to the court. This will avoid duplication of proceedings and Alistair will stand to recover a greater proportion of costs if successful.

'Clear'

Regarding 'Clear', Alistair should argue against registration under s 5(4) of the TMA 1994 on the basis that he has an earlier right in terms of good will that may be protected in an action for passing off. A stronger argument would be on the ground that the 'Clear' mark lacks distinctive character. Alternatively, if the mark has been registered, Alistair may seek to have the registration declared invalid. Section 47(1) of the TMA 1994 provides that a registration shall be liable to be declared invalid under s 3. Alistair's argument would be that 'Clear' is invalid by virtue of s 3(1)(b) of the TMA 1994, which provides an absolute bar on trade marks which are devoid of distinctive character. In *WG Du Cros Ltd's Applications* (1913), it was held that in determining whether a mark is distinctive, it must be considered quite apart from the effects of registration. 'The question therefore is whether the mark itself, if used as a trade mark, is likely to become actually distinctive of the goods of the person so using it ... the applicant's chance of success in this respect must ... largely depend upon whether other traders are likely, in the ordinary course of their business and without proper motive, to desire to use the mark, or some mark nearly resembling it, upon or in connection with their goods'. In *Blue Paraffin Trade Mark* (1977), Whitford J observed, 'the more apt a word is to describe the goods of a manufacturer, the less apt it is to distinguish them: for a word that is apt to describe the goods of A, is likely to be apt to describe the similar goods of B'.

Section 47(6) of the TMA 1994 provides that where registration of a trade mark is invalid to any extent, the registration shall to that extent be deemed never to have been made. Support for Alistair can lie in the view expressed in *Shell-Mex and BP Ltd and Aladdin Industries Ltd v R W Holmes* (1937). If other traders in the same line of business are likely to wish to make use of a mark and there is no reason why they should be inhibited from doing so, then the mark cannot be adapted to distinguish the applicant's goods from the goods of other traders. In *W & G Du Cros Ltd* (1913), Lord Shaw stated, 'I should describe the duty of the Registrar as this: that in examining the particular facts, he has also to survey the possible confusion or difficulties, and the possible impairment of the right of innocent traders to that which, apart from the grant of the trade mark, would be their natural mode of conducting their business'.

Since the nature of the goods and their respective marks will be the same, and sold through the same trade channels, there will be a risk of confusion. In *Daiquiri Rum* (1969), it was held that rum and rum cocktails were the same class of goods.

Furthermore, Alistair may argue that the mark is being registered in bad faith under s 3(6), with the sole intention of harming his business at the Hot Rum Bar.

In *British Sugar plc v James Robertson & Sons Ltd* (1996), the court removed the registration for the mark 'treat' because it was devoid of distinctive character, consisting exclusively of a sign to designate the kind, quality and intended purpose of the product under s 3(1)(c).

Magika will not have a case against Alistair over the word 'Clear' and would be advised to settle. The word clear is being used in its descriptive sense rather than as a trade mark or sign in trade use.

The verbal order

The verbal use of Magi and Clear by an employee would also be caught by either s 10(1) or (2) of the TMA 1994 (given that the goods might be identical or similar goods). The use is clearly in the course of trade and Magika Rum Ltd may rely on s 103(2), which covers use of a trade mark other than by graphic representation.

Origins Natural Resources Inc v Origin Clothing Ltd (1994) it was held that the TMA 1994 'requires the court to assume the mark of the plaintiff is used in a normal and fair manner in relation to the goods for which is registered, and then to assess a likelihood of confusion in relation to the way the defendant uses its mark discounting added matter or circumstances'.

Nonetheless, it will be worth Alistair defending the infringement action given all the circumstances, since the grant of an injunction is an equitable matter. If wrongful conduct has played a part in making use of the mark deceptive, historically the Court of Chancery would not grant an injunction against infringement. This was part of the general equitable doctrine that he who seeks equity must come with clean hands. As the grant of an injunction is discretionary, the court may look to earlier authorities where injunctive relief has been denied.

The court may consider that the use of the 'Magi' trade mark was as a result of Magika Rum Ltd's use of the mark, or an isolated instance as in *Ford v Foster* (1872), that the test in deciding whether 'the use of it [the mark] by other persons is still calculated to deceive the public, whether it may still have the effect of inducing the public to buy goods not made by the original owner of the trade mark as if they were his goods. If the mark has come to be so public and in such universal use that nobody can be deceived by use of it ... the right to the trade mark must be gone'.

Even if the mark is valid, Alistair may still be preserved by *Leahy, Kelly and Leahy v Glover* (1893) where the court refused an injunctive relief where a transaction was an isolated one and there was no reason to believe that would be repetition.

Question 28

Explain the benefits of a Community trade mark. What rights does a successful applicant enjoy?

Answer plan

A question which requires an access to Council Regulation No 40/94.

The issues to be considered are:

- Community Trade Mark Registration – origins
- Who may apply?
- Rights of proprietor
- Licensing
- Interplay with UK domestic law

Answer

European Council Regulation No 40/94 established the Community trade mark registration system. Issued on 20 December 1993, the regulation came into force on 15 March 1996, and the Community trade mark registration system became operational from 1 April 1996, registrations having been accepted from 1 January 1996. The regulation follows closely the provisions of the Harmonisation Directive which led to the Trade Marks Act 1994, approximating national laws.

The Community trade mark system provides protection for the whole EU. It enables trade mark owners to submit a single application for registration. Community trade mark applications are classified by the International System into 42 areas of goods and services.

Previously, the holder of a trade mark under domestic law was forced to register the mark in every country in each national system and was powerless to restrain a competitor from using a mark in another jurisdiction. Now with a Community trade mark, the mark is protected throughout all the countries of the EU, and enforceable under the legal systems of Member States. As with marks under the TMA 1994, a Community trade mark must be capable of distinguishing and be capable of representation in graphical form.

Benefits of the Community trade mark are numerous to a successful applicant. In addition to saving money, time and the prospect of litigation within differing jurisdictions, the registration on a European-wide basis overcomes a variety of related problems. Entry on the register confers a Community-wide proof of title and national variations in the registerability of marks and the scope of protection allowed are avoided. Barriers to trade arising from the application of national law to prevent imports are overcome along with the problem of conflicting marks in different States. The regulation is extremely comprehensive, covering the rights of proprietors, the registration procedure, challenges, the conversion of national marks to Community trade marks and *vice versa*, costs, administrative and budget matters for the Trade Mark Office and much besides. Article 97 provides that any matters not covered are to be determined by the application of national law and national rules of procedure. In the UK, this would include the amended RSC Order 100 and parties might also have regard to foreign law by virtue of Part III of the Private Internal Law (Miscellaneous Provisions) Act 1995, which will allow UK courts to look only at the law of another relevant country without deciding that there was a similar law in the UK.

Those trade mark proprietors who already have registration in some of the Member States of the EU will be able to retain the seniority of the earlier registration. Priority can be claimed for an earlier date if an application is made for a Community trade mark within six months of the previous date (the earliest possible date for a filing being 1 October 1995). The registration system operates through the Office in Alicante, Spain.

Article 16 provides that a Community trade mark will be treated as if it were a national trade mark registered in the particular State in which the proprietor is established. Recital 5 of the Regulation provides that the system replaces trade mark laws in Member States and proprietors retain the right to elect to have their mark protected only at a national level.

Article 5 provides that natural and legal persons may be proprietors of Community trade marks if they are: (a) nationals of Member States; (b) nationals of States that are parties to the Paris Convention; (c) nationals of States that are not parties to the Paris Convention who are domiciled or have industrial or commercial establishments in either the EU or a Paris Convention country; or (d) nationals who are trade mark holders from countries which are not parties to the EU but nonetheless afford protection to EU citizens and recognise the registration of Community trade marks. Refugees are also included.

Article 9 provides that the rights conferred by a Community trade mark are enforceable against third parties, which is analogous to s 10 of the TMA 1994, restricting the use of signs which are identical or similar to the mark for signs which are identical or similar, or the use of signs which are identical or similar for goods or services which are not similar where the later has a reputation and use of the sign takes unfair advantage of or is detrimental to the character or repute of the Community trade mark. These rights arise from the date of publication of the registration of the trade mark. However, 'reasonable compensation' may be claimed in respect of matters which would be prohibited where the mark has been published but not registered, where the acts complained of would otherwise amount to infringement, but the court must not determine the matter until after the registration is published. A crucial date is therefore the date of publication under Article 40.

A Community trade mark is renewed every 10 years under Article 47 on request by the proprietor of the mark. An application for renewal must be commenced within six months of the expiry date. As a Community trade mark will be cheaper to maintain than concurrent multiple registrations the proprietor will enjoy a corresponding saving on renewal costs.

As with trade marks under the TMA 1994, it is possible to assign or license a Community trade mark to different parties in different countries. Under Article 23, such transactions have to be recorded in writing to be effective against third parties. A single recording in writing at the Community Trade Mark Office will be sufficient. Under Article 22, exclusive and non-exclusive licences are possible and can be granted with respect to some of the goods and services for which the mark is registered. If a licensee breaches the terms of the licence, the proprietor can invoke the rights conferred by the registration. The splitting of licences for different licensees in different territories is subject to EU law which applies to the division of territories and markets.

If a Community trade mark is not used within the five years following the registration, the proprietor of the mark will be subject to sanctions with respect to the mark (Article 15). Registration should be secure providing the mark has been used in at least one Member State in the five years. Use of the mark includes 'in a form differing in elements which do not alter the distinctive character of the mark in the form in which it was registered' (reg 15(2)(a)), or 'affixing the mark to goods or to the packaging in the Community for the purposes of export' (reg 15(2)(b)).

A Community trade mark shall not entitle the proprietor to stop a third party from using in the course of trade: (a) his own name or address; (b) indications concerning the kind, quality, quantity, intended purpose, value, geographical origin, the time of production of the goods or of rendering of the service, or of other characteristics of the goods or service; or (c) the use of the trade mark where it is needed to indicate the intended purpose of a product or service, in particular accessories or spare parts.

Article 52 gives wider grounds for declaring invalid a Community trade mark than exists for challenging a national trade mark registered under the TMA 1994. A mark shall be declared invalid on application to the Office or on the basis of a counterclaim in infringement proceedings. A Community trade mark shall be declared invalid on application to the Office or on the basis of a counterclaim, where the use of a mark may be prohibited pursuant to the national law governing the protection of any other earlier right and in particular: (a) a right to a name; (b) a right to personal property; (c) a copyright; or (d) an industrial property right. This is arguably wider than the grounds for refusal of registration under the TMA 1994.

By s 6(1)(c) of the TMA 1994, a Community trade mark has effect in the UK with regard to any subsequent national applications. Thus, registration can be refused for marks which are identical or similar to a Community trade mark or where use could be detrimental to the reputation of a mark, pursuant to s 5. The criteria for absolute grounds of refusal and infringement are identical to those of the Directive. Under s 52(3), the threats, customs and anti-counterfeiting provisions of the TMA 1994 apply equally to a Community trade mark.

Under s 52(2) of the TMA 1994, the Secretary of State for Trade and Industry may by regulation make such provisions as he considers appropriate in connection with regulation, including regulations covering applications for Community trade marks through the Patent Office, the conversion of Community trade marks into trade marks under the TMA 1994 and the granting of jurisdiction to the UK courts to determine issues.

On paper, at least, the Community trade mark system has a number of attractions, if registrations proceed without any obstacles or opposition. Whether it will prove initially to be advantageous to any but the largest undertakings remains to be seen (since the mark may well have already been registered under national systems) but its significance is bound to grow with the expansion of international markets for many undertakings.

Chapter 4

Passing Off

Introduction

Passing off questions are popular with students. They are sometimes referred to by examiners in terms of the 'common law rights' of parties in problem questions. Actions in passing off should be understood as actions to protect unregistered trade marks. In a number of areas, there are overlapping principles with trade mark law. Questions should be approached by students as with questions on other aspects of the law of tort, where the prime remedy sought is an injunction rather than compensatory damages. Although the demise of passing off has been predicted in light of the expansion of what may be registered as a trade mark under the Trade Marks Act 1994 it seems likely to remain a part of the law – and hence syllabuses – for years to come. Examiners are looking for the essential elements of the claim and their application, followed by the application of more specific authorities.

The elements of the tort of passing off are the principles set out by Lord Diplock in *Erven Warnink BV v Townsend Hull* (1979) and *Reckitt and Coleman Products v Borden* (1990) ('jiff lemon'). If possible, each element should be set out in the answer with supporting authority. Passing off is a topic which lends itself to essay questions, the topic being open to evolution and redefinement as part of the common law. The essay questions here cover discussions of the elements of an action, particularly with regard to damage, a topic which is relevant to both essay questions and to problems. The wide range of authorities gives a student plenty of material to discuss.

Problem questions in passing off are relatively straightforward and involve setting out the elements of the tort and then identifying whether they are there in the problem.

A suggested approach to problem questions is as follows:

- Give the definition of passing off
- Does the plaintiff have a 'get up', name or mark?
- Does the plaintiff enjoy good will – defined in *IRC v Muller* (1901) as the attractive force which brings customers – and identify any limitations (eg territorial, time-related)

- Identify the misrepresentation
- Is the misrepresentation likely to mislead?
- Is there any evidence of confusion or customers being misled?
- What is the target audience and has it any special features?
- Exceptionally stupid people will be disregarded (*Morning Star v Express Newspapers* (1979) 'moron in a hurry')
- Is there any defence based upon a name? – care must be taken with personal names
- Identify the damage. If no damage can be found no action will lie. List possible heads of damage
- Consider the balance of convenience as to whether the injunction should be granted or refused. If the passing off is small or the risk of damage slight, relief may be declined

Most cases involve names and it is recommended that questions involving the use of personal names as a defence should be addressed with particular care. The most important case to refer to is *Parker Knoll v Knoll International* (1962) and the need for care leads to the issue also being dealt with as an essay.

In view of the flexibility of passing off, it should not be forgotten that it may provide an alternative right of action in cases involving copyright or even design rights (see Chapter 2).

Checklist

Students should be familiar with the following areas:

- *Annabel's Club Ltd v Schock* (1972)
- *Birmingham Relish v Powell* (1893)
- *Chelsea Man v Chelsea Girl* (1987)
- *Erven Warnink BV v Townend (Hull)* (1979)
- *IRC v Muller* (1901)
- *Lego v Lemelstrich* (1983)
- *Office Cleaning Services v Westminster Window and General Cleaners Ltd* (1946)
- *Parker Knoll v Knoll International* (1962)

- *Reckitt v Coleman* (1990)
- *Spalding v Gamage* (1916)
- *Wotherspoon v Currie* (1872)

Question 29

Outline the elements of an action in passing off.

Answer plan

This seems to be a relatively straightforward question where a student may find a generalist tort text book of greater assistance initially than a more specialised intellectual property text. Here the problem the student faces is the wide and diverse range of cases which have accumulated over the years under the heading of 'passing off'.

The issues to be considered are:

- Function of passing off
- *Spalding v Gamage* (1915)
- *Erven Warnink BV v Townsend* (1979) (Advocaat case)
- *Reckitt v Coleman* (1990)
- Good will
- Common field of activity
- Damage

Answer

Passing off protects the property in the good will of a business from erosion arising from misrepresentations made by others. Closest to an action for registered trade marks infringement, an action for passing off enables a trader to claim against another (usually a competitor) who by way of misrepresentation seeks to unfairly appropriate or damage the good will which the first trader enjoys. Whilst legitimate competition is acceptable, a trader must not '... sell his own goods under the pretence that they are the goods of another man' (*Perry v Truefitt* (1842)). This is the basis of the common law tort of passing off. As part of the common law its principles are open to evolution and restatement, so no precise definition can be formulated. The history of passing off shows that it is adaptable to a wide variety of situations and, as long ago as *Spalding v Gammage* (1915), it was recognised that the range of circumstances to which a trader may have recourse to such an action cannot be exhausted.

Nonetheless, three common elements can be detected as general principles underlying the action. As a prerequisite, it must be shown that the plaintiff's business has acquired a reputation in the market and is recognised by the public by a distinguishing feature or 'get up'. Secondly, the defendant must have said or done something amounting to or giving rise to a misrepresentation, or which is likely to deceive actual or potential customers. Thirdly, it must be shown that the plaintiff will suffer damage by deception.

The classical form of passing off was enunciated by Lord Parker in *Spalding v Gamage* (1915) that 'no person is entitled to represent his goods as those of another'. More recently, the courts have attempted more specific formulations. The essential elements of passing off were identified by Lord Diplock in *Erven Warnink BV v Townend & Sons (Hull) Ltd* (1979) as: (1) a misrepresentation; (2) made by a trader in the course of trade; (3) to prospective customers of his or ultimate consumers of goods or services supplied by him; (4) which is calculated to injure the business or good will of another trader (in the sense that this is a foreseeable consequence); and (5) which results in damage to a business or good will of the trader or is likely to do so.

The alternative formulation proposed by Lord Frazer was: (1) a trader's business; (2) that the class of goods is clearly definable and that they are distinguishable in the minds of the public by way of trade name from other goods; (3) because of the reputation of the goods there is good will attached to the name; (4) that the plaintiff, as a member of the class of those who sell the goods, is the owner of the good will in England which is of substantial value; and (5) that he has suffered or is likely to suffer substantial damage to his good will.

Subsequently, as observed by Oliver LJ in *Anheuser Busch Inc v Budejovicky Budvar NP* (trading as Budweiser Budvar Brewery)

(1984), these two statements of principle compliment one another, Lord Diplock's statement 'emphasising what has been done by the defendant to give rise to the complaint and Lord Frazer stating what the plaintiff has to show as the prerequisite of complaining', *per* Lord Oliver.

Since then these extended definitions have further been honed to three basic elements. In *Reckitt & Colman v Borden* (1990), Lord Oliver stated that passing off must establish three elements:

- good will or reputation attached to the goods or services supplied with an associated 'get up';
- demonstrate a misrepresentation by the defendant to the public leading or likely to lead to the public believing that the goods or services offered by him are those of the plaintiff;
- demonstrate that he suffers or is likely to suffer damage by reason of the erroneous belief engendered by the defendant's misrepresentation.

As with other common law torts, formulations for passing off are open to re-interpretation because of their Lordships' inherent power to depart from previous decisions. Decisions of the House of Lords need not be treated as the equivalent of statutory formulae (see *Cassell v Broome* (1972)).

Subsequently, the Court of Appeal in *Consorzio del Proscuito di Parma v Marks & Spencer* (1991) and *Harrods v Harrodian School* (1996) have endorsed the 'classical trinity' of: (1) reputation (or good will) acquired by the plaintiff in his goods, name or mark; (2) misrepresentation by the defendant leading to confusion (or deception); and (3) damage to the plaintiff.

Good will and 'get up'

Good will that constitutes the property right is 'the attractive force which brings customers in' (*IRC v Muller* (1901)). In an action for passing off the plaintiff must prove that the good will is associated in the public mind with a 'get up' – a distinctive mark or name. Thus, where the words 'Yorkshire Relish' were recognised as referring to a sauce manufactured by the plaintiff in *Birmingham Vinegar Brewery Co v Powell* (1897), the plaintiff could claim against an imitation of the name, even though customers were not aware of the plaintiff's precise identity. Names, fancy or invented words, shapes and colours can all constitute a 'get up' which can be attached to the plaintiff's good will. Seperation of the mark from the good will results in no action being possible in passing off (*Star Industrial v Yap Kwee Kor* (1976)). The good will may be geographically limited (*Chelsea Man v Chelsea Girl* (1987)). The reputation normally has to be in the UK (*Alain Bernadin et Cie v Pavillion Properties* (1967)), although the trade can actually take place abroad. For example, in *Maxim v Dye* (1977), the owner of the restaurant Maxim in Paris sought an injunction to restrain the defendant from opening a French restaurant in Norwich under the same name. The Norwich restaurant did not operate to the same standard as the French restaurant in Paris. The plaintiff obtained an injunction, even though he did not have a business in this country, because the defendant could harm the good will in Paris.

Good will can exist for a business even if operating for a short period (*Stannard v Reay* (1967)) but, if no business has been commenced at the same time, it is possible that there was no established reputation to be protected (*Compatibility Research Ltd v Computer Psyche Co Ltd* (1967)).

Deception

Mere confusion between businesses is not enough; it is essential for the plaintiff's proprietary right and good will in the name in question to be made out and affected (*Marcus Publishing v Hutton-Wild* (1990)). For deception to be proved, it is sufficient that 'a false representation has in fact been made, whether fraudulently or otherwise, and that damage may probably ensue. However, the complete innocence of the party making it may be a reason for limiting the account of profits to the period subsequent to the date at which he becomes aware of the facts', *per* Lord Parker in *Spalding v Gamage* (1915). As a result, a misrepresentation can be deliberate, reckless or innocent – in each case a plaintiff may have a claim.

The vast majority of cases involve names or an invented word coined by the plaintiff. Use of a plaintiff's name calculated to deceive and 'so to divert business from the plaintiff to the defendant' or 'to occasion a confusion between the two businesses' (*per* Astbury J in *Ewing v Buttercup Margarine Co Ltd* (1917)) will be actionable.

Examples of activities within the doctrine of passing off include misrepresenting inferior makes of goods as those of a higher quality (eg misrepresenting 'seconds' (*Spalding v Gamage* (1916); suggesting second hand goods are new (*Westinghouse Brake etc v Varsity Eliminator Co* (1935) or suggesting stale goods are fresh (*Wiltshire United Dairies v Thomas Dairies* (1957)). The tort may also be used in cases of titles where copyright is not of assistance.

Common field of activity

The doctrine that a common field of activity must exist between plaintiff and defendant arose in the decision in *McCulloch v Lewis A May Distributors Ltd* (1947) where the radio presenter, 'Uncle Mac', had no common field of activity with the manufacturer of breakfast cereal who adopted the name. In *Rolls Razors Ltd v Rolls Lighters Ltd* (1949), it was held that no confusion was likely because the respective products sold by the parties were not likely to be confused. The same principle was applied in *Wombles Ltd v Wombles Skips* (1977), where the proprietors of the children's' characters were held to be a separate field of activity to the defendant who manufactured rubbish skips. However, on occasion, the courts have found that good will extends beyond the products with which it is associated. In *Lego Systems Aktieselskab v Lego M Lemelstrich* (1983), the makers of the well-known toy bricks were able to prevent the defendants entering the UK gardening and irrigation market using their name.

Sufficiency of deception

Mere likelihood of confusion on the part of a small number of customers is not enough to sustain a claim for passing off. The plaintiff must show that a substantial number are likely to be deceived. Any special features of target customers will be considered, such as language barriers (*White v Asian Trading Organisation* (1964)), or who they may be, eg 'washerwomen, cottagers and other persons in humble station' *per* Lord Gorrell in (*'Dolly Blue') William Edge & Sons v William Niccolls & Sons* (1911), although the court will not have regard to unusually stupid people (*Morning Star v Express Newspapers* (1979)). Equally, the court may consider a more informed and astute category where appropriate, for example, health care professionals (*Hodgkinson & Corby Ltd v Wards Mobility* (1994)).

Damage

Proof of damage is an essential element in every case. The plaintiff must show that he has either suffered damage or that he is likely to suffer damage caused by the misrepresentation that the source of the goods or services is the same as those of the plaintiff. Actionable damage can take a wide range of potential forms including a diversion of sales, damage to reputation (*Annabel's Club v Schock* (1972)) and loss of a licensing opportunity (*Lego v Lemelstrich* (1983)). The courts are likely to refuse interlocutory relief where damage is speculative.

Question 30

Discuss how the courts have dealt with damage as an essential element of passing off.

Answer plan

The issues to be considered are:

- Definitions – need for damage
- Good will
- Loss of sales
- Damage to reputation
- Injurious association
- Confusion as damage

Answer

As part of the law of tort, proof of damage is an essential element in a successful action for passing off. Any misrepresentation by a defendant, such as to cause substantial damage to the good will of a business or the likelihood of such damage, will be potentially actionable, but the damage must be more than minimal (*per* Lord Frazer in *Erven Warnink BV v Townsend* (1979)).

As no tort of unfair competition exists in the UK, a plaintiff must establish that he or she has suffered damage of a type and in such circumstances for which the law will grant a remedy. Ordinary competition is not a basis for passing off. For example, in *Singer v Loog* (1882), a trader has a right to make and sell machines that are similar to another. A trader may refer to his rival's machines and his rival's name, providing he does so fairly.

In *Monodraught Flues Ltd v Nonfumo Flue Systems Ltd & Another* (1995), Laddie J reminded potential plaintiffs that, '... it is permissible to winkle out the established trader and replace his goods by new ones; that is what we call competition. It is only when the new entrant goes further and by imitating the established product's name or 'get up' so as to give rise to confusion and thereby cause or facilitate substitution or acquisition of customers who would otherwise not belong to the new entrant' that the law will grant a remedy. Arguably, the categories of damage are broader than Laddie J suggests and the key test for plaintiffs (or their lawyers) is to identify those forms of damage of which a plaintiff can and cannot complain.

In passing off claims, actionable damage can basically be divided into three categories: diversion, damage to reputation and dilution, as set out in *Taylor Brothers Ltd v Taylors Group Ltd* (1988). Each type of damage was identified as aspects of damage to good will, differing only in type as follows: 'Diversion is an appropriation of a part of a plaintiff's good will. Damage to reputation amounts to poisoning of the plaintiff's good will. Damaging by suggestion of association of the plaintiff's business amounts to a dilution of the plaintiff's good will. A plaintiff who is entitled in principle to the protection of his property right in good will is entitled to protection against all such forms of attack without nice distinctions being drawn'.

Direct loss of sales

In such cases, the two parties must normally be in competition with one another, and the damage will consist of the customers who have wrongly been acquired or diverted from the plaintiff as a result of the misrepresentation by the defendant. In this situation, the parties must usually be competitors to some extent or at least engaged in the same type of industry (eg *Albion Motor Car Co Ltd v Albion Carriage and Motor Body Works Ltd* (1917)). In *Draper v Trist*

(1939), it was held that if a plaintiff puts a quantity of goods on the market which are calculated to be taken as the plaintiff's, the court will generally infer that this will lead to some loss of sales, without the plaintiff necessarily providing actual proof of individual transactions.

Assessing the amount of actual damage may be problematic. Originally, it was held that to justify an interlocutory injunction, the risk of direction of customers must be direct and immediate (*Lyons Maid Ltd v Trebor Ltd* (1967)) but the risk of harm would now fall to be decided on *American Cyanamid* principles.

Losses may also be indirect. In *Hoffman La Roche v DDSA* (1969), there was held to be damage through the diversion of customers where the defendants imitated the colouring of tranquilising capsules. Arguments as to the scope of actionable damage can thus be potentially wide if they encompass customers who may be ignorant of the true identity of the manufacturer. In *Hoffman La Roche,* the court upheld the principle that goods of a particular 'get up' proclaim their origin just as much as if they had a particular name attached to them and, when goods are sold with a particular 'get up' for long enough to be recognised by the public as goods of a particular manufacturer it does not matter that the public does not know who the original manufacturer actually is. An earlier example is *Birmingham Vinegar Brewery Co Ltd v Powell* (1897).

Damage to reputation

In *Harrods Ltd v R Harrod Ltd* (1923), the business of the defendant as a money lender was held to be damaging to the good will of the well-known department store. The court held there was potential damage to the good will of Harrods and an injunction was granted. Warrington LJ stated that '... I think that under the word "property" may well be included the trade reputation of the plaintiffs, and that, if tangible injury is shown to the trade reputation of the plaintiffs, that is enough'.

Damage to reputation can arise from the defendant placing secondary or inferior goods on the market, purporting them to be the goods of the plaintiff (*AG Spalding & Bros v AW Gamage Ltd* (1915)). Injurious association with the plaintiff is another potential ground of damage, usually through the use of a trade name which either deceives or confuses. However, if the deception has gone on for many years and there is no evidence of any customers being misled or a decline in sales, no action will lie (*HP Bulmer Ltd v J Bollinger SA* (1961)).

Into this category may fall many types of claims in passing off, such as inducing a belief that one class of the plaintiff's goods are of another class or quality (*Teacher v Levy* (1905)); passing seconds as the prime item (*Gillette Safety Razor Co and Gillette Safety Razor Ltd v Franks* (1924)) or holding out stale goods as fresh ones (*Wiltshire United Dairy v Thomas Robinson & Sons Ltd* (1957)).

Injurious association

The basis of injurious association was set out by Lord Diplock in *Erven Warnink BV v J Townend & Sons (Hull) Ltd* (1979). Lord Diplock observed that damage to good will could lie through a defendant harming the reputation on which the good will is built and that an action may lie where 'although the plaintiff and the defendant were not competing traders in the same line of business, a false suggestion by the defendant that their business were connected with one another would damage the reputation and thus the good will of the plaintiff's business'. In *Annabel's Club v Schock* (1972), the plaintiffs complained of damage to the reputation of their night club by the opening of an escort agency also under the name of Annabel's.

Damage can be in the form of harm to reputation either in the eyes of the public or trade, sometimes by indirect means. In *Blazer plc v Yardley & Co Ltd* (1992), it was found that evidence was thin as to the effects of an association and did not suggest as a consequence that the public would think less of the plaintiff, let alone withdraw their custom.

If a damage is too trivial or speculative no action will lie. In *Stringfellow v McCain Foods (GB) Ltd* (1984), a final injunction was refused where damage was speculative and the argument that licensees might be put off by associating with oven chips was rejected. Such cases rarely go beyond the interlocutory stage.

Confusion

Generally confusion between two businesses which are operating legitimately is not enough to constitute actionable damage. In *Marengo v Daily Sketch and Daily Graphic Ltd* (1947), Lord Greene MR referred to the fact that parties must put up with 'the results of the confusion as one of the misfortunes which occur in life' where the confusion arises from the collision of two independent rights or liberties.

However, on occasion the courts have referred to confusion between parties on the part of the public as though it were an actionable form of damage. For instance, in *Ewing v Buttercup Magarine Co Ltd* (1917), the court stated that two types of damage could follow from the misleading use of a company's name, being either 'to divert business from the plaintiff to the defendant' or 'to occasion a confusion between the two businesses' (*Parker Knoll v Knoll International* (1962)). In *Chelsea Man Meanswear Ltd v Chelsea Girl Ltd* (1987), the Court of Appeal referred to the 'injury which is inherently likely to be suffered by any business when on frequent occasions it is confused by customers or potential customers with a business owned by another proprietor or is wrongly regarded as being connected with that business'.

Other categories

Since the outer limits of the tort of passing off cannot be defined, new forms of actionable damage are likely to emerge, although each can probably be classified as a variant of the three categories identified. In *Walter v Ashton* (1902), the owner of a bicycle shop passed off his business as a branch of *The Times* newspaper, selling 'The Times' bicycles. It was held that the possibility of *The Times* being wrongly exposed to litigation by dissatisfied customers was sufficient potential damage.

Loss of a licensing opportunity was considered in *Lego v Lemelstrich* (1983) by use of the well-known toy brick manufacturers' name, even though there was no common field of activity on the part of the defendant. On this basis, it will also be possible to predict new forms of action such as the loss of chance as recoverable damage (*First Interstate Bank v Cohen & Arnold* (1995)). The requirement of damage ensures that frivolous cases are not brought before the courts and that the tort is not abused by traders seeking a monopoly position, and free competition is promoted.

Question 31

To what extent is a person allowed to use their own name as a defence against a claim of passing off?

Answer plan

This is an area where the law suffers from a lack of clarity, and an inadequate awareness of the various aspects of the rules on the student's part may lead to inaccurate answers in essays. Passing off questions may often include the possibility of a person using their own name, and all too often students set boundaries of this defence far too widely in their answer.

The issues to be considered are:

- Legal property in names – no copyright
- Non-commercial use
- *Rodgers (Joseph) & Sons v WN Rodgers* (1924)
- *Parker Knoll Ltd v Knoll International* (1962)

Answer

Whilst no one can claim monopoly rights under copyright in a single word or name (T*averner Rutledge Ltd v Trexapalm* (1975)), it is possible to restrain the use of a name in business under the law of passing off. The one exception is with what has been called the right of a person to use their own name in business, but an analysis of this proposition in the light of decided cases shows that its operation has been increasingly hedged with restrictions.

Strictly speaking, no absolute right of property exists purely in a name and no action can lie for restraining non-commercial use. In *Cowley v Cowley* (1901), it was held that Lord Cowley could not prevent his former wife using the title Lady Cowley after their divorce. In business, however, it has long been possible to seek to protect a name and the good will associated with it. In *Du Boulay v*

Du Boulay (1869), it was held that where a trader has used a name, 'any person using that name, after a relative right of this description has been acquired by another, is considered to be guilty of a fraud, or at least, of an invasion of another's right, and renders himself liable to an action or he may be restrained from the use of the name by an injunction'.

Both corporate and legal persons have on occasion claimed the benefit of a defence in their own name. In *Montreal Lithographing Co v Sabiston* (1899), the Privy Council held that a company, which was the transferee of the assets and good will from a dissolved company, could not sue the respondents for carrying on the business under the name of a dissolved company or any other so framed as to lead to a belief that the business was a successor. In the absence of any representation, an injunction would not lie against the use of a mere name. However, this was subject to the restriction that a company must use its name without abbreviation, addition or other modification (*Saunders v Sun Life Assurance Company of Canada* (1893) which was later reflected in decisions on personal names).

Even fictitious names can be protected on occasions. In *Hines v Winnick* (1947), the plaintiff claimed rights in the name of his band and performances under the stage name of 'Dr Crock and the Crackpots'. It was held that the name had become part of his stock in trade and the defendants could be restrained from making use of it. He was able to restrain misleading use of the name in recordings made by the BBC.

The relative right referred to in *Du Boulay v Du Boulay* (1869) was qualified by the important exception widely upheld in the 19th century that a person must not be restrained from using their own name and that this was an inherent natural right.

In *Burgess v Burgess* (1853), the plaintiffs who were the manufacturers of fish sauces, failed to obtain an injunction to restrain the defendant from selling 'Burgess's Essence of Anchovies'. The court held a person selling an article in his own name could not be restrained by another who also sold under the same name unless there was proof of fraud. Similarly, in *Turton v Turton* (1889), it was held that, although there was a probability that the public could occasionally be misled by the resemblance in names, no injunction would lie to prevent Thomas Turton & Sons, as opposed to John Turton & Sons, from trading in their own name. Lord Esher MR stated 'that if all that a man does is to carry on the same business, and to state how he is carrying it on – that statement being the simple truth – and he does nothing more with regard to the respective name, he is doing no wrong'. A similar approach can be detected in *Massam v Thorley's Cattle Food Co* (1880) in which the court held, 'A surname is not a man's legal property, or conferred upon him by law in any particular way, it is gained by reputation'.

The right to trade under one's own name does not extend to the right to use one's name as a trade mark, if the result will be confusion (*Ronson Products Ltd v Ronson Furniture Ltd* (1966)) although under s 11 of the Trade Marks Act 1994 use of a real name will be defence for an action for infringement by the holder of an identical mark.

In *John Brinsmead & Sons Ltd v Edward George Stanley Brinsmead* (1913), a case involving pianos of differing qualities, it was held that, if a man uses his own name so as to be likely to deceive and divert business from the plaintiffs to the defendants, he will be restrained.

The key question in each case seems to be whether the use of a name is calculated to deceive the public unless precautions are taken. Confusion is not sufficient. In *Rodgers (Joseph) & Sons v WN Rodgers* (1924), the court considered the doctrine further. The proposition in law that no man is entitled to describe his goods so as to represent that those goods are those of another was held to have only one exception; a man is entitled to carry on a business under his own name so long as nothing more than confusion is caused with the business of another, and so long as the name is used honestly.

To be able to raise a plea of use of one's own name, the defendant would have to fulfil a number of conditions:

- there must be full use of his own name by the defendant;
- he must do nothing more than cause confusion;
- in general he must be a natural person;
- he must act honestly;
- he must be using the name so as to describe the goods.

The criteria set out by Lord Romer have been followed closely in subsequent decisions. It should therefore be stated that whilst English law does allow a person generally to use their own name honestly in the market or use it as part of a business name, such use may nonetheless be restrained if it leads to deception.

In *Parker Knoll v Knoll International* (1962), the House of Lords upheld an injunction to restrain the defendants from using their own name. Reviewing the authorities, their Lordships differed in their opinions; the minority (Denning and Devlin LJJ) holding (*obiter*) that use of a full name should not be restrained unless there was a deception. Mere confusion was not enough. Lord Devlin took the view that where there was no question of fraud, a false representation could be made even if literally true; it did not matter whether the name is an actual or fictious one. It may be concluded from the decision of *Parker Knoll* that a person may be restrained from using his or her name if it is used in circumstances which will naturally and plainly refer to some other person, unless steps are taken which distinguish it. If a person makes a statement which is true but carries a false representation then it will be possible to restrain it.

What is clear from the decision is that the use of a name on goods in a trade mark sense is no defence even if *bona fide*. What is left unclear is whether use of a business name can be a defence, particularly in cases where use of the name results 'in causing confusion' as opposed to 'deceiving'. The position is further complicated by the fact that the courts have held confusion between businesses to be a form of damage (*Chelsea Man v Chelsea Girl* (1987)). This requires the plaintiff to produce proof of the state of mind which follows from a representation which is recognised as possible under the law of misrepresentation; 'the state of a man's mind is as much a matter of fact as the state of a man's digestion' – *Edginton v Fitzmaurice* (1885). The end result to be considered would be an actual deception. A state of confusion on the part of a customer who is still able to ascertain the true position will not count.

Nicknames have produced a variety of opinions. In *Jays Ltd v Jacobi* (1933), no passing off was proved as the first defendant had acquired the name Jay by reputation and was entitled to trade under it, the names were not the same and the plaintiff had an apostrophe before the 's'. The action failed as no dishonesty was established. However, in *Biba Group v Biba Boutique* (1980), a nickname was no defence to an action for passing off. In *Parker Knoll*, Denning LJ gave the example that a man called William John Pears cannot set up a soap business and call his soap 'Pears Soap'. He is not entitled to abbreviate his own name so as to deceive.

The law thus appears to be that restraint will lie if there is deception as to a name applied to goods but, if in the course of trade some confusion arises from the use of the same business name, 'that is a lesser evil than that a man should be deprived of what would appear to be a natural and inherent right' (*Marengo v Daily Sketch* (1947)). The intention of the party using his or her own name can therefore be crucial and if a deception arises then an action will lie.

Question 32

Toby Parkinsons Ltd are an established retailer in products for babies and children under the age of three. They have an established 'get up' of blue goods for male children and pink ones for female ones, marked with a 'TP' logo and sometimes accompanied by pictures of cherubs. They also sell goods as 'Parkinsons' and mark some of their range with the name.

Tracy Parkinson is an entrepreneur who decides to open her own baby clothing shop. She too adopts the tradition of blue goods for male infants and pink goods for females. She decorates items with her own name and initials as the whim takes her and she calls her shop Tracy Parkinson's or TP's. Toby Parkinsons Ltd are concerned about their trade reputation as they view Tracy's goods to be of inferior quality. They also believe there will be a diversion of trade. Advise Toby Parkinsons Ltd of their common law rights.

Answer plan

A relatively straightforward question – except the use of a personal name. Questions are sometimes phrased in terms of common law rights rather than passing off, but it is passing off that the examiner is getting at. (Another alternative which also raises the issue of passing off is where the question involves the holder of an unregistered trade mark.) Care is needed with any consideration of the use of a person's personal name. Too superficial a study of the subject will suggest that all may be well if a person trades under their own name. Regrettably the issue is not that simple.

The issues to be considered are:

- Definition of passing off
- Use of initials
- Use of own name
- Confusion
- Common field of activity
- Damage

Answer

The common law rights of Toby Parkinsons Ltd lie in the right to bring an action for passing off against Tracy. To sustain a claim, Toby Parkinsons Ltd must prove the necessary elements of the tort. Classic passing off was defined by Lord Halsbury in *Frank Reddaway & Co Ltd v George Banham & Co Ltd* (1896) as the principle that 'nobody has any right to represent his goods as those of somebody else'. In *Erven Warnink BV v J Townend and Sons (Hull) Ltd* (1980) (the 'Advocaat' case), five elements were identified: (1) a misrepresentation; (2) made in the course of trade; (3) to prospective customers in the course of trade; (4) which is calculated to harm the business reputation or good will of the plaintiff; and (5) damage. Subsequently, in *Reckitt & Coleman v Borden Ltd* (1990), these were reduced to the classic trinity of three elements: (1) a misrepresentation; (2) made in the course of trade; and (3) damage.

Toby Parkinsons and Tracy are both trading in the same field and Tracy is using a name, initials and goods which resemble those of Toby Parkinsons. To succeed in an action, it is essential that Toby Parkinsons have 'good will' in their business which is associated by the public with their mark. Good will was defined in *IRC v Muller* (1901) as 'the attractive force that brings customers in'. If the public are moved to buy at source by name or 'get up', this should be sufficient to establish good will. There is no necessity in a passing off action that the customers deceived should be aware of Toby

Parkinsons' precise identity, provided they are accustomed to buy the plaintiff's goods and are deceived by a misrepresentation (*Birmingham Vinegar Brewery Co Ltd v Powell* (1897)). Whilst it is possible to have good will associated by the public with colours used in the course of trade, the courts have generally been reluctant to protect unregistered trade marks which derive solely from eye appeal or visual appearance.

Arguably, the use of the colours blue and pink and images of cherubs are too commonplace and banal to be associated in the public mind with Toby Parkinsons' good will. If there is nothing distinctive, then a claim based upon this resemblance alone will fail. Toby Parkinsons Ltd will be on much stronger ground with the use of their name and initials. The words and initials do not have any descriptive function and clearly relate to source.

Initials and combinations of letters may be restrained, so it is possible for a claim to lie in the use of 'TPs' by Tracy. In *Birmingham Small Arms Co Ltd v Webb & Co* (1906), Parker J held that BSA could be distinctive of the plaintiffs with regard to the sale of spanners and was infringed by a defendant who used BAS. Similarly, in *Du Cros v Gold* (1912), the letters W & G displayed on the doors of taxi cabs was infringed by the defendants who used M & G, although in *IDW Superstores v Duncan Harris* (1975), it was held that the court should be slow to restrain the use of a trading name merely because the words which constitute the name bear initials which make up the name under which a plaintiff is trading (*per* Megarry J). If the use of the name and initials by Tracy is likely to deceive customers, then the element of misrepresentation will be established.

Even though the question indicates that there are differences in the goods which are stocked, it is unlikely that a defence of a non-common field of activity will be available to Tracy. Lack of a common field of activity has been grounds in the past for refusing relief (*Harrods Ltd v Harrodian School* (1996)). However, in other cases where a name has been distinctive, relief has been granted even if the activities are not the same (*Lego v Lemelstrich* (1983)). Here, a common field of activity clearly exists between the two businesses, although some of the goods may not be precisely the same, and it would be reasonable to expect a common connection between them. In *Dunlop Pneumatic Tyre Co Ltd v Dunlop Lubricant*

Company (1889), although the Dunlop Tyre company was not selling heating oils, there was a sufficiently allied field between the two activities. The inference will be that confusion is likely to follow.

Mere confusion between the two businesses will not be enough, there must actually be an effect or likely effect on Toby Parkinsons' proprietary right and good will (*Marcus Publishing v Hutton Wild* (1990)). Simple confusion does not necessarily mean misrepresentation (*My Kinda Town (t/a Chicago Ribstack) v Dr Pepper's Store* (1983)). However, there is no need to prove that anyone has actually been deceived (*Bourne Swan v Edgar* (1903)). There is nothing to suggest that Tracy has done anything further to distinguish her goods.

Tracy may raise the defence that she is entitled to use her own name and seek to rely on the authorities that the law will not restrain her own name in business. Unfortunately, the more modern authorities are against her.

In *Turton v Turton* (1889), it was held to be a general rule that natural persons could trade under their personal names and could not be restrained by another trader using the same name. The same principle was expressed in *Marengo v Daily Sketch* (1948), where the view was taken that 'a man must be allowed to trade in his own name and, if some confusion results, that is a lesser evil than that a man should be deprived of what would appear to be a natural and inherent right'.

Following various decisions by the courts, however, Tracy cannot claim an absolute right to her own name. *Rodgers (Joseph) & Sons v WN Rodgers* (1924) imposed a number of important qualifications. If a person uses a personal name so as to be likely to deceive and divert trade from the plaintiff's business to that of the defendant, an injunction will lie. A defence can be raised only where a person is using their own full name honestly, doing nothing to create confusion and using the name to describe the goods. In *Parker Knoll v Knoll International* (1962), it was further held that if goods are marked with a name and there is a likelihood of deception, then no defence can be raised. In addition, Tracy is also using an abbreviated version of her name not her full one – the defence is thus not made out. Tracy's position is further undermined by the fact that the question states that TP is described as her nickname and as such it is unlikely to attract any protection (*Biba Group Ltd v Biba Boutique* (1980)).

An interesting and possibly rewarding course of inquiry for Toby Parkinsons to explore, before or at trial if an opportunity arises, would be to determine why Tracy has adopted the name and similarities in initials and 'get up'. This may be raised in cross examination should the case come to trial. A deception does not need to be deliberate or reckless to be actionable in a passing off action – it can be entirely innocent. Any answers elicited from Tracy might be revealing if she is deliberately attempting to trade upon Toby Parkinsons' good will. If a defendant has deliberately adopted a name or 'get up' with an intention to deceive, the court is liable to presume that they will have succeeded.

In determining the likelihood of confusion, the name and appearance may be taken together to assess whether the imitation amounts to passing off (*Lever v Goodwin* (1887)). The court will take the position of the ordinary customers buying goods in the circumstances of trade. Tests have included whether the imitation would deceive a person of ordinary intelligence (*Buttons Ltd v Buttons Covered Ltd* (1920)) and the court will disregard particularly unobservant or stupid individuals in the market place (*Morning Star v Express Newspapers* (1979) – 'moron in a hurry').

Damage or a likelihood of damage must be proved. In *Chelsea Man v Chelsea Girl* (1987), it was held that damage could take a number of forms including: (a) the diversion of trade from the plaintiffs; (b) injuring the plaintiff's trade reputation by marketing goods of a different quality; and (c) the damage caused to the business by confusion on frequent occasions by traders or customers between the two businesses.

A further heading of damage may be the dilution of good will if Toby Parkinsons' enjoys a particularly exclusive reputation and Tracy's goods are of inferior quality. If a name is adopted with fraudulent intent, the court will readily infer damage. (*Harrods Ltd v R Harrod Ltd* (1923)).

The only point which seems to be in Tracy's favour is that Toby Parkinsons have delayed in seeking an interlocutory injunction. The court will consider such an application on the principles of *American Cyanamid v Ethicon* (1975). Since it may well be impossible to quantify the amount of lost trade, this may be a factor that the court will consider. Since Tracy's business developments are at a relatively early stage, Toby Parkinsons should seek an injunction, although it is too late to apply on *a quia timet* basis. Toby Parkinson's activities are far in advance of the plaintiff's and as being the first on the market will mean that they have far stronger rights to the exclusive good will.

Furthermore, Tracy's activities may lead to the undermining of Toby Parkinsons' good will, given that the goods sold by Tracy are cheaper (*Taverner Rutledge v Trexapalm Ltd* (1975)). The advice given to Toby Parkinsons should be to act as quickly as possible. A suitable form of injunction might restrain Tracy from using the name Parkinsons or her initials in her business.

Question 33

In 1995, Hoskins Films made a moving and reverential film concerning a 19th century character known as the 'Rhino Man' who suffered from a rare medical condition but who overcame social prejudice and disability to become a respected member of society. In the early part of his life, the Rhino Man wore a mask, hat and cape to disguise his appearance from hostile crowds, and images of these appeared on the posters and promotional material for the film. The film was released on video in 1996 and there was an accompanying book.

In 1997, Hoskins Films are appalled to see an advertisement in New Musical Express for a recording by Row Records of the obese rap singer Reggie 'Rhino' Murray who advertises a rap record with a chorus of 'Rhino-Rhino-Gut' to a repetitive beat. Hoskins Films send an order to Row Records asking for the Rhino Man recording as advertised and are sent a copy.

Hoskins Films are further appalled to discover that Bad Taste Biscuits have brought out a novelty Rhino Man biscuit which feature drawings of the mask, hat and cape on the wrapper.

In the interests of human dignity and their commercial reputation, Hoskins Films wish to restrain both the record advertisement and the biscuits from using the image. Advise Hoskins Films as to their common law rights.

Answer plan

This question is based upon the unreported decision in *Thorn EMI Films v Arista Records* (1983) in which film makers sought to bring an action to restrain the passing off of a record advertised with imagery derived from the plaintiff's film *The Elephant Man*. Vice Chancellor Megarry held that damage had to be established, which the plaintiff failed to do.

The issues to be considered are:

- Elements of passing off
- Concept of 'get up'
- Common field of activity
- Trap order
- Damage

Answer

The common law rights referred to in this question are the right of Hoskins Films to bring an action for passing off. However, given the stated circumstances, they are unlikely to be able to succeed against either defendant.

The basis of an action in passing off is that the defendant, through a misrepresentation, has harmed the good will of the plaintiff resulting in damage. Two formulations of the elements in passing off are to be found. In *Erven Warnink BV v Townend* (1979), Lord Diplock stated that a plaintiff had to prove five elements as a necessary part of any claim: (1) a misrepresentation; (2) made in the course of trade; (3) to prospective customers of his or ultimate consumers of goods or services supplied by him; (4) which is calculated to injure the business or good will of another trader (in the sense of a reasonably foreseeable consequence); and (5) which causes actual damage to a business or good will of the trader by whom the action is brought, or will probably do so. In *Reckitt and Coleman v Borden Inc* (1990), Lord Oliver reduced these elements to the classical trinity of: (1) misrepresentation; (2) the existence of good will; and (3) damage caused to the good will. However, as Lord Diplock stated, the fact that these elements exist does not mean that damage has actually been suffered and in the absence of any proof of damage, no remedy will lie. From the facts stated in the question, an action for passing off would not succeed given that Hoskins Films would have to prove the existence of good will in the 'get up' of the artwork and title of the film 'The Rhino Man'. Good will is the attractive force which brings customers in (*IRC v Muller* (1901)) and there is nothing to suggest that Hoskins Films have used 'The Rhino Man' as an unregistered trade mark or that they have any distinctive 'get up' in it.

Neither Reggie 'Rhino' Murray nor Bad Taste Biscuits are passing themselves off under the name Hoskins Films. Whilst copyright does not protect titles, an action in passing off can be an alternative. According to *Lever Brothers Ltd v Bedingfield* (1898), deliberate copying will not be sufficient if there is no probability of deception. A soap manufacturer had a distinctive label, and from the evidence it was obvious that there was copying of some parts of it. However, what was taken was not sufficient to constitute an infringement of copyright but it could sustain an action in passing off.

There is no need to allege or prove fraud in a passing off action, or that anyone has been deceived (*Bourne v Swan & Edgar* (1903)), as the court can act where it is satisfied that the resemblance is such that one mark will be mistaken for the other.

In *LPC Music Magazines Ltd v Black and White Music* (1983), the plaintiffs were the producers of a comic called 2000 AD which featured a character called Judge Dredd. The two defendants were responsible for bringing out a record called 'Judge Dredd' celebrating the character from the comic. The plaintiffs claimed that damage could result to their good will on the basis of: (1) the lack of fame of the artists; (2) the quality of the record; (3) words in the song impugning Judge Dredd; and (4) the encouragement to others to make unlicensed songs. The court rejected these claims on the basis that any such damage was entirely speculative. The court found it unlikely that the two enterprises would be associated in the public's mind. The position of Hoskins Films is arguably even weaker since the Rhino Man in the question is not conceived as an original creation of the plaintiffs but as a historical character. In any event, cases involving character merchandising have been largely unsuccessful in the English courts. In *Taverner Rutledge v Trexapalm* (1975), it was held that no person could have a monopoly in the name Kojak for use on lollipops. In *Lyngstad v Annabas Products Ltd* (1977), the defendants had an existing business in a field which the plaintiff wished to enter. The defendants put pictures of the pop group Abba on to T-shirts but no passing off was proved as the plaintiffs did not have an established market in the UK. Here, Hoskins Films are unlikely to be able to show that they wish to enter into either the biscuit manufacture or record business.

Although Reggie 'Rhino' Murray could not claim the protection of using his nickname (*Biba Group v Biba Boutique* (1980)) there is seems to be little danger of association as it seems unlikely that people buying either the record or the biscuit would automatically associate them with the plaintiffs and Hoskins Films. Mere confusion between the two undertakings is not sufficient to found an action in passing off.

Sending out an order may not in itself constitute passing off. In *Re Wilson & Mathieson Ltd's Application* (1929), the use of a swan mark was not calculated to deceive the trade into believing that taps with that mark were made by the plaintiff, who manufactured baths. The plaintiffs had sent a test order, receiving a tap in response, and tried to use this as a basis for a court action. Tomlin J found there was no likelihood of confusion. He could find no evidence of a deception and the sending of the tap was a *bona fide* response to the order. The goods were of a type to which the plaintiffs had never applied their mark. The court will in any event scrutinise a trap order with special severity. A person executing a trap must act with scrupulous fairness and do nothing to ensnare the other party into the trap (*Procea Products Ltd v Evans & Sons Ltd* (1951)).

Questions of bad taste or morality will not be considered by the court as a basis for passing off. In *Miss World (Jersey) Ltd v James Street Production Ltd* (1981), the Court of Appeal considered a claim brought by the plaintiff who were the proprietors of the good will in the Miss World Contest. The defendants were the producers of an Alternative Miss World film, an event featuring drag artists and transvestites. Although the court indicated no approval or appreciation of the defendants' film, there could be no danger that the two events would be associated and there was no damage.

In an earlier case, *Morecambe & Heysham Borough v Mecca Ltd* (1962), the plaintiffs had run a contest entitled Miss Great Britain since 1946. The defendants ran a contest where the winner was entitled Miss Great Britain. The court declined relief on the grounds that such confusion as existed arose not from the names of the contests but from the similarity of the titles. Words had to be given an ordinary meaning and were not descriptive of the winner of the contest. There were also substantial differences.

As Hoskins Films do not share a common field of activity with the record company or with the biscuit makers, it will not be possible to show a loss of direct sales to customers which could provide a basis for damage. Although there have been cases such as *Lego v Lemelstrich* (1983) where protection has been given where there was no common field of activity, Hoskins Films go by their own name, not that of the Rhino Man. Even in the event of the use of a 'character name' no action may lie. In *Wombles Ltd v Wombles Skips Ltd* (1977), the proprietors of book and television rights in the Wombles were regarded as not having any common field with the operators of rubbish skips. With no direct competition between the two, there will be no damage.

An alternative claim might be that the record, by way of its advertisement, has damaged the reputation of the plaintiff. In *Annabel's (Berkley Square) Ltd v Schock* (1972), the court found that the relevant association between the fields of activities was such that it was impossible to say that the public would not be misled into thinking that the two enterprises were connected. No evidence is adduced to show that anyone has associated the Hoskins Films with either the record company or the biscuit manufacturers. (Evidence of confusion was present in *Annabel's Berkley Square Ltd v Schock* (1972).)

In any event, in recent years the courts have tended to move away from this basis of an action in the absence of any other damage. In *Blazer v Yardley* (1992), evidence was thin as to the effects of an association, and did not suggest that in a consequence the public would think less of the plaintiff, let alone that they would remove their custom from the plaintiff.

In the Court of Appeal decision in *Harrods v Harrodian School* (1996), Millet LJ expressed the view that although a business name 'may be universally recognised, the business with which it is associated in the minds of the public is not all-embracing. To be known to everyone is not to be known for everything'.

In view of the current position of the law of passing off, Hoskins Films will not have a case against either of the putative defendants and should be advised not to pursue any action.

Question 34

The extension of what can be registered as a trade mark under the Trade Marks Act 1994 is likely to relegate actions for passing off to a historical curiosity. Discuss.

Answer plan

The issues to be considered are:

- Section 2(1) of the TMA 1994
- The elements of passing off as a common law tort
- Advantages of a trade mark
- Sections 5 and 11 of the TMA 1994
- Practice in pleading – claims in the alternative
- Situations where trade mark protection do not assist

Answer

The Trade Marks Act 1994 makes express provision to preserve the right to bring an action under the common law tort of passing off. Section 2(1) states that no damages will lie under the TMA 1994 to prevent or recover damages for infringement of an unregistered trade mark, 'but nothing in this Act affects the law relating to passing off'. Yet the wide range of what may now be registered as a trade mark under s 1(1) of the TMA 1994 has led to predictions that actions for passing off will become increasingly infrequent as traders protect their marks by registration.

The TMA 1994 broadens the basis of what may be registered to include shapes, colours, packaging and anything which is capable of distinguishing the goods or services of one undertaking from those of another, provided they can be represented graphically (s 1(1)). Previously, these features were not capable of registration under the TMA 1938. An action in passing off lay to protect non-registerable characteristics such as shapes as with a dimple whisky bottle in *John Haig & Co v Forth Blending Co* (1953) or the 'jif' lemon in *Reckitt and Coleman Ltd v Borden & Co* (1990) or packaging in *William Edge & Sons Ltd v William Niccolls & Sons Ltd* (1911) ('Dolly Blue' washing powders). Colours could in certain cases be capable of protection as in *Hoffman La Roche v DDSA* (1969).

In passing off actions, it is necessary to prove the existence of a 'get up' where an unregistered mark does not depend on a name. Plaintiffs have been successful in relatively few cases. Neither was it possible under the TMA 1938 to register descriptive or geographical names (*York* (1984)) and prior to 1986 it was not possible to register trade marks for service. Another restriction was the requirement of the TMA 1938 that marks had to be applied to goods of the same description. A defendant could not be restrained from applying a mark to goods of another description unless there was an overriding public interest which could be identified. In such situations, passing off provided a measure to protect a reputation. Personal names and nicknames can be protected as trade marks, whereas the protection of name marks can be problematic under the tort of passing off. Established reputations in marks may be protected under s 10(3) of the TMA 1994 even with dissimilar goods, allowing for the development of brand names on a wide range of goods, and potentially infringing marks can be prevented from registration (s 5(3)). Section 10(3) of the TMA 1994 will also make it possible to claim in cases where a defendant might otherwise escape liability in a passing off action on the basis that the plaintiff and defendant do not share a common field of activity (*Harrods Ltd v Harrodian School* (1996)).

The protection conferred by registration of the mark will operate through the UK or, in the case of a Community trade mark, throughout the European Union. This protection is far wider than that which may exist under passing off, where the extent of good will may be held to be confined to certain geographical areas (*Chelsea Man v Chelsea Girl* (1987); *Anheuser Busch Inc v Budejovicky Budvar NP (t/a Budweisr Budvar Brewery NP* (1984)).

In *Mercury Communications v Mercury International* (1995), Laddie J commented on the power and value of a registered trade mark '... registration gives a true monopoly. Subject to certain statutory defences, the proprietor will be able to restrain any trader who uses the same or a sufficiently similar mark'. This indirectly and succinctly expresses the disadvantage of an unregistered mark in that in an action for passing off the mark holder has to prove the existence of a reputation in the mark with potential customers. The reputation has to be maintained and, as Laddie J observed, 'in the majority of cases this means that his common law rights will wither and disappear unless he continues to market and advertise his goods under the mark'. A trade mark can be kept in force indefinitely, providing registration fees are paid and there is an intention to use the mark (s 32). Rights are breached through any use of the mark in the course of trade whether by graphic representation or otherwise (s 103(2)). In an action for passing off, the rights of a trader can only be upheld if there is or is likely to be substantial confusion in the market place which will cause damage.

An action for the protection of an unregistered mark requires the proprietor to prove every element of an action in passing off, but unfortunately this can be a task akin to hitting a moving target. As a common law tort, the essential elements are susceptible to evolution and change. Historically, the tort has been applicable to a wide range of situations, but the precise limits have not been defined. Examples vary from Lord Parker's view in *AG Spalding v Gamage* (1915) that the categories of passing off were not closed and it was impossible to list all the situations, to Lord Diplock's concept of 'the undivided middle' in *Erven Warnink v Townend* (1979), to 'outer limits' of passing off, referred to in *Hodge Clemco Ltd v Airblast Ltd* (1995). The lack of clarity in some situations often makes the litigant's precise position uncertain. Examples where passing off has been proved have included passing off goods of one manufacturer as those of another (classic passing off as in *Spalding v Gamage* (1915)), selling 'seconds' as being of prime manufacture, the selling of stale goods as fresh and others. Whatever the cause of complaint, the proprietor of the good will has to prove, according to Lord Diplock's formula: (i) a misrepresentation; (ii) made in the course of trade by the trader; (iii) to prospective customers or ultimate consumers of the defendant's goods or services; (iv) which is calculated to injure the business or goodwill of another; and (v) which causes actual damage. Alternatively, the formula was expressed by Lord Oliver of Aylmerton in *Reckitt & Colman Products Ltd v Borden Inc* (1990): (a) reputation of good will established by the plaintiff; (b) a misrepresentation by the defendant; and (c) damage. Whereas the proprietor of a registered trade mark only has to show his or her mark is on the register, the plaintiff in a passing off action has to prove each of these elements in order to succeed. A measure of uncertainty will necessarily attach to each, because these elements are open to re-interpretation and qualification, even if a judgment emanates from the House of Lords. It was stated by the House concerning its judgments in *Cassell v Broom* (1972) that the definitions of a tortious cause of action are not to be treated as the equivalent of statutory formula. As a result, uncertainty for the litigant is a feature of a passing off action.

With these drawbacks, has passing off now lost all relevance, given that a trader who is serious about protecting his mark will achieve far better protection by registration as a trade mark? Firstly, there may be a number of undertakings which, because of their scale or the nature of their activities, do not wish to acquire registered trade mark status with commercial connotations, eg charitable or religious bodies and certain voluntary bodies. Nonetheless, they may wish to protect their name and reputation, and passing off would remain a potential cause of action. Amongst traders motivated by commerce, passing off will also still remain relevant as the astute applicant for a registered trade mark will be aware that passing off is still relevant to the operation of trade mark registration. Under s 5 of the TMA 1994, when considering an application for a trade mark, the Registrar may have to consider the rights of the proprietors of earlier unregistered marks. Section 5(4) provides that a mark shall not be registered if its use in the UK is likely to be prevented by any rule of law or passing off. According to *Road Tech Computer Systems Ltd v Unison Software (UK) Ltd* (1996), the existence of such rights may be a mandatory ground for the Registrar to refuse an application to register a new mark, provided all other requirements are proved.

Under s 11 of the TMA 1994, passing off considerations are also involved where a trader uses his or her own name. Section 11 provides that the use of a registered trade mark cannot prevent a trader applying his or her name to a business, but such use could still be restrained through a passing off action. Similarly, the preservation of certain earlier rights in a particular locality under s 11 will retain passing off considerations in the application of trade mark law.

Since the infringement provisions of s 10 have yet to be fully tested in the courts, and because of the surprise that was expressed at the judgment of Laddie, J in *Wagamama Ltd v City Centre Restaurants* (1995) in rejecting the concept of 'likelihood of association' giving rising to an action in trade mark proceedings, it is likely that a claim of passing off will be featured in most pleadings in the alternative. (It would also be a wise precaution in case an action for trade mark infringement is met with a claim that the mark is invalid or should be revoked.)

Finally, passing off may continue to provide a cause of action in situations to which registered trade marks may not extend, such as where a defendant does not actually use the trade mark but nonetheless damages the good will of the plaintiff. An example is in deceptive responses to ordering such as that postulated as long ago as in *Carr & Sons v Crisp & Co Ltd* (1902) by Byrne J, as 'a man who goes into a public house and asks for a glass of Bass, and is served with something else'. This example remains just as valid today, for although the deceptive trader has not personally used the trade mark, he will nonetheless be liable in passing off.

Chapter 5

Patents

Introduction

No one would suggest that the law of patents is easy. It is difficult for everyone and covers such a volume of material that it would be possible to devote an entire Question and Answer book to it. It is therefore not surprising that many students avoid questions on the protection afforded to inventions by patents despite some of the fascinating issues that are involved. In order to develop a knowledge of intellectual property law, it is essential to have some knowledge, if only in outline, of the patent system.

At the level of general intellectual property courses, students are expected to have a basic knowledge of the patent system and the requirements to patent an invention. To answer questions effectively, a student must seek to develop an overview of the patent systems. Novelty, inventive step, industrial applicability and excluded matter are issues which may arise in almost all problem questions, if only in outline. Ideally, a student should have some knowledge of patent applications, excluded material and the rights of inventors. Since few inventors are now lone individuals, the position of inventor-employees is an important area and may appeal to those with a knowledge of employment law. Students with a technical background may also be attracted to the law of patents. Questions on the construction of patents usually relate to the 'pith and marrow' approach as opposed to the purposive approach proposed by Lord Diplock in *Catnic Components v Hill* (1982).

Inevitably, answers to patent questions will be longer than for other topics and reference must be made to the Patents Act 1977 and to pre-1977 case law. The questions and answers which follow can only supply the broadest of approaches suitable to answering questions for examinations and assessed work.

Checklist

Students should be familiar with the following areas:

- Sections 1–3 of the Patents Act 1977
- RSC Order 104 – Patent Court
- Exceptions to patentability
- *Molins v Industrial Machinery Co Ltd* (1938)
- *Windsurfer GB v Tabur Marine* (1985)
- *American Cyanamid v Ethicon* (1975)
- *Hickman v Andrews* (1983)
- *Quantel v Spaceward Microsystems* (1990)
- *Van Der Lely v Bamfords* (1963)

Question 35

How do the courts determine the presence of the 'inventive step' necessary for patentability under the Patents Act 1977? Are the tests adequate?

Answer plan

Given that the courts have found it difficult to formulate what constitutes an inventive step, a student should not feel too perturbed if difficulties are encountered. The important thing is to illustrate a breadth of knowledge, the most important case being *Windsurfer*, and the tests developed before and after.

The issues to be considered are:

- Section s 1(1) of the Patents Act 1977
- Section 32 of the Patents Act 1949
- *Windsurfer Int v Tabur Marine SA* (1985)

Answer

Section 1(1) of the Patents Act 1977 stipulates the essential prerequisites for a patent claim to be valid: novelty, industrial application and inventive application. Only if these conditions are satisfied may a patent be granted. Of these requirements, the inventive step – the essence of making an invention in the popular mind – has generated the greatest divergence in judicial approach and hence uncertainty in patent law. 'Invention' is not defined by the PA 1977, but under s 3 an invention shall be taken to involve an inventive step if it is not obvious to persons skilled in the art, having regard to any matter which forms part of the state of the art. The state of the art comprises all matter before the priority date made available to the public by written or oral description, by use or in any other way (see s 2(3)).

The patent represents the reward for creating a product or process which has not hitherto been part of human knowledge and which had not been devised by anyone else. A further justification for imposing the test of an inventive step was stated by the Court of Appeal in *PLG v Ardon International* (1995), that the public should not be prevented from doing what was an obvious extension from existing technical knowledge, if sufficiently interested. For an old patent, (ie before 1 June 1978) a claim is invalid if what is claimed 'is obvious and does not involve any inventive step, having regard to what was known or used before the priority date of the claim in the UK' (s 32 PA 1977). The courts have taken the view that the two terms are synonymous.

The presence of an inventive step is a question of fact to be decided in every case. 'What would the document in fact convey to those interested in the art?' (*British Thompson-Houston v British Insulated Cables* (1925)). Because inventions can vary widely, the courts have developed a variety of approaches, as appropriate tests for one invention may not be applicable. Obviousness can be determined at trial by the evidence in chief and cross examination of expert witnesses. If the claimed invention would have been obvious to a man skilled in the art, then there will be no inventive step. The courts are conscious that it is easy to be wise after the event, since viewing with hindsight can lead to unfairness to inventors (*Non Drip Measure Co Ltd v Strangers* (1943); *British Westinghouse Electric & Manufacturing Co Ltd v Braulik* (1910)).

The level of invention need only be very low. Often quoted is the mere requirement of 'a scintilla of invention' in what is claimed, or the way it is practically applied to reach anything within the claim (*Parkes v Crocker* (1929)). If this is detected, the subject matter of the claim involves an inventive step. In *General Tire and Rubber Co v Firestone* (1972), Graham J reviewed previous authorities on obviousness, holding it relevant to take into account the following: (1) whether the invention has a technical or commercial value; (2) the history of the matter which might throw light on obviousness particularly where there were a limited number of directions in which the notional skilled man might go; (3) the qualifications the notional skilled man would be deemed to possess; (4) the nature of the problem; and (5) the meaning of the words under s 32(1) of the PA 1977 then governing applications. The court observed that the view taken of any particular claim necessarily depends upon the precise nature of the evidence and upon the manner of presentation. Simplicity of invention does not mean a lack of inventive step.

The clearest modern test for determining the presence of an inventive step is that made by the Court of Appeal in *Windsurfing International v Tabur Marine (Great Britain)* (1985). The case involved the patentability of a navigational boom for a windsurfer. The court set down a four-fold test: (1) identifying the inventive concept in the patent; (2) imputing to a normally skilled but imaginative addressee what was a common general knowledge in the art at a priority date; (3) identifying the differences if any between the matter cited and the alleged invention; and (4) deciding if those differences viewed without any knowledge would have constituted steps which would have been obvious to the skilled addressee or whether an inventive step was necessary. This case was decided under s 32 of the PA 1949, providing a fact-finding tribunal with a structured approach when inquiring as to inventive step. In *Windsurfer*, the appellants argued that the requirement of a skilled man had to be realistic rather than hypothetical. Effectively, the courts apply the same test and degree of knowledge of prior art as for novelty, and do not limit prior art to what was or ought to have been known by the diligent searcher, holding 'All factual knowledge is relevant in deciding whether a skilled man would have considered the invention obvious'.

Under step (1), the task is to identify the inventive step in the claim, distinguishing between the parts which are crucial and the parts that are merely limitations on the scope of the claim (*Unilever v Chefaro* (1994)), as opposed to seeking a generalised inventive concept from the specification. Features of an invention which are not features of the claim are irrelevant in determining obviousness.

The third task of the *Windsurfer* case is to identify the differences between the pleaded prior art and the alleged invention. If documents are put before the court, it must decide what they disclose and then identify the differences. A document which discloses an invention but contains a specific teaching that it will not work, will not render it obvious (*Nestle Products Limited's Application* (1970)).

Suggestions that the skilled man would not read some material were rejected, the assumption being that the notional skilled man is sufficiently interested to apply himself (*Proctor & Gamble v Peaudouce* (1989)).

The most difficult of the *Windsurfer* tests is step (4), whether, viewed without any knowledge of an alleged invention, those differences constitute steps which would have been obvious to the skilled man or whether they require any degree of invention.

In *Molnycke AB v Proctor & Gamble Ltd* (1992), the *Windsurfer* principles were re-stated more succinctly: (1) What is the inventive step? (2) What was the state of the art at the priority date? (3) In what respect does the step go beyond or differ from the state of the art? (4) Would the step be obvious to a skilled man?

However, other approaches have been adopted in the past and depending on circumstances some may remain relevant. In *John-Manville Corp's Patent* (1967), Diplock LJ stated that, 'The correctness of a decision upon an issue of obviousness does not depend upon whether or not the decider has paraphrased the words of an Act in some particular verbal formulas. I doubt whether there is any verbal formula which is appropriate to all classes of claims'.

Indeed, a review of authorities shows different tests have been applied to obviousness over the years. In *Hickman v Andrews* (1983) (which involved the 'work-mate' invention consisting of known devices), the inventiveness may reside in the formulation of the problem to be solved and the inventive application of known features. In *Beecham Group's (Amoxycillin) Application* (1980), the selection of the area of research could amount to inventiveness.

The commercial success of an invention has sometimes been proposed as a test for obviousness. In *Parks-Cramer v Thornton* (1966), the Court of Appeal held that in spite of the simplicity of the invention, the fact was that it was a commercial success in the context of failed attempts to achieve the same result was evidence of an inventive step.

In *Technograph Printed Circuits Ltd v Mills and Rockley (Electronics) Ltd* (1972), 'But it is only because the invention has been made and has proved successful that it is possible to postulate what stating point and by what particular combination of steps the inventor could have reached his invention'. However, the fact that an invention has merit is in no way determinative of it being a commercial success (*Longbottom v Shaw* (1891)). It should also be noted that the Court of Appeal also departed from the view that commercial success in the *Windsurfer* case and rejected suggestions that commercial success could be equated with inventive step, stating that merely making an obvious or anticipated idea was not inventive. For example, heavy investment in advertising may be responsible for the success.

Another early test is whether the invention satisfies 'a long felt want' (*Longbottom v Shaw* (1891)). If the invention does this, the court may infer that the product or process was not obvious because no one else made it determinative. In *Parkes v Crocker* (1929), Tomlin J stated in a case where 'the problem has waited solution for many years', and where the device is novel, superior and widely used, this could be taken to rebut a claim that a patent lacked inventiveness. When skilled individuals fail to come up with an answer, it is impossible to suggest obviousness (*Intalite International v Cellular Ceilings (No 2)* (1987)).

Given the range of tests available and applied by the courts and the divergence of approaches, it can therefore be argued that there is no one adequate test, and it may be that an attempt to reach all-embracing formulas is doomed to failure because of the huge differences in subject matter which different patent applications involve. Certainly, there must be doubt as to the applicability of 19th century approaches as technology progresses. Indeed, it was recognised in general that traditional patent concepts may not be applicable on the microscopic or molecular scale. As Lord Mustill commented in *Genentech*, 'a prime reason why these questions are so hard to formulate is that the structure and philosophy of the Act are not appropriate'. Although a more standardised approach has been taken in recent years following the decision in *Windsurfer*, findings as to an inventive step remain difficult to predict. This situation suggests that there is no one adequate test which can achieve certainty.

The fact that two independent persons arrive the same route is an indication that it was obvious (*Johns Electric Ind Mfy Ltd v Mabuch 1 Motor KK* (1996)). The European Patent Office has adopted a test of problem/solution by ascertaining the prior state of the art, discerning the technical problem to be solved, seeing what the solution proposed is and deciding if clearest is obvious.

Question 36

What factors can effect whether an invention is new for the purposes of the Patents Act 1977?

Answer plan

The issues to be considered are:

- Definition of novelty under the Patents Act 1977
- State of the art – s 2(1) and 2(2) of the PA 1977
- Prior publication
- Disclosure to the public by use
- Secret use
- Mosaic

Answer

Under s 1 of the Patents Act 1977, an invention has to be new, a requirement also referred to as 'novelty'. This has long been a requirement but the PA 1977 defines novelty for the first time in a statute relating to patents, despite it being a long-standing requirement for obtaining a patent. As long ago as the *Clothworkers of Ipswich* (1614), the grant of letters patent was held to be wrong in principle where a matter was already known, since the monopoly right of a patent would prevent a person from lawfully using that which they already possessed. In *Manton v Manton* (1815), a case involving a new firing mechanism for guns, it was said, 'The question will be, whether this is a new invention, or whether it has existed from an antecedent time? In the later case, the plaintiff can claim no merit, for that which was invented before never can become the subject of a patent'. Historically, the reward for inventiveness was the patent monopoly.

Under s 2(1) of the PA 1977, an invention shall be taken to be new if it does not form part of the state of the art. By s 130(7), ss 2–6 PA 1977 are drafted so as to have the same effect in the UK as the various Patent Conventions to which the UK is a party.

Under s 2(2), the state of the art in the case of an invention shall be taken to comprise all matter which has at any time before the priority date of that invention been made available to the public, whether in the UK or elsewhere by written or oral description, by use or in any other way. Within the term state of the art, in s 2(2), is all knowledge which exists anywhere in the world, as contrasted with those things which have been kept hidden (*Quantel Ltd v Spaceward Microsystems Ltd* (1990)).

Novelty is of crucial significance to a patentee. Once a patent has been granted, the revelation that it is not novel will be a defence to infringement proceedings, the well-known 'Gillette' defence (*Gillette Safety Razor Co v Anglo-American Trading Co Ltd* (1913)) and is likely to lead to revocation. If a patent does not appear to be known or if it cannot be inferred that it is so, the patent will be classed as new (*Molins v Industrial Machinery Co Ltd* (1938)). Effectively, the question to be determined is one of fact. However, the requirement does not necessarily entail that the invention has literally never being conceived before; rather, it has a technical meaning.

A test of novelty was set out in *General Tire v Firestone* (1972), of whether the prior proposal contains a clear description of, or clear instructions to do or make something that would infringe the patent if carried out after the grant of the patentee's patent. The instructions must show something which falls within the claims, not which might be an infringement. In *General Tire v Firestone,* 'A signpost, however clear, upon the road to the patentee's invention will not suffice. The prior inventor must be clearly shown to have planted his flag as the precise destination before the patentee'. Similarly, in *E I Du Pont De Nemours & Co (Witsiepe's) Application* (1981), the disclosure of a prior invention does not amount to prior publication if the former 'merely points the way which might lead to the latter'. Furthermore, the disclosure must be an enabling one; details stating that an invention would not work will not be an anticipation, nor will it be if the alleged anticipation is capable of more than one interpretation (*General Tire v Firestone*). In such a case, the court is unlikely to be satisfied on the evidence that the invention is anticipated.

A collection of old integers that do not interact to produce a novel product lack the necessary novelty (*Pugh v Riley Cycle Co* (1914)), nor will finding a new application for a known product (*Isola v Thermos* (1910)) which concerned domestic use for laboratory cooling devices). However, in a case where the old intergers interact in some way, the result may be a product which is novel (*Martin and Biro Swan Ltd v H Millwood Ltd* (1954)). In *Hickman v Andrews* (1983) the invention was the 'work-mate', a collection of known features combined together but was nonetheless new because it could be said to function in a new manner. Technical terms will be considered in the light of their meaning at the time.

Failure on grounds of novelty depends on whether the invention has been disclosed to the public, whether deliberately or inadvertently. Disclosure may take place through either the invention being part of the prior state of the art (typically described in a document) or through it being known to the public before the priority date, in the sense that members of the public could have known of the invention, whether they took advantage of the knowledge or not. The principle that once an invention has been entered into the public domain it cannot be patented is a long-standing one (*Patterson v Gas Light and Coke and Co* (1877)). Whether a document discloses an invention is a question for the court, guided by expert evidence as appropriate. In considering disclosure, the court looks at the document with the eyes of the appropriately skilled man, with special rules for photographs (*Van der Lely (C) NV v Bamford Ltd* (1963)).

When assessing whether a prior publication anticipates the invention, the prior art must: (i) give clear and unmistakable directions to do what the applicant has invented; and (ii) have the result that if the instructions in the prior art are carried out the later invention would be infringed. The receipt of a single specification by a patent agent in the UK was held to be a sufficient publication (*Bristol-Myers Co's Application* (1969)). Even if the document is published abroad in a foreign language, this will be a disclosure which undermines novelty. In determining novelty, an opponent is not entitled to make a 'mosaic' of existing documents and then claim that the invention is disclosed. Although mosaicing is possible in determining obviousness and whether an invention involves an inventive step, novelty will not be undermined.

Disclosure to a single individual who is not bound by any duty of confidentiality will be sufficient to constitute disclosure to the public and thus undermine novelty. In *Bristol-Meyers*, a prior disclosure took the form of one document reaching an employee of a third party company which was free to use the information as it saw fit. This amounted to a disclosure. A similar approach is taken by the European Patent Office in that a single sale of a patented product may undermine novelty (*TELEMECHANIQUE/Power Supply Unit (T482/89)* (1993)).

The courts will discount disclosures in breach of confidence. The possibility of a breach of confidence will not be sufficient for the purpose of s 2(2) of the PA 1977. The breach must be established (*Microsonics Corpn's Application* (1984)). Alternatively, prior to the date of the patent application, carrying out the instructions of a prior publication would have resulted in the production of the product claimed there is anticipation. But where there is no prior publication in situations where the product claimed as the subject of the patent is occasionally produced there may not be (*Bristol-Myers (Johnson's) Application* (1971); *Letraset Ltd v Rexel Ltd* (1974)).

Prior use of an invention does not invalidate it if it is secret or uninformative. A prior use will undermine novelty if it is a use from which knowledge could be derived which could enable the invention to be performed. In *Milliken Denmark As v Walk Of Mats Ltd* (1996), it was held that a machine could be treated like a book in that it can be examined and the information gleaned written down. If it was possible to discern the information in the claim then novelty would be undermined. In *Quantel v Spaceworld Ltd* (1990), although a computer had been used in public, the novel features which constituted the invention were internal and therefore had not been revealed. An important characteristic is that the invention has been made available to the public

In view of the requirement that the invention must have been made known to the public, proceedings may seek to determine whether this could have taken place. Laboratory use and testing in secret do not undermine novelty. In *Windsurfer v Tabur Marine* (1985), it was considered that use of a device in circumstances where it was possible for anyone to see it was a disclosure to the public, even if the numbers were limited and the audience were unaware of the significance of what they were actually seeing. Providing that the disclosure is open to someone, somewhere, to make use of, it is irrelevant that no one has appropriated the idea. In *Windsurfer*, the use of a crude prototype by a 12-year-old child off Hayling Island was a disclosure of the plaintiff's patent.

Question 37

When will an invention be denied a patent? Answer with reference to the Patents Act 1977.

Answer plan

Although requiring a lengthy answer, this is a straightforward question which simply requires a student to review the Patents Act 1977 for exclusions and cite relevant examples.

The issues to be considered are:

- Sections 1(2) and 1(3) of the Patents Act 1977
- Patentability of:
  - Theories
  - Industrial application
  - Schemes and presentation of information
  - Medical treatment
  - Life forms

Answer

Although all new technological processes (whether chemical, mechanical or electrical, machines, devices, articles, products or composition) are inherently patentable, s 1(2) and (3) of the Patents Act 1977 precludes certain material from being the subject of a patent. The Act also allows the Secretary of State for Trade and Industry to vary what may be patented (s 1(5)).

The legal protection of a patent – which amounts to a complete monopoly – does not extend to matters which fall more clearly within the ambit of other forms of intellectual property rights, such as literary, dramatic, musical and artistic works and aesthetic works, which are the subject of copyright (s 1(2)(b)). Other exceptions in the PA 1977 are derived originally from the requirements that a patent must involve a new manner of manufacture, under previous legislation, or are included in the European Patent Convention. The PA 1977 itself requires that inventions must be of industrial applicability. The exceptions to patentability consist of matters which cannot meet these criteria or, alternatively, are designed to protect society by the preventing the patenting of inventions detrimental to society and its moral standards.

Section 1(2) of the PA 1977 has been described as 'a non-exhaustive catalogue of matter or things, starting with "a discovery", which as such are declared not to be inventions' (*Gale's Application* (1991), Nicholls LJ). In *Merrill Lynch Inc's Application* (1988) Falconer J held that if anything in the excluded categories constituted the inventive step, then no patent could be granted regardless of how a claim was drafted. The exceptions come from the substance of the patent, not what the applicant claims, preventing clever wording from avoiding the exclusions. In *Lux Traffic Controls Ltd v Pike Signs Ltd; Lux Traffic Controls v Foronwise Ltd* (1993) it was said, 'It is clear from both the decisions of the European Patents Office and judgments of the Court of Appeal that the form of the claim in a patent cannot be decisive as to whether or not the invention relates solely to the excluded matter'.

Attempts to patent an item falling within s 1(2) in the guise of another item will be rebuffed. In *Merill Lynch's Application*, '... it cannot be permissible to patent an item excluded by s 1(2) under the guise of an article which contains that item – that is to say, in the case of a computer program, the patenting of a conventional computer containing that program'. The exclusion from patentability is a matter of substance not form' (*Fujitsu Ltd's Application* (1996)).

The industrial application restriction

The requirement that a patent must be capable of industrial application (s 4) precludes discoveries and theories in the abstract (s 1(2)(a)–(e)). In *Young v Rosenthal & Co* (1884), Grove J held, 'An invention of an idea or mathematical formulae or any of that sort, could not be the subject of a patent'. Similarly, in *Lane Fox v The Kensington and Knightsbridge Electric Lighting Company* (1892), Lindley LJ stated, 'When Volta discovered the effect of electric current from a battery on a frog's leg he made a great discovery, but no patentable invention'. What can be patented is the incorporation of that discovery into technology. Something more than excluded matter is required to enable an invention to be patented – a technical contribution to the art.

In *Gale's Application* (1991), Nicholls LJ stated that it is 'Helpful to have in mind principles of patent law, well established before the Act, that an idea or discovery as such is not patentable. It is the practical application of an idea or discovery which leads to patentability. It leads to patentablility even if, as frequently happens, the practicable application of the discovery is inherent in the discovery itself or is obvious once the discovery has been made and stated'.

In *Vicom Computer Related Invention* (1987), it was stated that 'Decisive is what technical contribution the invention makes to the known art'. Thus, anti-matter may exist in advanced theoretical physics but will remain unpatentable as a theory. However, if ever anyone devised an anti-matter engine, beloved of science fiction writers, this would constitute a patentable invention.

Schemes, methods and computer programs and presentation of information

Schemes, rules or methods for performing a mental act, playing a game or doing business, or a program for a computer and the presentation of information are excluded. Again, it is possible to find cases where the presence of a technical element has made a difference (s 2(1)(c)). Diverse examples include camouflage painting (*T's application* (1920)); a method of arranging buoys for navigational purposes (*W's application* (1914)); an installation for distributing utilities services on a housing estate (*Hillier's*

Application (1969)); or a new pack of cards for Canasta (*Cobianchi's Application* (1953)).

A method of flying an aeroplane was not patentable in *Rolls Royce Ltd's Application* (1963). Section 1(2)(d) of the PA 1977 excludes anything which consists of the presentation of information, going further than the old law which allowed the patenting of novel methods of presenting information (*Nelson's Application* (1980)). The application was for a patent in method the of carrying an instructional message using a visual message with verbal and humorous reinforcement. Whitford J held that the method solely consisted of matter having intellectual, literary or artistic connotation and was not a manner of new manufacture.

Pitman's Application (1969) involved a method of teaching the pronunciation of language by showing the reader visually the correct stress and inflection of words and phrases in a text, in conjunction with a reading machine. The Patents Appeal Tribunal held that, because of the presence of a mechanical element, it could not be regarded solely as an intellectual or literary arrangement of matter.

Patents can be properly refused on the grounds that only visual material is involved but a distinction is made if printed on a sheet to serve a mechanical purpose (*Fishburn's Application* (1940)). Purely abstract and intellectual developments (*IBM Corp/Document* (1990)), the technical Board of Appeal rejected an application for a patent related to a method of automatically abstracting and storing documents in an information storage and retrieval system and for similarly retrieving it.

Gale's Application (1991) concerned a computer-related invention, a read-only memory ROM providing means to evaluate square roots of numbers. The instructions were recorded on a disk or ROM and the Patents Court held it was a patentable invention. The Comptroller appealed to the Court of Appeal under the PA 1977, citing s 1(2) and the European Patents Convention, Article 52(2)(3). The court held that instructions to be used in a computer were not patentable. Instructions had to be recorded on a disk or ROM, which was no more than a known device in which instructions were imbedded. A claim could not be made for the instructions incorporated on the disk or ROM.

If a claim is clearly directed to a method involving the use of apparatus modified as programmed to operate in a new way, it should be accepted (*Burroughs Corpn (Perkins') Application* (1974)). Computer programs which have the effect of controlling computers to operate in a certain way, where such programs are in physical form, are proper subject matter for letters patent.

Medical treatment

Different considerations apply in the exclusion of methods of medical diagnosis or treatment. The exception was stated in *John Wyeth & Brothers' Application: Schering's Application* (1985), '... the use in practice by practitioners of such methods of medical treatment in treating patients should not be subjected to possible restraint'. The justification is that no one should have a monopoly in mechanisms which relieve human suffering. However, the exemption is not as wide as is often imagined.

In *Schering Akt's Application* (1971), processes for the medical treatment of human beings or cure or prevention of diseases are excluded from the PA 1977. However, a method of contraception by the suppression of ovulation by use of a known substance did not fall within the exception – pregnancy was not a disease. Similarly, a method of taking oestrogen pills was not a method of treatment (*London Rubber Industries Ltd's Patent* (1968)). In a decision by the High Court of Australia, a cosmetic process for improving the strength and elasticity of hair was the proper subject of a patent (*Joos v Comptroller of Patents* (1973)). Hairdressing is a field of economic endeavour and has commercial significance and these expressions ought to be understood in relation to the grant of patents.

Public order and biological inventions

Anti-social inventions or those contrary to public order are excluded under s 1(3) of the PA 1977. The basic position is that animals and plants cannot (and in the view of the writer should not) be the subject of a patent under s 1(3) (based upon Article 53(b) of the European Patent Convention). (See, however, *Harvard/Onco Mouse (T19/90)* (1990) EPOR 501 European Patent Office.) To some extent, the position for plant breeders is ameliorated by rights given to them under the Plant Varieties and Seeds Act 1964. However, not all forms of biotechnology are excluded and it is clear from s 1(3)(b) that microbiological processes and products may be patentable (for example, for use in waste disposal). The requirement for an invention to have industrial application is assisted by the definition including agricultural processes (s 4(1)). The precise boundaries between microbiological and biological processes have not been defined. DNA sequences and fragments may be patentable (*Genentech Inc's (Human Growth Hormone) Patent* (1989)). To date, moral arguments have not carried any weight in the European context. In *Greenpeace v Plant Genetic Systems* (1995), there was opposition to a grant of a patent for plant life forms, citing environmental risk. The European Patent Office rejected the immorality argument, finding no grounds to refuse on abstract or ethical grounds; only where there is an overwhelming consensus will that be the case. A subsequent appeal (1995) modified the original decision to restricting the patent to the plant cells which had been genetically engineered, but without consideration of the moral issue.

Arguably, the patent system is inappropriate in the area of life-forms because of conceptual difficulties which arise in applying a framework derived from the protection of macroscopic mechanical and industrial processes to the complexities of biochemistry (*Genentech* (1989)).

Question 38

Ricardo develops a new type of solar cell and wishes to patent it in the UK. He seeks your advice.

Answer plan

A question which requires a knowledge of the stages involved in applying for a patent.

The issues to be considered are:

- Sections 1 and 7 of the Patents Act 1977
- Sections 14–29 of the PA 1977
- Patents Rules 1990 SI 2384

- Patentability
- Right to apply
- Contents of specification
- Priority date
- Examination
- Amendments
- Grant
- Duration

Answer

In order to be granted a patent, the solar cell invention must satisfy the requirements of s 1(1) of the Patents Act 1977 in being new, involving an inventive step, being capable of industrial application and not excluded. As Ricardo's invention does not fall into the excluded categories, it should qualify if novel (it will be new if it does not form part of the state of the art (s 2(1)) and involves an inventive step.

The procedure for patentability is set out by the PA 1977 and rules made thereunder. Application may be made to either the European Patent Office or the British Patent Office, and the right to apply for a patent is open to anyone regardless of nationality or residence. A British resident is obliged to file first in the UK for national security. If document turns up later, the security of a patent can only be preserved if amended.

The only restriction is that the application is made by the inventor or joint inventor (s 7(2)(a)). As inventor, Ricardo qualifies. Ricardo should be advised to retain his notes and details of his experiments. In *SKM SA and Another v Wagner Spraytech UK Ltd* (1982), it was observed that on the issue of obviousness the evidence of the inventor is admissible and may be material or even critical. The inventor's notes and experiments are relevant to pleadings either as part of the inventor's evidence or as a means of checking it.

The inventor is defined as the devisor of the invention (s 7(3)), so Ricardo, being self-employed, will therefore qualify. The Patent Office assumes that the person making the application is so entitled to the patent. The stages are set within a timetable, the preliminary examination being within a year, publication within 18 months and final decision within four years.

Contents of the application

The application must be in English (*Rhode and Schwarz's Application* (1980)). Applications must fulfil the requirements of s 14(2) of the PA 1977, in containing a request for the grant of a patent, a specification containing a description of the invention, a claim or claims, and any drawing mentioned in the description of any claim and an abstract. Rules 19(1) and (2) require the abstract to commence with a title for the invention. The abstract shall contain a precise summary 'drafted in such a way which allows clear understanding of the technical problem to which the invention relates, the gist of the solution and principal use or uses of the invention'. Speculative material and alleged means or value are not to be included.

Ricardo must bear in mind that the body of the specification must disclose the invention in a manner that is clear and complete enough for the invention to be performed (s 14(3)). The patent specification is the most important document and Ricardo must ensure that it contains a comprehensive technical description of the invention and ends with a list of claims which define the legal scope of the patent. There will be a preamble, background and brief technical description, and a full technical description made with reference to the drawings. Ricardo should avoid leaving potentially invalid claims in the specification. If he leaves them in he may be required to give a specification (*Wilkinson Sword v Cripps & Lee* (1982)). If the specification of the patent does not disclose the invention clearly or completely enough for it to be performed by a person skilled in the art, it may risk revocation under s 72(1)(c) of the PA 1977. The body of the specification may consist of assisting the construction of the claims.

A set of legal claims will be included, and care will be needed in the drafting, as Ricardo will be setting out the limits of his claimed patent monopoly. The claims that Ricardo makes must define what the invention actually does, and the matters for which he seeks protection must be clear and concise, and be supported by the description. There is no requirement to describe every possible way in which the invention is to be performed (*Quantel Ltd v Spaceward Microsystems Ltd* (1990)). There is a requirement that the language be clear so that others can use it when the patent expires (*Edison and Swan United Electric Co v Holland* (1889)). The claim must state what the invention claimed is (*Ingersoll Seargant Drill Coy v Ashai Kasei Kogyo KK'S Application* (1990)). Extensions for new applications may be made under Rule 26 of the Patent Rules.

Under s 125 of the PA 1977, the extent of the invention is that specified in the claims of the specification 'as interpreted by the description and any drawings contained in that specification'. There are no special rules for the construction of a patent, rather the normal canons of construction should be employed (*Daily v Etablissements Fernand Berchet* (1992)). The claims and the specification are to be read together. One factor is that the claims would be expected to be consistent with the specification and with each other (*Brugger and Others v Medic Aid Ltd* (1996)). If Ricardo selects to define the claim in narrow terms, the court should not rewrite it in broader language simply because it thinks a wider form of wording would have been easy to formulate. Equally, if the wording is too wide, Ricardo's claim may risk attack on the basis of lack of novelty or obviousness, since it is more likely to fall into the prior art or may have been disclosed, or be an obvious extension of the prior art.

Filing

Under s 5(1) of the PA 1977, the date of an invention is the date on which Ricardo files it with the Patent Office. If Ricardo's claim discloses more than one invention, then each may have a different priority date. At least one claim, and a request for a preliminary application must be made (s 15(5)) within 12 months (s 15(5); Patent Rules 1990 r 25). He must ensure that the variants are dealt with (s 5(2)(b)). Infringement proceedings may arise from this date. Ricardo may be advised to employ a patent agent or patent attorneys given a right of audience. They may conduct a prior art search. The application may cover variations and modifications of the solar cell.

Publication

Within 18 months, the application must be published by the Patent Office, allowing public inspection of Ricardo's claim. The publication will be filed, subject to the discretion of the Comptroller not to publish material disparaging to any person, or material that would be expected to encourage offensive or anti-social behaviour (s 16). Publication is carried out by the Patent Office under s 16(1). Publication takes place through the government printer and is dispatched worldwide.

Examination and search

Within six months of publication, Ricardo should request an examination and search. A fee is payable and the Patent Office will undertake a search of technical literature. An examination is also conducted to ensure that the application fulfils the legal requirements of patentability. Under s 17(4) of the PA 1977, the examiner must make such examination as in his opinion is reasonably practicable. Ricardo could also find it useful to have one carried out independently. Initially, the date of filing is the only matter disclosed (*Asahi Kasei Kogy KK's Application* (1991)). Nothing in the provisions about late filing or non-filing of drawings affects the Comptroller's power under s 117(1) to correct errors or mistakes with respect to the filing of drawings.

Where a preliminary examination has taken place, a request for a substantial examination should be made. Under s 17(2) of the PA 1977, the examiner investigates to such an extent as he considers necessary in view of the examination and search carried out under s 17 and the rules, and shall determine that question and report his determination to the Comptroller.

The examiner will raise any objections with Ricardo and allow time for any amendments to overcome those objections. If agreement cannot be reached an appeal lies to the Comptroller, then to the Patent Court and the Court of Appeal. Ricardo may expect to enter into negotiation and correspondence. Patent applications are usually filed with claims which are likely to be honed down and subject to various protection amendments, and variations restricting the monopoly. If the examiner raised any objections to granting a patent, the applicant is given the opportunity to argue his or her case and to make certain amendments. This must be done within four years and six months of the initial application, unless an appeal to the Patents Court is involved.

Grant

As soon as practicable after a patent has been granted, the Comptroller must publish (in the Official Journal (Patents)) a notice that it has been granted. A patent is granted on the date of publication of the notice, and the owner or proprietor of the patent must be sent a certificate in a prescribed form. The effect of the grant puts an end to all pre-grant procedures (*ITT Industries Inc's Application* (1984); *Ogawa Chemical Industries Ltd's Application (1996)).*

If the patent is granted, Ricardo will enjoy a monopoly for 20 years from the filing date (s 25), providing that he keeps up the payment of renewal fees.

Question 39

Albert seeks to patent a canoe which can double as a glider over rapids. Using hydrofoils which can extend as wings, the innovation allows a canoeist approaching a large waterfall to glide over to the next stretch of calmer water. Albert wants to patent his invention, which he believes may help surveyors and travellers in remote areas, and to sell it as the first gliding canoe.

A search by the Patent Office reveals a photograph of an Aztec carving which shows a winged canoe similar to the plans put forward by Albert, published in a book in Germany, 'Did God Fly A Canoe?' The author of the book, Eric Von Kontrick, claims that Earth was once visited by aliens who arrived by flying canoes. Eric Von Kontrick further claims that indigenous tribes along the Amazon basin make their own gliding canoes for use in secret religious ceremonies. Eric also claims to have made a gliding canoe himself which he used on an uninhabited stretch of the Amazon. Unfortunately his only model sank.

Advise Albert as to the patentability of his invention.

Assuming the patent is granted, what should Albert do if he discovers that Eric is seeking to import potentially infringing gliding canoes via Hodge Ferries, who have a shipment coming to Britain? Advise him as to the steps he should take to protect his patent.

Answer plan

The issues to be considered are:

- Section 1(1) of the Patents Act 1977
- Novelty
- Disclosure through photographs
- Disclosure through use in public
- Obviousness
- *Windsurfer v Tabur Marine* (1985)
- Infringement through importation – s 60(1) of the PA 1977
- Meaning of imports

Answer

To constitute a patentable invention, it is necessary for the invention to satisfy the requirements of s 1(1) of the Patents Act 1977. Section 1(1) requires an invention to be the result of an inventive step, to be novel, capable of industrial application and not be excluded. In the question, there is nothing to suggest that the patent will fail through it involving any excluded matter or lack of industrial application – the gliding canoe could be made the subject of manufacture.

The evidence uncovered by the Patent Office may threaten the potential patentability because Albert's invention may fail for novelty, in that it has been disclosed, or for obviousness. Under s 2(1) of the PA 1977 an invention is taken to be new if it does not form part of the state of the art. Under 2(2), the state of the art comprises all matter (whether a product, a process, information about either, or anything else) which has been made available to the public whether in the UK or elsewhere. A mere suggestion in a previously published work is immaterial (*Re Woodcroft's Patent* (1846)). Under s 3, the book must actually disclose the invention by means of the photographs and description. An invention is taken to involve an inventive step if it is not obvious to a person skilled in the art, having regard to any matter which forms part of the state of the art by virtue only of s 2(2) above. This follows Article 56 of the European Patent Convention. Eric's book may be one way in which the invention may be disclosed.

Normally, prior disclosure which undermines novelty is through publication in a document. The construction of each document is for the court, which will apply the ordinary rules of construction in each case, guided by expert and technical evidence as appropriate. However, the question specifically refers to a photograph of Aztec carvings and the courts have stated on occasion the need to take a different approach with photographs. In *Van der Lely (C) NV v Bamford Ltd* (1963), Lord Reid stated that whilst lawyers are expected to be experts in the use of the English language, a different approach was needed when considering photographs. It was not simply a matter of how the court would construe the image. The view to be taken is with the eye of the person with appropriate engineering skill and experience and what such a person would see in the photograph. Evidence must be called as to the significance of the photograph's contents. Whilst decisions are for the judge, the judge should not attempt to evaluate or construe the photograph, 'He looks at the photograph in determining which of the explanations given by the witnesses appears to be the most worthy of acceptance'.

Separate to the question of disclosure in a prior publication is disclosure through use in public. If a prototype is used in public and its workings can be deduced by examination, then the invention will fail for lack of novelty (*Lux Traffic Controls Ltd v Pike Signals Ltd* (1993)). In *Quantel v Spaceward* (1990), it was held that the use of a computer in public was not a disclosure of the claimed invention contained in the internal workings of the computer which was concealed from members of the public.

It is essential that the invention has not been disclosed to the public before. Disclosure would also be an issue as regards possible prior use of the flying canoe as alleged by Eric. Leaving aside the alleged use by the aliens as claimed in Eric's book (who are unlikely to be classed as a section of the public), the claim of use by tribes in the Amazon is more open to verification. According to the question, the ceremonies are secret so arguably there will have been no disclosure to the public. Alternatively, the claim will have to be considered in the light of evidence given by Eric. The court will assess Eric's evidence and credibility like that of any other witness. If he repeats his claim to have invented the winged canoe, thus undermining novelty and perhaps obviousness, the fact that the only working model sank might lead to a finding that Eric's model was a 'near miss' but does not undermine obviousness.

It will be essential that the invention involves an inventive step. Would Albert's invention be obvious to a man skilled in the art? The question of obviousness will be determined by the court applying the *Windsurfer v Tabur Marine* (1985) tests. *Windsurfer* proposed a four-fold test involving: (1) identifying the inventive concept embodied in the patent; (2) imputing to a normally skilled but imaginative addressee what was common general knowledge in the art at the priority date; (3) identifying the differences as may exist between the material cited and Albert's alleged invention; (4) deciding whether those differences, viewed without any knowledge of the alleged invention, constituted steps which would have been obvious to the skilled man or whether they required any degree of invention.

The third step in the *Windsurfer* case is to identify the differences between the pleaded prior art and the alleged invention. If documents are put before the court, the court must decide what they disclose and then go on to identify the difference. It is presumed a sufficiently skilled man is sufficiently interested to read the material (*Proctor & Gamble v Peaudouce* (1989)).

This will rebut any suggestion that a notional skilled man would not actually read Eric's work, instead applying his mind to the subject and to considering the practical application of the information which he has. The fact that the book is in German is not an exception (see *JAPAN STYRENE PAPER/Foam particles* (1991)).

Infringement through importing

It is an infringing act to import a patented product into the jurisdiction (s 60 of the PA 1977). Similarly, in *Elmsie v Boursier* (1869), manufacture and importation of a patented product will be an infringement. Eric Von Kontrick could be restrained by an injunction. However, infringement proceedings will not extend as far as Hodge Ferries. Although s 60(1) of the PA 1977 is broadly worded and covers infringement 'where the invention is a product he makes, disposes of, offers to dispose of, uses or imports the product or otherwise', liability has been held not to extend to carriers such as airlines. In *Smith Kline and French v Harbottle* (1980), the expression 'keeps it whether for disposal or otherwise' was considered by Oliver J, examining Articles 29 and 31 which gave rise to s 60 of the PA 1977, and looking at the dictionary definitions of 'keep'. In his judgment, 'keep' was taken to mean 'keeping in stock' as in the sense of keeping goods for sale. Applying the authority of *Gartside v Inland Revenue Commissioners* (1968) that 'It is always proper to construe an ambiguous word or phrase in light of the mischief which the provision is obviously designed to prevent, and in light of the reasonableness of the consequences which follow from giving it a particular construction', he ruled that stronger and more positive language would have been used to impose liability on mere carriers. The section is designed to catch 'keeping' in the context of the PA 1977, keeping for a purpose other than that of a 'mere custodian or warehouseman'.

Offering to dispose was considered in *Kalman v PCL Packaging* (1982) in light of the equivalent Article 29(a) of the Community Patent Convention: 'dispose of must include selling and that the sale of an article is included in the definition. It does not go as far as the delivery outside the jurisdiction'.

Alternatively, under s 60(2) of the PA 1977 so-called contributory infringement is added if an unauthorised person supplies or offers to supply any means relating to an essential element of the invention for putting the invention into effect, when he knows or it is obvious to a reasonable person in the circumstances that those means are suitable and are intended to put the invention into effect in the UK. Knowledge includes the state of mind of a person who shuts his mind to the obvious.

The most attractive remedy available to Albert will be interlocutory injunctive relief whereby Albert can keep Eric off the market until the trial of the action. It is likely that Albert will be required to give a cross undertaking to damages as a condition of obtaining the injunction. If Eric were an innocent infringer, the extent of remedies that may be applied will be restricted. Remedies may differ in that an account of profits will not be available for innocent infringement (*Gillette v Edenwest* (1994)).

Damages may be refused if Eric can show he acted in innocence of Albert's patent. This may be hard for Eric to establish since claims of naiveté and ignorance will be scrutinised by the court (*Lancer Boss v Henley Forklift* (1975)). A factor will be whether Albert grants licences but does not manufacture. If so, he will find it hard to establish that damages will not be an adequate remedy (*Fleming Fabrications Ltd v Albion Cylinders Ltd* (1989)).

Question 40

What defences exist to a claim of patent infringement?

Answer plan

A question which requires a review of relevant defences and will be an issue to consider in problem questions on infringement. The object in answering is to demonstrate a breadth of knowledge of the possible defences, arising from s 60 of the Patents Act 1977 and otherwise.

The issues to be considered are:

- Invalidity
- Lack of title
- Licence
- Repairs
- Prior use
- Exhaustion of rights
- Accidental infringement
- Public policy

Answer

Like the claims in a patent itself, defences to a patent act must be very strictly drawn, otherwise patent monopoly rights are diluted.

Defences include denial that the acts complained of were committed by the defendant or that such acts (if committed) did not amount to an infringement. Whether or not acts have been committed by a defendant is a question of fact. Whether the acts complained of are infringements is a matter of law. Thus, certain technical defences may arise from the language of the PA 1977, subject to construction by the court.

Acts which do and do not amount to infringements are specifically set out in s 60, including six statutory defences under s 60(5)(a)–(f). If a defendant is sued for infringement, he or she is required to serve a defence and counterclaim, and particular objections must be served within 42 days of service of the statement of claim under RSC Order 104.

Invalidity of the patent

In defending infringement actions, defendants will frequently commence invalidity proceedings and a counterclaim for revocation. After complete specifications are construed and the exact nature and scope of inventions ascertained, the court considers the validity of the patents. Where defendants claim anticipation by prior publication, disclosure of the time, name and place of publication will be ordered and defendants will be required to give specific information to identify the details relied upon under RSC Order 104. The court may order further particulars to be given as necessary. Defendants are not allowed to stray outside the particulars of objections, so far as the grounds under which validity is challenged are concerned; nor are defendants allowed to call evidence in support of any of the other grounds, unless the evidence is clearly within the particulars given under the ground of the objection.

Lack of title

Revocation can be commenced on grounds that the person granted is not the person entitled or that the protection conferred by the patent has been extended by an amendment which should not have been permitted. Lack of title is a defence which may be raised effectively, denying that the plaintiff has a right to sue. Other than a licensee holding a compulsory licence or a licence of right, an action cannot be maintained unless one or more parties are registered as owners of the patent. This may be determined by production of certified copies of entry in the register. The certificate of the Comptroller is *prima facie* evidence of the entry. However, if a document of title is not entered on the register, title cannot be proved unless the court otherwise directs.

Licence

It is a complete defence to an infringement action to prove that the act complained of was done by leave or licence of the patentee. With two or more registered owners, a licence will be effective only against those who actually granted the licence and those who have acquiesced. With patents held by co-owners, licences must have been granted with the consent of all the co-owners. Therefore, if A and B are registered owners of a patent, and B sues C for infringement, it is no defence for C to show that he has a licence from A, unless he also shows that B consented to or acquiesced in the licence. This principle is known as non-derogation from grant, and was relied upon by the House of Lords in *Leyland Motor Corporation Ltd v Armstrong Patents Co Ltd* (1986), which involved copyright in technical drawings.

The defendant must show that the act complained of as an infringement comes within the ambit of any licence in respect of the duration, the area concerned, the extent, and all other limits of the licence. There is a fundamental difference between an assignment of a patent, or an application of patent and a licence. An assignee is free to do as he or she wishes (*Allen & Hanburys v Generics (UK) Ltd* (1986)). A non-exclusive licensee, on the contrary, is merely entitled to do acts that would be prohibited but for the licence.

An example would be a licence purporting to be for three years from the date of the patent. No defence will lie to an alleged act of infringement committed four years after that date. Similarly, a licence limited in territorial terms (or any part thereof) will not excuse an infringement in any other geographical area not included within the scope of a grant. (However, geographic limitations may fall foul of the Treaty of Rome on barriers to free competition; see also Regulation No 2349/84.) A licence may also be restricted in terms of the activities which the licensee may undertake.

It does not matter whether the licence is express or implied. An express licence is made either orally or in writing. The terms of an oral licence must be ascertained from the evidence of witnesses; a written licence will be construed from the written instrument alone and the circumstances in which it was made. A licensee under an express licence is estopped or debarred from disputing the validity of the patent, unless it is an expressed term of the licence that there is permission to do so.

For example, a licence to use a patented article will not be a defence to an action brought for an alleged manufacture or disposal of an article. A licence to repair an article may be implied where a purchaser gives the item to a third party to repair. In *Sirdar Rubber Co Ltd v Wallington Weston Co* (1907), Lord Halsbury stated that the principle is that 'you may prolong the life of a licensed article but you must not make a new one under cover of repair'. In *Solar Thompson Engineering v Barton* (1977), it was stated that if there are no general restrictions, the customer can use the item in any general way. A person cannot claim a defence in manufacturing a new article, and whether a repair has taken place is a matter of fact.

Where a patented article is manufactured or sold (either in the UK or elsewhere) by or with the consent of the patentee, a purchaser of the article may exercise all the rights of an owner, including re-sale, unless prior notice has been given (*Incandescent Gas Light Co v Cantelo* (1895)). Where such a defence is raised, the patentee must prove that he or she did not manufacture the article (*Betts v Wilmott* (1871)).

Where a defendant claims the protection of a licence, he may be expected to produce it at an early stage in proceedings 'and not to occupy large amounts of public time in attacking a patent under which they claim to be in the position of licensees' (*British Thomsom-Houston C Ltd v British Insulated and Helsby Cables Ltd* (1924)).

Linked to the question of licences is the defence that the patentee has granted licences with prohibited conditions, available by virtue of s 44 of the PA 1977. A defendant may claim that the patentee has imposed on licensees, purchasers or hirers certain conditions in restraint of trade attaching to a sale or use of the invention. Such conditions may be in a contract between the plaintiff and the defendant or with a third party.

Exhaustion of rights

Section 60(4) of the PA 1977 puts into effect the doctrine that once a patented product has been put on the market in any EC country by or with the express consent of the proprietor of the patent, the disposal will have exhausted his or her rights and no subsequent disposal will infringe. Section 60(4) states that without prejudice to s 86 (relating to the implementation of the Community Patent Convention), s 60(1) and (2) do not apply to any act which, under any provision of the CPC relating to the exhaustion of the rights of the proprietor of a patent, cannot be prevented by the proprietor of the patent. It does not apply to goods imported from EC countries where there is no licence, or from non-EC countries (*Re Tylosin* (1977)).

Prior use

Prior use by a defendant may also be pleaded as a defence. It is a long-standing principle that a person cannot be restrained from continuing to do what has hitherto been done. Section 64, as amended by Schedule 5, para 17 of the Copyright Designs and Patents Act 1988, provides that prior users may continue to enjoy protection, notwithstanding that such use would *prima facie* undermine the validity of the patent in terms of novelty and inventive step.

Accidental infringement

Innocent infringement is not a defence to an infringement action (s 59(1) of the PA 1949; *Wilbec Plastics Ltd v Wilson Dawes Ltd* (1966)). However, in some cases an accidental use or manufacture may be a defence. In *Reymes-Cole v Elite Hosiery Co Ltd* (1965), Lord Diplock observed that it would be odd if a patentee could stop a manufacturer from making products which had an accidental element of manufacture. Similarly, an infringement in relation to the accidental or temporary entry of a foreign registered aircraft or vessel into the UK will not be actionable.

There is a limited exception for liability for activities started before the commencement of the PA 1977 (ie before 1 June 1978) under Schedule 4, para 3(3). This applies to acts commenced before that date which did not infringe, and were continued to be done after the commencement date. The construction of the word 'continued' was considered in *Rotocrop v Genbourne* (1978).

Miscellaneous

Certain public policy defences are also recognised. It will not be an infringement of a patent where the act complained of is done for a non-commercial purpose, such as education in private (s 60(5)(a)) or for experimental purposes (s 60(5)(b)). The third statutory provision is for the extemporaneous preparation in a pharmacy of a medicine for an individual in accordance with a prescription given by a registered medical or dental practitioner, or dealing with a medicine so prepared.

Question 41

Ronnie and Sue are employed by Benjy's Nightwear who make pyjamas and dresses. Ronnie works in the marketing department and Sue works in the textile quality control department.

One evening at home, whilst examining some rejected samples Sue had saved from being dumped, they try making some experiments with some hologram designs that Benjy's picked up at a marketing seminar. They have the idea of applying holograms. Sue, drawing on her knowledge of quality control, concludes that this can be done by heating the material and the holograms. Over a period of months they refine the idea. Through experimentation, they perfect the process of heat treating the holograms and the clothing so the holograms can be applied to the textiles. They then resign from the company and seek a patent for the process. Their contracts of employment with Benjy's Nightwear do not mention inventions.

What would your advice be if the court held that the patent belonged to Benjy's Nightwear and proved commercially successful?

Answer plan

Section 9 of the Patents Act 1977 specifically deals with the position of employee/inventors such as Ronnie and Sue, building on the common law principles. Both the statute, the rules and the case law need to be applied.

- Section 39 of the PA 1977
- *Re Harris's Patent* (1985)
- *Electrolux v Hudson* (1977)
- *Glasgow Board of Health's Application* (1996)
- Compensation – s 40 of the PA 1977
- Patents Rules 1990

Answer

In this question, Sue and Ronnie seek to patent their invention. The process would fulfil the requirements of s 1(1) of the Patents Act 1977 and will be of industrial application. They are entitled to make a joint application for a patent under s 7(1) of the PA 1977. Section 7(2)(a) states that the application should be the inventor or joint inventor. Section 7(3) states that the inventor is the person who devised the invention. However, an important exception is to be found in s 7(2)(b) which provides that any person entitled to property in the patent is entitled to claim. Although s 7(4) presumes that the person making the application is the person entitled, an employer, such as Benjy's Nightwear, may seek to claim the invention under s 39.

Disputes as to ownership of patents may be considered at first instance by the Comptroller and then by the courts. The onus of proof will be on Sue and Ronnie to establish ownership. (*Staeng Limited's Patents* (1996)). However, the invention made by Ronnie and Sue is closely connected to the line of business in which Benjy's Nightwear is engaged and involves materials originally derived from them, so the circumstances will necessitate close scrutiny by the court.

The court will consider the contract or job description under which Sue and Ronnie are employed. In resolving an issue, the evidence of documents described as job description and terms of employment are normally likely to be decisive. As there are no specific clauses relating to a specific duty to invent or ownership of any inventions which may result from employment, the court may look to equitable principles and implied terms. Certainly, Benjy's Nightwear are likely to argue vigorously that a term should be implied which results in Benjy's being the legal and beneficial owners of the patent.

The absence of a term or a condition in the contract does not prevent an employer being able to claim a patent for an invention devised by an employee. Both common law and statute could be raised by Benjy's Nightwear. Although it was well established that in the absence of an express condition relating to an invention by employees, there could be implied into a contract of employment a covenant that inventions so made in the course of employment should be held by the employee on trust for the employer. However, in *Electrolux Ltd v Hudson and Others* (1977) it was held that because the first employee was not employed to invent and had made no use of materials, and the invention was outside work, the patent could not be claimed by the employer.

Where an employee, in the course of his employment, has made an invention which it was part of his or her duty to make, the law imports into the employment contract a term that the invention, and hence any patent, is the property of the employer. The term can only be altered by an express agreement that the ordinary relationship between employer and employee does not apply and the parties have contracted on some other basis. Employer's rights are paramount (*Patchett v Stirling Engineering Co Ltd* (1955)) and if the employer obtains a patent, it will be deemed to be held on trust.

Benjy's Nightwear may also cite *Triplex Safety Glass Co v Scorah* (1938) as to whether anything may be read or implied into the first contract of employment any agreement not to take part in activities harmful to the plaintiff. The only implied term was that he would serve his employer with good faith and fidelity.

However, the mere fact that the invention was made in the employer's time, and with the employer's materials, so that the employer – with the inventor's consent – has been using it is not necessarily determinative. In *Mellor v Beardmore* (1927), Art (9), the court held that the mere existence of a contract of service in no way disqualifies a servant from taking out a patent in his own name and entirely for his own benefit – and that notwithstanding the fact that he has used his employer's time and materials to aid him in completing his invention, either express or implied, to communicate the benefits of his invention to those who employ him.

In order to determine ownership of the patent between Sue and Ronnie as opposed to Benjy's Nightwear, the Comptroller or the court will apply s 39 of the PA 1977. Under s 39(1), inventions made in the course of employment belong to the employer in three situations. The court must determine whether the invention was made; (a) in the normal course of the normal duties of the employee; or (b) in the course of duties falling outside his normal duties but specifically assigned to him, and the circumstances in either case were such that an invention might reasonably be expected to result from the carrying out of his duties. Under s 39(1)(b), where the invention is made in the course of the duties of the employee and, at the time of making the invention, because of the nature of his duties and the particular responsibilities arising from the nature of his duties he had a special obligation to further the interests of the employer's undertaking.

Section 39 declares what had formerly been common law. The court will take the approach laid down in *Harris's Patent* (1985) to determining ownership of inventions made by employees. In *Harris*, in considering the relevant circumstances under s 39(1)(a), the 'circumstances referred to the invention in suit' – not to any invention. It was held that if an invention meets s 39(1)(a), it will fulfil s 39(1)(b).

In addressing s 39(1)(a), the court will accordingly consider a number of factors. First, it is necessary to decide what constitutes inventing. Normal duties or alternatively what duties lying outside that category that were 'specifically assigned to him'.

Secondly, it is necessary to decide what circumstances in either case were such that an invention might reasonably be expected to result. The court will closely consider the duties that Ronnie and Sue are engaged upon, looking for innovative and developmental aspects of their duties. In this question, the duties of Ronnie consist of marketing existing products and keeping an eye on lines brought out by rival manufacturers. His duties do not seem to involve inventive features and reporting on the activities of competitors. Whilst the discovery might lie in the field of work, Ronnie and Sue do not have a duty to invent. It does not matter that Ronnie and Sue have made their invention at home. The precise location of where the invention was made is irrelevant. (*Harris's Patent*.)

As it seems unlikely that s 39(1)(a) can apply, the next question were duties such as to place in s 39(1)(b). Again, much will depend on the nature of Sue's work. Is she employed to protect the nature of existing products or to improve them? It might be more problematic since Sue is in quality control which might involve improving products – her work could be interpreted as involving a special obligation to further the interests of Benjy's Nightwear.

In *Glasgow Health Board's Application* (1996), the court had to determine whether an invention was solely owned by a hospital employee who had devised an optical spacing device for use with an indirect opthalmoscope. The employee had clinical responsibilities and participation in teaching. He was not contracted to research. It was a fallacy to assume that his duty to treat patients extended to devising new ways of doing so. The circumstances of making the invention had nothing to do with carrying out duties. Whilst the invention might be a useful accessory to his contractual duties, it was not really part of it. Jacob J found the application for a patent should proceed in the employees name alone.

If neither circumstances are satisfied under s 39(1), the invention will belong to Ronnie and Sue by virtue of s 39(2).

Compensation

Alternatively, if the court determines the issue against Ronnie and Sue, they could seek to make an application under s 40 of the PA 1977 for compensation if the invention proves commercially successful.

Where the patent belongs to the employer, the compensation scheme may be theoretically used to remunerate inventor employees where the patent is of outstanding benefit. Under s 40, Ronnie and Sue would be entitled to claim a fair share taking into account the nature of their duties and existing remuneration.

The Patent Rules (1990) govern the application procedure. Section 59(1) states that an application to the Comptroller under s 40 for an award of compensation shall be made on the appropriate form. The prescribed period for making the application is the period which begins when the relevant patent is granted and which expires the year after it has ceased to have effect.

Under Rule 59(3), the Comptroller will send a copy of the application to the employer who has two months in which to file a counter statement if he wishes to oppose the claim beginning with two months from which the statement is sent. The Comptroller will then send this to the employee, who will have an opportunity to file evidence in support of his case, as will the employer, and evidence in reply within two months. It will be important that they put in all evidence. The Comptroller may give such directions as he may think fit with regard to subsequent procedure. No further evidence may be supplied without leave (Rules 59(7) and (8)).

Question 42

Discuss the 'pith and marrow' and the purposive approaches to patent claims.

Answer plan

The issues to be considered are:

- Pith and marrow doctrine
- Purposive approach
- *Catnic Components v Hill* (1982)

Answer

The construction of a patent is of great importance to its proprietor, since it defines the exact scope of the monopoly that the proprietor enjoys. A patent specification is divided into two parts, the general description and the claims under s 14(5) of the Patents Act 1977.

In cases of disputes over the nature, area and protection which a patent afforded, the courts formerly applied what is termed as the 'pith and marrow' construction to patent claims. The 'pith and marrow' approach effectively considers that certain essential parts of an invention constitute the patent which may be infringed.

The first case in which the term 'pith and marrow' approach appears is *Clark v Addie* (1877). The patent related to improved apparatus for clipping and shearing horses. The court upheld the view that a patent may be granted not only in respect of the whole and complete invention described, but also in respect of a subordinate integer part. However, the patent must be described so as to make it clear in respect of what the patent is granted, and the failure to properly explain or describe the claim as a result of the specification was defective.

In *Clark v Addie,* the court found (*per* Lord Cairns) that it was necessary for the tribunal to determine in what way the patent would be infringed. One approach would be to take the whole instrument. A second would be to decide whether an infringer had taken parts of the invention which could be said to be the 'pith and marrow' of the invention, although the infringer might not have taken all of the parts.

The construction of a specification, as for all other instruments, is a matter for the court to decide, but explanations of the words or technical terms of art are matters of fact upon which evidence may be given (*Hill v Evans* (1862)). With a 'pith and marrow' doctrine, the court has to find that the infringement falls within the text of the claim.

In cases hinging on construction, the onus lies on the applicant to satisfy the court or tribunal that a matter falls within the specification. In order to judge whether something falls within a claim, it is necessary to ascertain the essential substance of the claim. Something not mentioned in the claim cannot be included by an infringer and will infringe even if he does not take every integer of the claim. Vagueness in a patent claim can arise from the use of an ordinary word in the English language such as 'pad' (*Re Weber's Patent* (1946)), or 'hub' (*Raleigh Cycle Company Ltd v H Miller & Company Ltd* (1946)).

In *Proctor v Bennis and Others* (1887), the court used the alternative phrase 'colourable variation'. The court was determining the liability of the defendant where the defendant, although not taking the exact combination of a machine, has taken the essence of it, and therefore his machine would be called a colourable variation, ie an infringement. A colourable variation is where a man makes slight differences in the parts of his machine, although really he takes in substance those of the patentee and gives colour to the suggestion that he is not infringing the patented machine when he is really using mere substitutes for portions of the machine so as to get the same result for the same purpose.

Thus, prior to the PA 1977, the law was such that the approach was to construe literally and if the alleged infringement did not textually infringe, to consider whether the alleged infringement took the substance of the invention, ie the 'pith and marrow' of the claim.

An example of the approach is found in *Rodi & Wenenberger v Henry Showell* (1969), where Upjohn LJ stated that the court must ascertain what are the essential integers of the claim – a question of construction on general principles. Once the essential integers are identified, the court had then to consider the alleged infringing article. To constitute an infringement, the infringer had to be found to take all the essential intergers. If non-essential parts were taken there was no infringement.

The purposive approach

When ascertaining the extent of the monopoly claimed, the courts had in mind that the purpose of the claims was to give the patentee protection and at the same time to give a reasonable amount of certainty to the public. In *Catnic Components Ltd v Hill & Smith* (1982), the House of Lords considered a claim involving a lintel used in load bearing. The defendants used a similar lintel, differing in the angle of alignment. The defendants claimed that their variant was not an infringement of the patentee's claim of a vertical lintel if construed literally, since their lintel stood at a slight angle. They also denied 'pith and marrow' infringement since the perpendicular stance was a functional requirement of any lintel. The House of Lords in considering the matter found the patent infringed on the basis that the term 'vertical' meant 'vertical or sufficiently close to vertical to be able to perform the same functions as it would have done if it were vertical'.

Lord Diplock stated that 'The question in each case is whether persons with practical knowledge and experience of the kind of work in which the invention was intended to be used would understand that strict compliance with a particular descriptive word or phrase appearing in a claim was intended by the patentee to be an essential requirement of the invention so that any variant would fall outside the monopoly claimed, even though it could have no material effect upon the way the invention worked'. The purposive approach takes the view of the limits of the claim depending on the reader, rather than exactly marking out the boundaries.

In *C Van der Lely NV v Ruston's Engineering Co Ltd* (1985), the plaintiffs claimed a patent in a rotary cultivator. Three patents were alleged to be invalid on the basis that none were sufficiently and clearly defined (ambiguity) and that they were not fairly based on the matter disclosed in the specification. The Patents Court found against the plaintiff who appealed. In dismissing the appeal, the court held that it was necessary to construe claims in the context of and with reference to the specification. However, it was not a legitimate approach to limit the scope of the claim merely because the invention was described in the specification in more restricted terms or by reference to some limitation not expressly or by inference reproduced in the claim itself.

Following *Catnic Components Ltd v Hill & Smith Ltd* (1982) the courts have taken the view that the way to determine the ambit of the monopoly set out in a claim was to apply the principle of purposive construction set out by Lord Diplock. His approach was subsequently taken to have provided the three 'Catnic questions' as set out in *Improver Corporation v Remington Consumer Products Ltd* (1990) by Hoffman J to aid purposive construction and determine the width of a patent monopoly. Firstly, the court should consider whether the variant put forward has a material effect upon the way in which the invention works. If the answer to this question is yes, then the variant is outside the patent claimed. Secondly, if the answer to the question is no, the court must consider whether this would have been obvious to a reader skilled in the art. If no, the variant is outside the claim. If yes, the court must thirdly consider whether a reader skilled in the art would nevertheless have understood from the language of the claim that the patentee intended strict compliance with the primary meaning as an essential requirement of the invention. If yes, the variant is outside the claim.

In *Daily v Establissements Fernand Bercket and Others* (1992), Balcombe LJ stated that, (notwithstanding the mystique with which some patent lawyers appear to surround the exercise of their expertise,) the approach of the court in infringement cases is first to construe the specification, using canons of construction that are to be applied to every written instrument construed by the court. He affirmed that this must be the purposive approach taken in *Catnic* rather than the literal approach (*Glaverbel SA v British Coal Corp (No 2)* (1993) – a patent is to construed in the way it would have been done at the time of filing the specification by those skilled in the relevant field). In interpreting this, the court may have regard to Article 69 of the European Patent Convention (*per* Mummery J). In *Assidorm v Multipack* (1995), Aldous J held that the purposive approach fits squarely with the Protocol Guidelines on interpretation. The Protocol on Article 69 provides that it shall not be interpreted so that the extent of the protection given by a European patent is to be understood as that defined by a literal meaning of the wording used in the claims, with the drawings and the descriptions being used only to determine any ambiguities. Similarly, the claims are not reduced to mere guidelines, allowing the patentee to obtain protection for what he thinks has been obtained. Effectively, the approach of interpretation is to navigate between two extremes, combining a fair protection for the patentee and a reasonable degree of certainty for the public.

Question 43

Holbrook was an employee at Projections Corporation, a business concerned with making laser systems and searchlights for projecting images on clouds. Whilst he was an employee, Holbrook helped develop a new sky-writing device which Projections have sought to patent in their own name. Shortly after making the application, Projections dismiss Holbrook and he finds a job with BrightSky Ltd who are in the business of luminous advertisements and sky-projection themselves.

Shortly after Holbrook's departure, staff at Projections Ltd are shocked to see in Bang! magazine, a journal for fireworks manufacturers, a promotional offer for sky-writing equipment. The magazine is promoting an exhibition with the offer of a reduced price laser projector for Bang! subscribers, supplied by BrightSky. Further inquiries reveal that BrightSky are marketing their laser projector with a special launch event at a site in Battersea, London. Projections Corporation instruct their legal department to write as follows to BrightSky, the magazine and the site owner:

> Take notice that we shall take all necessary steps to protect our patent. We trust that you will govern yourself accordingly and withdraw your plans for the exhibition as described in the recent edition of Bang! Should it not be possible to reach a settlement proceedings may issue.

The letter is marked 'without prejudice'.

Projections Corporations also place an insert in Bang!, advertising their product and stating their intention to protect their patent, and have the same displayed at their Web-site. The insert includes a statement that 'because of the value of this item, our rights will be enforced'. Exhibitors withdraw from the event and it has to be cancelled.

One exhibitor, Charlie, who had hoped to invest in a laser projector wishes to clarify the position and telephones Projections Corporation. An employee tells him, 'Withdraw from this or you may get caught up in legal action'. Charlie is worried by this and withdraws from the exhibition.

Answer plan

Threats to sue for patent infringement are actionable unless they can be justified. This is in an important aspect in advising a party in a patent question to ensure their rights are not stated too widely, thus exposing the party to a theoretical claim for threats. Similar provisions apply under the Registered Designs Acts 1949 and have recently been extended to the Trade Marks Act 1994.

The issues to be considered are:

- Section 70 of the Patents Act 1977
- Meaning of 'aggrieved'
- Section 60 of the PA 1977
- Section 69 of the PA 1977
- *Brian v Ingledew Brown Bennison & Garrett* (1996)

Answer

Under s 70 of the Patents Act 1977, it is an actionable wrong to issue groundless threats of proceedings. Section 70 provides that if any person (whether or not entitled to any right in a patent) issues threats for patent infringement, a person aggrieved by the threats (whether or not the person to whom they were made) may bring an action against a person issuing them.

In each of the cases, the parties must be persons aggrieved. Whether a person is aggrieved is a matter of law but whether a person is actually aggrieved is a matter of fact (*Brian v Ingledew Brown Bennison & Garrett* (1996)). The term was considered by Lord Denning in *Attorney General (Gambia) v N'Jie* (1961): 'The words "person aggrieved" are of wide import and should not be subjected to a restricted interpretation. They do not include, of course, a mere busybody who is interfering in things that do not concern him; but they do include, of course, a person who has a genuine grievance because an order has been made which prejudicially affects his interest'.

Threats may be justified under s 70(2)(a) which enables a threatener to avoid liability. To fall within the protection of s 70(2), Projections Corporation will have to show that the respects in which the threat of proceedings was issued would constitute an infringement of a patent under s 60. Section 70(4) provides that an action will not lie for a threat of proceedings for an alleged manufacture or importation of a product or of using a process. A threat of proceedings for manufacture or importing the sky-writer based on laser beams could thus fall within the exception under s 70(4). In *Therm-A-Stor Ltd v Weatherseal Windows Ltd* (1981), Oliver LJ stated, *obiter*, that the word 'product' was a perfectly general word apt to describe any article, and there is nothing in s 70(4) which confines it to an item which is the subject of a patent.

The solicitor's letter

The letter from the solicitor will be an actionable threat, and liability could attach to both Projections and the solicitors concerned, despite marking it 'without prejudice', a step which normally ensures correspondence aimed at settlement cannot be raised in proceedings. A letter marked 'without prejudice' can be a threat since the words do not protect the maker of the threat, as in *Kurtz & Co v Spence & Sons* (1887). In *Cavity Trays Ltd v RMC Panel Products Ltd* (1996), Aldous J held that a patentee can make a threat against a person that he will be sued for manufacturing products for disposal once the product has been made. A patentee can give adequate warning of intended proceedings by alleging that the manufacture of a product will infringe. Here Projections have gone much further. The defence under s 70(4) is limited and does not extend to threats involving exhibitions, promoting or marketing, such as would be involved in the trade fair.

As the defendant to proceedings, Projections Corporations, in pleading any threat justifiable must give particulars identifying the acts relied upon as being infringing acts by the plaintiff in respect of which proceedings were threatened (*Reymes-Cole v Elite Hosiery Co Ltd* (1961)). Since a defendant can be any person who has issued the threat, irrespective of whether they have an interest in the patent, the solicitors could be personally liable for the threats that have been issued (*Benmax v Austin Motor Co Ltd* (1953)).

The advertisement

The PA 1977 uses the words 'circulars, advertisements or otherwise', and both the insert in Bang! and the message being displayed on their Web-site would fall within this definition. The words 'or otherwise' are not construed *ejusdem generis* with the preceding words (*Driffield & East Riding Pure Linseed Cake Co v Waterloo Mills Cake Warehousing Co* (1886)).

A general warning which does not suggest the goods of any particular person was held not to be a threat in *Challender v Royle* (1887). Here the wording goes beyond a general assertion of rights and has caused exhibitors to cancel. Given the broad definition of the term 'aggrieved', customers who had been prompted to withdraw might well be able to issue proceedings, so the potential for a claim against Projections could be very wide.

Statement to Charlie

The statement made to Charlie will also amount to an actionable threat, even though it is not, from the words used, directed at him personally. Generally, a threat will be actionable if it is a statement that would be reasonably believed by the person to whom it is addressed to be a threat of proceedings for infringement of a patent (*CP Developments Company (London) Ltd v Sisabro Novelty Co Ltd* (1953); *Wills & Bates Ltd v Tilley Lamp Company* (1944)). The position is not altered by the fact that Charlie is not the subject of the threat, as patent threats need not be directed at the person threatened (*John Summers & Sons Ltd v Cold Meat Process* (1947)).

In each of these cases, an aggrieved person may seek an injunction to prevent the continuation of the threats and may recover damages for any loss that has resulted from the threats. Alternatively, the court will restrain a patentee from issuing further circulars and notices threatening legal proceedings unless he undertakes to commence proceedings to assert the validity of the patent.

Since the question states that the patent has not yet been granted, problems could ensue. If BrightSky or Holbrook bring a claim for threats, Projections Corporation could seek to justify their threats in terms of patent infringement. This, however, will not be a bar to BrightSky and Holbrook's claim (*CE'SNOA Ltd v Poseidon Industrie AB* (1973)). BrightSky and Holbrook and any other party would be entitled to bring revocation proceedings to have the patent declared invalid (*John Summers & Sons Ltd v Cold Metal Process Co* (1947)).

If Projections have yet to obtain the patent, the court would have to consider their position in relation to their rights under s 69 of the PA 1977. Section 69 provides that where an application for an invention is published, the applicant has the same rights subject to s 69(2) and (3) as if the patent had been granted on the date of publication. Under s 69(2)(a), this includes the right to bring proceedings in respect of any act, and under s 69(2)(b) if the act would, if the patent had been granted on the date of publication of the application, have infringed not only the patent but also the claims (as interpreted by the description and any drawings referred to in the description or claims) in the form contained in the application prior to publication by the Patent Office.

In *Brian v Ingledew Brown Bennison & Garret* (1996), the Court of Appeal held that a threat made in respect of s 69 rights could be an actionable threat under s 70. However, the Court of Appeal differed in its views as to whether it was possible to justify such a threat under s 70(2) in the same way as if the patent had already been granted. Aldous J took the view that it was illogical to construe s 70 as giving rights to a person threatened with proceedings for infringement of a patent in respect of actions before the grant, if it was not open to the threatener to be able to justify the threats as proper.

There will be no difficulty for Projections Corporation provided their patent in the sky-writer is granted before trial. The view taken by Aldous J was that s 70(4) allows a threatener to avoid liability if the acts giving rise to the proceedings constituted or would constitute an infringement of the patent under s 60, read in conjunction with s 69. No difficulty would arise in deciding whether the threats can be justified provided the patent is granted before trial of the threats action, although in a case of delay a court would determine the question of whether the patent would be valid based upon the balance of probabilities. However, Hobhouse LJ did not share this view. Whilst agreeing that the threats concerning s 69 rights were actionable and that the person making the threat was required to prove under s 70(2)(a) that the alleged acts complained of would constitute an infringement of the patent, his view was that the threatener would have to overcome a high burden of proof in demonstrating this, since the criteria in s 70(2) are 'absolute and objective'. It was therefore no defence to the person making the threat to say that he had a *bona fide* belief that he would be granted the patent, nor that he had reasonable grounds to believe that he probably would be, nor that the patent would probably be sufficiently wide to justify the threats.

Given this uncertainty in the law and the potential liability to threats proceedings, it might be advisable for Projections Corporation to reach a licensing agreement or settlement with BrightSky.

Question 44

Irvings Chemical Co and Stokers Chemicals Ltd are both producing chemical products and carrying out research in similar fields. Irvings Chemical Co seek to obtain a patent for a chemical substance they have developed which aids the clotting of blood. What are the chances of obtaining a patent if related results could have been predicted by Stokers Chemicals Ltd, who have been working in a similar branch of chemistry but did not make the substance or anticipate the effect that the chemical could have on the blood?

Assuming the patent is granted and Irvings Chemical Company discover that Stoker Chemicals are now manufacturing the patented substance without licence, advise what Stokers Chemicals Ltd on the tactics they might use in their defence. What would be the position if Stokers Chemicals subsequently discovers further evidence that impugns novelty after the court has decided the issue in Irving Chemical Co's favour?

Answer plan

This question looks at chemical patents, revocation proceedings and the doctrine of *res judicata*.

The issues to be considered are:

- Obviousness
- Infringement
- Revocation
- *Res judicata*

Answer

Irvings' patent must comply with s 1(1) of the Patents Act 1977 in being novel, involving an inventive step, being capable of industrial application and not falling into an excluded category. Patents may be granted in chemical substances, wherever the chemical substance is not part of the prior art, and treated like any other article.

Irvings' application will be considered in light of the state of the art, defined under s 2(2) of the PA 1977 as comprising all matter which has been made available to the public '... by use or in any other way'. The court will consider the evidence contained in the documents which Stokers will seek to raise. Under s 3, the invention must actually be disclosed to undermine novelty, and such disclosure must be an enabling disclosure allowing the manufacture of the product and the availability of any particular materials (*Asahi KKK's Application* (1991)).

The question of whether an inventive step is involved will vary from case to case and much will depend on the evidence placed before the court (*General Tire and Rubber v Firestone Tyre* and *Rubber Co Ltd* (1972)). The presence of an inventive step has often been a complicated issue in chemical patent cases and a variety of tests may be applied. A test often used in the past was an adaptation of the 'Cripps question' first propounded in *Sharp & Dohme v Boots* (1928). The patent involved the use of higher alkyl resorcinols which were alleged to be especially valuable as germicides. The question was, 'Was it for all practical purposes obvious to any skilled chemist in the state of chemical knowledge existing at the date of the patent, which consists of the chemical literature available ... and his general chemical knowledge that he could manufacture valuable therapeutic agents by making the higher alkyl resorcinols?' If the answer was yes, the patent would fail for obviousness.

In *May & Baker and Ciba Ltd's Patent* (1948), it was held that an invention consisting of the production of new substances from known materials by known methods cannot be held to possess subject matter simply on the basis of being new. If the substances are useless, no invention will follow. However, an invention may be patentable where it consists of substances which are new or if the substance is a selection patent – one obtained from a known series of compounds. Even where an invention consists of the production of further members of a known series whose useful attributes have already been described or predicated, it may possess sufficient subject matter to support a valid patent provided that the conditions in *IG Farbenindustrie AG's Patents* (1930) are fulfilled in producing a substantial advantage to that known before.

A more recent test in *Olin Mathieson v Biorex* (1970) was whether a notional research group at the relevant date, in all the circumstances, which include a knowledge of all the relevant prior art and of the facts of nature and success of a particular chemical compound, would be led directly to try and produce an alternative in the expectation of producing a useful alternative. In *Beecham Group Limited's (Amoxycillin) Application* (1980), Buckley LJ held that choice of a particular line of research could be taken as evidence of the necessary inventive step.

Since Irvings' patent has a biological use, it may be necessary to consider obviousness from the point of view of a notional expert in two disciplines. In *Boehringer Mannheim GmbH v Genezyme Ltd* (1993) *per* Aldous J, it was held that the notional skilled addressee might be a person with a degree in chemistry and experience in enzymology and carbohydrate chemistry. In practice, the court recognised the 'skilled person' would be a team including an enzymologist and a carbohydrate chemist.

In *Windsurfer v Tabur Marine* (1985), a four-fold test for obviousness was laid down: (1) identifying the inventive concept; (2) imputing to a normally skilled but unimaginative person knowledge that was the state of the art; (3) identifying the difference between the prior art and the invention in suit; and (4) deciding whether the differences, viewed without hindsight of the invention, constituted obvious steps or required a degree of invention.

An invention can be old without being obvious where an earlier inventor has missed the significance or failed to disclose the features now contained in Irvings' patent.

In *Du Pont v Akzo* (1981), the Court of Appeal considered that a substance that had never been made could not have been used and thus could not properly be described as 'known'. Although a compound was chemically predictable as a formula, it was not a known substance until Irvings made it. Similarly, in *Beecham v Bristol (Patent Licence Agreement)* (1978), a patent for a semi-synthetic penicillin Amoxycillin could not be said to have been invented until first manufactured. In *Du Pont (Witsiepe's) Application* (1982), the House of Lords considered that as a general rule a patent cannot be claimed in discovery of a new quality in a known substance. This does not apply, however, when the new quality or use is discovered in or for a product or process which is merely a member of a class. If the special qualities were unknown until Irvings revealed them and the document did not predict that it might have them, this may be sufficient to rebut a claim of obviousness. The mere fact that the formula is mentioned in an earlier reference will not invalidate the claim if it is based on an unexpected new property from one of a class.

Since the substance has an effect on the clotting of the blood, the patent may be open to attack on the grounds that it involves a form of medical treatment. Irvings will have to take particular care with drafting the claims. No patent will be allowed in a method of treatment. Section 4(2) of the PA 1977 precludes an invention of a method of treatment of the human or animal body by surgery or therapy, or of diagnosis from being capable of industrial application.

Infringement and defences

The monopoly granted by a patent can only be infringed if one or more claims of the complete specification are infringed. This will depend upon whether Stokers has committed an act in relation to the Irvings' patent prescribed by s 60. If the patent is valid, Stokers will be liable for infringement under s 60(1)(a) of the PA 1977 if he goes ahead and manufactures the substance. If Irvings' patent is valid, two alternative forms of action may be brought depending on the stage which Stokers' manufacture has reached. In *Shoe Machinery & Co Ltd v Cutlan* (1896), Romer J stated that there are two kinds of action which can be brought by a plaintiff patentee, 'that the defendant has infringed before action is brought, and in respect of this the plaintiff is entitled to claim damages, or an account, and an injunction to prevent similar infringement in future. The other action is based on the fact, not that the defendant has infringed but that he threatens and intends to infringe; and in this case the plaintiff may claim an injunction'.

In either case Stokers may enter a defence and commence revocation proceedings. A defendant is required to serve defence and counterclaim and particulars of objections, which must be served within 42 days of service of the statement of claim (RSC Order 104). In objecting to the validity of a patent under s 72, Stokers will have to serve particulars of the objections to Irvings' patent with the petition.

A denial of infringement by Stokers will put Irvings to proof that Stoker has: (a) committed the acts complained of in the breaches, and (b) that such acts are an infringement of the patent. Depending on the evidence, Stokers could allege want of novelty or lack of inventive step, and in the particulars specify the name of every person alleged to have made such a use, whether it continued to the priority date and, if it is not possible to state this, the earliest and latest occasion on which use took place. Particulars should contain drawings as necessary (Order 104(2)).

Stokers' citation of a formula in earlier documents may not be prejudicial to patentability. As the first makers, Irvings may still retain the chance of successfully defending revocation proceedings. Section 63 of the PA 1977 provides for the eventuality of a patent being held to be partially valid. As a condition of relief under s 63(3), the court or the Comptroller may direct that the specification of the patent shall be amended to its or his satisfaction. Having regard to the court's discretion, should the patent specification be amended as sought? Was the specification for the patent framed in good faith and with reasonable knowledge and skill?

Under s 62(3), no damages shall be awarded in proceedings for infringement of the patent committed before the decision to allow the amendment, unless the court or the Comptroller is satisfied that the specification of the patent as published was framed in good faith.

If Stokers fail to revoke the patent but subsequently discover new evidence which impugns novelty, it is unlikely that he will be able to issue fresh proceedings. The doctrine of *res judicata* applies in patent actions as much as in any other branch of civil law. In *Shoe Machinery Co Ltd v Cutlan* (1896), the discovery of fresh evidence did not entitle a party to re-litigate. When the question of the validity of a patent is brought before the court, a litigant 'is bound to put his whole case before the court; if he does not do so, it is his fault or misfortune'. (This was subsequently applied in *Chiron Corporation v Organon Teknika Ltd* (1994).)

Chapter 6

Confidential information

Introduction

Confidential information is protected by way of an action in equity. Essay questions will typically relate to the elements of the action, or the public interest defence which has developed particularly in the last 30 years. The public interest defence is one which may also be cited in copyright cases.

In a problem question, a tie up with copyright or patents can be expected and a discussion of the balance of convenience in granting an injunction and Anton Piller order is also expected. Problem questions may frequently involve an employer/employee situation and a knowledge of *Faccenda Chicken v Fowler* (1985) is therefore important.

It should also be noted that confidential information is a way of protecting ideas which cannot be protected by copyright. See *Frazer v Thames Television* (1984).

Checklist

- *Coco v A N Clark* (1969)
- *Faccenda Chicken v Fowler* (1985)
- *Gartside v Outram* (1857)
- *Initial Services v Putterill* (1967)
- *Lion Laboratories v Evans* (1984)
- *Seager v Copydex* (1967)

Question 45

Confidential information

Outline the elements and scope of the doctrine of confidential information.

Answer plan

A straightforward question. As many cases involve the duty of confidentiality in the context of employer-employee relationships, a knowledge of these principles is important.

The issues to be considered are:

- Basis of claim
- *Coco v A N Clark* (1969)
- Public interest
- Application to ideas

Answer

The publication and dissemination of true and accurate information may be actionable at law if the information was originally received under a duty of confidence. The origins of breach of confidence lie in equity. Its exact basis is unclear, and foundations in contract, tort and common law have all been proposed. In *Frazer v Evans* (1969), the basis was proposed to be one of 'good faith' (*per* Lord Denning).

Elements of the action

The elements of an action were set out by Megarry VC in *Coco v A N Clark (Engineers) Ltd* (1969) as: (1) the information must have a necessary element of confidentiality – ie it is of a type to be protected; (2) the information was communicated in circumstances of an obligation of confidentiality; and (3) the information will be used in an unauthorised way, possibly resulting in damage.

In *Coco,* it was doubted whether equity would intervene in a case unless the circumstances are of sufficient gravity; equity ought not be invoked merely to protect trivial tittle-tattle, however confidential. Megarry VC suggested a 'reasonable man' test of 'if any reasonable man standing in the shoes of the recipient of the information would have realised that upon reasonable grounds the information was being given to him in confidence, then this should suffice to impose upon the equitable obligation of confidence'. The Law Commission (Report 110) rejected this test, but it has continued to be applied in subsequent decisions. The reasonable man may be expected to have a knowledge of intellectual property rights. In *Carflow Products (UK) Ltd v Linwood Securities (Birmingham) Ltd and Others* (1996), which involved showing prototypes for a design, the view was taken that a reasonable man would not look at transactions without having an awareness of other intellectual property rights and would not expect to be under an obligation of confidence.

Types of information protected

Although the courts have protected a wide range of material under the doctrine of confidential information, to succeed in a claim the plaintiff must be concerned with information having certain characteristics. The courts have applied it to personal relationships (*Argyll v Argyll* (1967)) protecting marital confidences; commercial records (*Anton Piller KG v Manufacturing Processes Ltd* (1976)); trade secrets (*Seager v Copydex* (1967)) and government secrets (*AG v Jonathan Cape* (1976) and *AG v Guardian Newspapers* (1990)). Not every form of information, however, will be protected by the confidentiality tag. In *Saltman Engineering Co Ltd v Campbell Engineering Co Ltd* (1963), Lord Greene MR stated that information must have 'the necessary quality of confidence about it, namely it must not be something which is public property and public knowledge', and Megarry VC in *Coco* doubted, *obiter*, 'whether equity would intervene unless the circumstances are of sufficient gravity; equity ought not to be invoked merely to protect tittle-tattle, however confidential'. An injunction will only be granted if the confidential information can be defined with some precision (*Lock International plc v Beswick* (1989)). The fact that copied information could be pieced together legitimately is no defence (*Johnson & Bloy v Wolstenholme Rink* (1987)). Information that has been revealed in a court case ceases to be confidential (*Chantry Martin v Martin* (1953)). In *Attorney General v George Blake* (1996), it was held that former members of the secret intelligence service owe a lifelong duty to the Crown. Once information ceases to be secret the duty of confidentiality is extinguished.

In *Faccenda Chicken v Fowler* (1985), Goulding J held that information in the employment context could be divided into three categories: (1) information of a general or trivial type which was not confidential; (2) information that was the employee's stock in trade, working knowledge which remains confidential whilst the employment contract remains in force; this obligation ceases once it ends, and any restriction should be on the basis of an anti-competition clause; and (3) information that was so sensitive or secret (eg formulae, trade secrets) that it could never lose its designation as confidential information which can only be used for the employer's interests. The duty of confidentiality is wider while the employee is in post than when he or she leaves employment.

In *Hytrac Conveyors Ltd v Conveyors International Ltd* (1983), an Anton Piller order was obtained but no statement of claim made until 12 weeks after the issue of a writ. The court held that an action should not be started where the plaintiff was unable to identify the claim until an Anton Piller was issued. Where questions of copyright and breach of confidence are concerned the exact ambit of the plaintiff's claim should be declared.

The equitable basis of the claim should not be forgotten and cases may turn on their facts. Where information has been released into the public domain as in *Lennon v News Group Newspapers Ltd* (1978), where Lord Denning distinguished the protection of *Argyll v Argyll* (1967) to marital secrets, observing that the plaintiffs given their reported behaviour could not be said to have had 'much regard for the sanctity of marriage' and that through giving stories to the press they had placed themselves in the public domain.

An obligation of confidence arises in the employer/employee relationship to all confidential information derived from either a contractual term or alternatively as an implied term. In *Tipping v Clarke* (1843), Wigram VC stated, 'Every clerk employed in a merchant's counting house is under an implied contract that he will not make public that which he learns in the execution of his duty as clerk'. To the present, the courts have found that the employer/employee relationship can be the basis for an action for breach of confidentiality. Employees are under obligations to employers not to disclose confidential information obtained in the course of and as a result of employment. The obligation of confidence may arise from an implied term in a contract, quite apart from any express restrictive covenants (*Bents Brewery Co Ltd v Hogan* (1945)). In *Initial Services v Putterill* (1968), Lord Denning considered that only the person to whom a duty is owed can claim it.

Confidential information can protect ideas and thus confer protection where no other right is available. As in *Maudsley v Palumbo & Others* (1995), 'breach of confidence has mitigated the well established principle that in copyright there is no protection in ideas'. In *Gilbert v Star Newspaper Co Ltd* (1894), it was held that protection will lie for the plot and dramatic ideas in plays which remain unpublished in written form. There may be no breach of copyright but there can be an action for a breach of confidence. Section 171(1)(e) of the Copyright Designs and Patents Act 1988 states that nothing in the Act affects the operation of any rule of equity relating to breaches of trust or confidence.

The scope of confidential information is not unlimited and one of the important defences to an action for breach of confidence is the defence of public interest. Formerly this defence had largely been restricted to cases of 'iniquity' where a person would be justified in breaking a confidence. In *Lion Laboratories Ltd v Evans* (1985), the Court of Appeal in an interlocutory decision accepted the defence and refused an injunction in a case involving the exposure of a confidential report indicating defects in a new breathalyser which when used could ultimately result in wrongful conviction of motorists. Stephenson LJ outlined considerations a court should take into account, and stressing the judgment was not a 'moles' charter', the court hedged the defence with a number of important strictures, it being equally recognised that there is also a public interest in upholding confidentiality.

Remedies

The action must be for damages and not simply for restraint. Damages may be claimed for breach of confidence (*Seager v Copydex Ltd (No 2)* (1967)) on a tortious basis, and considered analogous on the same basis for the conversion of goods (*per* Lord Denning). This will only be effective if the information has not yet been released and an injunction will be sought on a *quia timet* basis.

When considering injunctive relief, the court weighs the two competing interests of confidentiality and disclosure. It is possible that the court will grant an injunction on some parts of the information and not others. At this stage, there will not be a full hearing of evidence or law involved, although the approach laid down in *Series 5 Software Ltd v Philip Clarke & Others* (1996) was that the court should rarely try to resolve complex issues of disputed fact or law but could look at the overall strength of each party's case.

Confidentiality may still be maintained even though the information has already been published. According to *Schering Chemicals v Falman Ltd* (1982), the wider interest in maintaining confidentiality must be weighed against the public interest in making the issue known at large. The plaintiffs obtained an injunction although the information had already been published in the press or on television because it 'included information which ... could not be republished without risk of causing further damage to Schering'.

If further material damage cannot be prevented, there will be no purpose in granting the injunction (*Lord Advocate v The Scotsman Publications Ltd* (1990)) and normally if information has been widely disseminated the injunction will be refused, although exceptions exist as in *AG v Guardian Newspapers Ltd* (1987), where an injunction restraining publication was upheld by a majority of the House of Lords even though the book was widely available abroad. (The injunction was subsequently discharged at trial.)

Question 46

Outline the scope of the 'public interest' in cases of breach of confidence. Is it correct to say that a defence has been established?

Answer plan

A question which requires consideration of a chain of judgements from *Initial Services v Putterill* (1967) to *Lion Laboratories v Evans* (1984).

Answer

Over the last 30 years, the courts have indicated that a claim of public interest may justify a breach of the obligation of confidence. Originally, this defence was termed the 'iniquity' rule but increasingly it has been recognised as the defence of public interest, and several cases overlap with copyright infringement actions, to which a specific public interest defence is now provided (s 171 of the CPDA 1988). What has been a live issue is the scope of this defence which may justify the breaking of otherwise confidential obligations and whether it is limited to the exposure of 'iniquities' or whether it embraced a wider concept of public interest.

Equity and common law recognised the obligation of good faith to an employer and in keeping with the *laissez faire* attitude of the 19th century, there was not a distinct defence of public interest. Rather, the courts' view was expressed in *Gartside v Outram* (1856) that, 'The true doctrine is, that there is no confidence as to the disclosure of an iniquity', Wood VC further adding that 'no private obligations can dispense with that universal one which lies on every member of society to discover every design which may be formed, contrary to the laws of society, to destroy the public welfare.' Originally the defence was raised in cases involving the exposure of unlawful acts by an employer.

Frequently, the courts have begun with the authority of *Gartside v Outram,* but arguably the birth of the public interest concept as a defence lies with decision in *Initial Services v Putterill* (1967). In *Putterill,* price-fixing agreements contrary to law were exposed in breach of an obligation of confidence but the Court of Appeal refused to strike out a defence of public interest. Lord Denning took the view that a defence to disclosure was not limited to cases of fraud or crime but extended to 'any misconduct of such a nature that it ought in the public interest be disclosed to others.' Lord Salmon also called into question the traditional concept of iniquity 'what was iniquity in 1856 may be too narrow or two wide in 1967'.

In *Frazer v Evans* (1968), Lord Denning considered that 'iniquity' was not the fundamental issue underlying the public interest but was only an example of a new test, stating that there were some things which may be required to be disclosed in the public interest which no doctrine of confidence could be used to conceal.

The defence of public interest was raised in *Hubbard v Vosper* (1972) where an appeal against an interlocutory injunction was upheld on public interest grounds, the harm to the public being the quack remedies being promulgated by the plaintiff which the defendant sought to expose. Following *Hubbard v Vosper*, in the case of *Beloff v Pressdram Ltd* (1973), Ungoed-Thomas J stated that the defence of public interest 'as now recognised by the law' but declined to allow the defendants to claim the benefit of it in a case involving a leaked memorandum from the *Observer* to the satirical magazine *Private Eye* where the information in question did not disclose any 'iniquity or misdeed'. Ungoed-Thomas considered that 'public interest' involved matters such as threats to national security, breach of the law, fraud, breach of statutory duty and matters medically dangerous to the public and 'doubtless other misdeeds of similar gravity.' The use of the term 'misdeeds' indicates that Ungoed-Thomas regarded the defence as being limited to cases of iniquities.

The reluctance to extend the public interest arose from the recognition that there is also a public interest in ensuring confidences are upheld, in preserving the doctrine of confidentiality and that there is a public interest in employees honouring their obligations. Just such a balancing exercise took place in *Distillers Co (Biochemicals) Ltd v Times Newspapers Ltd* (1975). In *Distillers,* the court took the view that the misdeeds contemplated in *Putteril* would include those which had yet to be committed.

In *British Steel Corporation v Granada TV* (1981), the media of information and the journalists who wrote for them had no immunity based on public interest which protected them from the obligation to disclose their sources of information in a court of law where the court in its discretion considered such disclosures necessary. In *British Steel Corporation v Granada Television* (1981), Lord Wilberforce and Lord Frazer were content to refer to the public interest exception as the 'iniquity' rule, but as an *obiter* statement it does not expressly rule out a wider concept of public interest.

In *Woodward v Hutchins* (1977), Lord Denning suggested that a wider basis could exist for public interest, including the alcoholic excesses and sexual behaviour of popular singers travelling on planes. Lord Denning took the view that such public figures could hardly complain if their activities were revealed. In *Khashoggi v Smith* (1980), an injunction was refused to Mrs Khashoggi to prevent an article in the *Daily Mirror* containing details from a former housekeeper, partly on the grounds that she had courted publicity. These may be distinguishable from public interest cases, however, and it may be that where the plaintiff has presented him or herself in a favourable light, the court will not see it as inequitable to restrain the release of information which shows an opposite view.

In *Malone v Metropolitan Police Commissioners* (1979), the plaintiff claimed that telephone tapping could result in the breach of confidential information. Megarry VC reviewing the authorities held that considerations such as confidentiality in cases of telephone interception were necessary in the detection of crime.

In *Cork v McVicar* (1984), the offences related to potential corruption by the police and this was held to be a situation where the passing of information to the press could be justified. *Francome v Mirror Group Newspapers* (1984), concerned an allegation that breach of jockey club rules should have been disclosed to the police or the jockey club. A release to the *Daily Mirror* was not acceptable destination for the information.

Lion Laboratories Ltd v Evans (1985) concerned the results of a laboratory test in a confidential report indicating defects in a new breathalyser. The *Lion* case is the first in which a public interest succeeded where an iniquity was not involved. The Court of Appeal recognised that there was a public interest in a serious issue affecting the life of citizens and the risk of wrongful convictions based upon the potentially unreliable recordings of the breathalyser, even though the information had been obtained in breach of confidence.

Stephenson LJ outlined considerations a court should take into account as follows: (1) the public may be interested in matters which are not their concern; (2) the media has its own interest (as stated in *Francome v Mirror Group Newspapers* (1984), '...they are particularly vulnerable to the error of confusing the public interest with their own interest.'); (3) the best recipient for information may not be the police or other responsible body.

In *Lion Laboratories v Evans* (1985), there was no evidence of 'iniquity' on the facts of the case, but a wider public interest could be identified in the proper administration of justice. *Malone* and *Francome*, both involved allegations of an iniquity. As part of the process, the Court of Appeal confirmed that there is a strong public interest in preserving confidentiality within any business and thus be able to rely on its employees. In *Lion,* the Court of Appeal attempted to give guidance and stated that a court must ask whether a serious defence of public interest may succeed at the trial.

Stephenson LJ took the view that the court should not countenance disloyalty or give its assistance to a breach of trust, whatever the motive of the informer. Griffiths LJ stated that the defence of public interest is not 'a moles charter' and with an admitted breach of confidence there is often a powerful argument in favour of maintaining the *status quo*. To allow to publish confidential information, the defendants must do more than raise a plea of public interest. It was necessary to show 'a legitimate ground for supposing it is in the public interest to be disclosed.'

In cases where a public interest defence is raised, Lord Denning in *Putterill* took the view that the recipient of confidential information must be someone who has a proper interest in its receipt. In some cases this could be the press. In *Francome v Daily Mirror* (1984), Donaldson MR acknowledged the part the media may play 'in exposing crime, anti-social behaviour and hypocrisy' but also stated that there was a danger in confusing the media's interest with the public interest, there being a profound difference being matters of public interest and issues which simply interest them.

The ruling by the Court of Appeal that the 'public interest' defence is not limited to cases to iniquity is in line with several judgments by Lord Denning (including that in *Frazer v Evans*) and with the recommendation of Law Commission (Report No 110). Taken together, the authorities establish a genuine defence which exists independently of the scope of the equitable conditions for granting or refusing the remedy of an injunction or damages. As with libel proceedings, the court treats the defence of public interest separately if there is a public interest in the information being disclosed. It would therefore be pleaded independently, before the court applies the normal tests of whether the injunction should be granted.

It is therefore correct to say that a defence of public interest has been developed. However, whilst approved by the courts, it nonetheless remains hedged with restrictions and to a large extent each case will be decided on its facts.

Question 47

The Softhead Users Group is a consultancy firm giving advice on the use and application of Softhead computer software. SUG issues a company newsletter and support service.

Frank is an employee of the Softhead Users Group who leaves after four years of employment. Frank decides to set up his own company Support For Softhead SFS.

Several of customers of the Softhead Users Group network receive brochures form the newly formed SFS which resemble those issued by SUG. This leads SUG to believe that Frank has copied material and taken a list of customers, although no lists are found to be missing. The Softhead Users Group are concerned that Frank will use his acquired knowledge in direct competition against them.

Advise the Softhead Users Group on their position.

Answer plan

- Copyright
- Confidential information
- Passing off
- Remedies – Anton Piller orders and injunctions

Answer

Copyright

The first question to determine is whether there is any copyright on which SUG can claim. Since protected works are not required to have any literary merit (*Exxon Corporation v Exxon Insurance Consultants* (1982)), it is likely that the brochure will be a protected original literary works under s 1(1)(a) of the Copyright Designs and Patents Act 1988. There is no copyright in information or ideas but only in the manner of expressing them. The list could be protected as a compilation under s 3(1) of the CDPA 1988 and there are a number of authorities which would support SUG having a claim provided that has been skill and labour in making the compilation is distinct from the labour and skill in ascertaining the information (*Waterlow Directories v Reed* (1992)).

Elanco Products v Mandops (Agrochemical Specialists) (1979), involved instructions for the use of herbicide which were in the public domain. A list of customers and supplies could amount to a copyright work. In *Collis v Cater* (1898), a chemist prepared a catalogue of articles and medicines arranged under various headings and sub-headings. A company carrying on several similar businesses copied the plaintiff's list from the catalogue omitting only two preparations. The argument that a mere dry list could not be the subject of copyright was rejected.

Having been in post for four years it would hardly be surprising if Frank had not remembered some names. In such situations, an inference cannot be drawn that Frank must have taken away a list of SUG customers or had consciously memorised the list before he left SUG. In *Coral Index Limited v Regent Index Limited and Another* (1970), Stamp J held that it was not right to draw an inference of improper copying or retention of lists where knowledge was equally explicable on the basis of employee experience.

In the light of all the evidence the court has to reach a conclusion as to whether the literature produced by SUG could be the subject of copyright, or whether it was merely something which gave news or information of which competitors were free to avail themselves.

Where a defendant sets up a case that his work is a fair compilation of others and is not a mere copy from anyone, it is of the highest importance that the defendant should produce his original manuscript.

In *Francis Day Hunter v Bron* (1963), the court looked at the similarities between the two. There must be two elements present (i) a sufficient objective similarly between the infringing work and the copyright work, or a substantial part of it; and (ii) the copyright work must be the source from which the infringing work is derived. The same case affirmed that subconscious copying or unconscious recollection can amount to infringement.

If copying can be established the court will then determine whether there has been substantial part amounting to infringement.

Copying the extract from the brochure is likely to amount to a substantial amount of the text and will constitute infringement under s 16(3). Frank's actions will amount to infringement in terms of reproducing the work in a material form and possibly making an adaptation of it, contrary to ss 16 and 21.

Confidential information

Equity provides some protection for confidential information on the basis that it is unconscionable for a person who has received information on a confidential basis to release that information (*Stephens v Avery* (1988)). Customer lists may be protected by the doctrine of confidential information (*Anton Piller Manufacturing v KG Processes* (1976)) but here it is not established that Frank has retained or copied one. (The high standard of proof and the need for potentially serious harm as prerequisites of granting the order would preclude SUG from obtaining an Anton Piller order in this case – see below).

However, here Frank has left and will therefore be subject to a less rigorous duty. In *Faccenda Chicken Ltd v Fowler* (1987), the Court of Appeal drew a distinction between confidential information binding a man only during his employment under an employed duty of fidelity or good faith, and confidential information of a more restricted class. In *Faccenda Chicken,* the court divided confidential information into three classes: (i) trivial or publically available information; (ii) information of a confidential nature but which remains in an employee's head and becomes part of his own skill and knowledge. Such information is confidential whilst employment continues but the obligation ceases on termination; (iii) certain trade secrets so confidential in nature that they cannot be disclosed to third parties or lawfully be used for the benefit of anyone else. On the facts, it seems such knowledge as Frank holds will fall into category (ii) which he may retain and use after employment ceases. It is not an actionable breach of duty of fidelity for an employee whilst he is still in employment to make plans or preparations for when that employment ends. Knowledge of who the customers may be falls into the category of information that is not confidential once employment has ceased.

The question does not refer to any covenant in the contract of employment restraining Frank but in any event such a clause if interpreted by SUG as grounds to restrain Frank might be vulnerable to a counterclaim of restraint of trade.

Passing off

A claim in passing off is unlikely to succeed, although both are operating in the same field of activity. The action in passing off does not seek to restrain fair competition, only misrepresentations that are made in the course of trading. In this case, the similarity in names between the two businesses is limited to the use of the word 'Softhead'. The use is descriptive indicating the type of business which Frank is seeking to carry on. Use of similar descriptive words without more will not be enough to generate a right to bring an action for passing off. It would be necessary to show that the name would have acquired a secondary meaning to indicate sources as distinct from its obvious meaning (*Wotherspoon v Currie* (1872)). Since Softhead does not make the software but simply provides a support service, no claim could be sustained on this basis.

SUG would have to show that Frank as a new entrant to the market was imitating the established company name or get up so that there was or was likely to be a deception of customers. If there was an acquisition of customers or if customers were induced to believe that there was an association between the two, an action might lie. Unless Frank has garnished the name in a script or similar get up there is unlikely to be passing off.

Whilst injurious association has been recognised as a type of damage for which an injunction can lie (*Annabel's Club v Schock* (1972)), the evidence available is that customers have realised the two are separate. In *Office Cleaning Services Ltd v Westminster Windows and General Cleaners Ltd* (1949), it was stated that 'in the case of trade names, the courts will not readily assume that the use by a trader as part of his trade name is likely to cause confusion and will easily accept small differences as adequate to avoid it'. Furthermore, the use of Softhead is a descriptive term. While a defendant who falsely applies a descriptive term to which he is not entitled is liable to an action in passing off by persons whose business goodwill will be damaged (*Erven Warnink RV v J Townend & Sons (Hull) Ltd* (1979)), it will be difficult to show actionable damage since no one seems to have assumed that there is a link between the two businesses and Frank has taken steps to distinguish his business. The title could not give rise to an action for passing off since it was what the magazine was about. The fact that customers have passed the brochures on to SUG without showing any confusion further suggests that there is no actionable misrepresentation.

Remedies

The court will consider an application for an injunction on the basis of the principles in *American Cyanamid v Ethicon* (1975).

In confidential information cases, the position for damages is complicated and since there appears to be no ground for an injunction, a claim for damages is also unlikely to succeed given that the basis of the claim lies in equity. If the plaintiff cannot succeed with a claim for injunction, the case for damages is negligible.

Similarly, a claim for an injunction to restrain passing off will fail since the elements of the tort have not been made out and there is no evidence of damage. Accordingly, there is no evidence of the high standard needed to justify the issue of an Anton Piller order. Orders for the seizure of documents are not to be granted to enable plaintiffs to go on 'fishing expeditions'.

However, an injunction will lie to restrain breach of copyright infringement. The claim for extensive losses caused by the copyright infringement and recoverable as damages is unlikely to succeed. The court is likely to follow the approach in *Work Model Enterprises Ltd v Ecosystems Ltd and Clix Interiors Ltd* (1996) and hold that the protection of copyright will not extend to everything which happens after appropriation and the court will only consider the value of what is taken.

Chapter 7

Character merchandising and malicious falsehood

Introduction

Chapter 7 is a miscellaneous chapter dealing with two other areas of intellectual property: character merchandising and malicious falsehood.

Question 48

Character merchandising

In the 1960s, Peter played a TV character 'Uncle Luke' in 'Luke's Wild Frontier', a TV series based on a 19th century novel set in the United States after the American Civil War. The series ended in 1972 but there have been regular re-runs on TV and Peter takes part in fan conventions.

Ollie wants to promote his chain of theme restaurants dedicated to American fast food and tripe. He secretly takes a photograph of Peter leaving a 'Luke's Wild Frontier Convention'. He cuts and expands the photograph and uses the cut-out of Peter's face in the hoarding of his new restaurant. Ollie makes further copies and sends them to his other outlets.

Some weeks later Peter is horrified to see his face adorning the decorations on the front of one of Ollie's restaurants, styling itself 'Uncle Luke's Dixie Fried Tripe'. Peter is appalled by the thought of his features being incorporated in an international food chain. Advise Peter as to remedies.

Answer plan

Character merchandising is an area where English authorities have shown a marked reluctance to expand intellectual property rights, although this has not been the approach in the Australian courts.

The problem question covers a range of remedies which may be invoked but none is absolutely certain.

A question which relates to a grey area of the law – the appropriation of 'personality'.

The issues to be considered are:

- Names and titles – copyright position
- Status of photographs in defamation
- Passing off
- Malicious falsehood

Answer

In this question, Peter seeks to restrain the use of his image in a photograph taken by Ollie for decorating a restaurant. Unfortunately, English law gives few remedies to persons who have their images appropriated without their permission and he is therefore not in a very strong position legally.

The TV company responsible for the original television series will own copyright as a literary work in the script and the images of the film under s 1(1)(a) of the Copyright Designs and Patents Act 1988, the film itself under s 4 and as a broadcast under s 7. Although the original series was broadcast in the 1960s, rights in the television show would be transformed into equivalent rights under the transitional provisions of the CDPA 1988. As Peter would have been an employee, it is likely that the first ownership in any copyright would be vested with the TV company (*Byrne v Statist* (1914)) unless the contrary can be shown by a contract of employment. Thus, only the TV company would be entitled to sue for infringement of any copyright in Uncle Luke but such a claim would be unlikely to succeed. The photograph is not a still from the film or broadcast, so there will be no infringement.

Firstly, other than the name Uncle Luke, Ollie has not appropriated anything from the show. There can be no copyright in names or titles (*Francis Day Hunter v Twentieth Century Fox* (1940); *Taverner Rutledge v Trexapalm* (1975)) being too short to constitute literary works.

A photograph is capable of being protected under s 4 of the CDPA 1988, being defined as a recording of light or other radiation on any medium on which an image is recorded. A still from a film is capable of copyright protection, as is a photograph taken from a television screen (s 17), with the exception of a photograph taken for private or domestic use.

However, the photograph which Ollie has taken does not come from any broadcast image but is a photograph of a living person, Peter. There is no direct causal connection between this work and any type of copyright work contained in the TV series. Ollie can claim to be the author for the purposes of s 9 of the CDPA 1988 as the person who has taken the photograph. He has therefore created an original work, not a copy.

The only viable claim that the TV company might attempt to bring would be to argue that there is a copyright in the character of Uncle Luke. This is further complicated by the fact that the TV company did not conceive of the character of Uncle Luke, and the original novel stated to be 19th century is likely to be out of copyright.

There is a limited right to privacy in certain photographs which prevents their display in public as part of the moral rights conferred by s 85(1)(b) of the CDPA 1988, but these are confined to specially commissioned photographs involving private occasions.

Defamation

Libel might provide a basis of a claim, but the jury would have to make the appropriate finding before an injunction would lie. In *Monson v Tussauds* (1894), the plaintiff had been tried and acquitted of murder. A wax model of him with a gun was displayed by the defendant. Collins J left open the question of 'whether a private person can restrain publication of a portrait or effigy of himself which has been obtained without his authority'.

In *Dockrell v Dougall* (1899), the plaintiff failed in a claim for an injunction where his name had been used in an advertising campaign for quack medicine but a jury had failed to find it libellous. It was necessary to show an injury to his name or profession which in the absence of a libel could not be done.

In *Sports and General Press Agency v Our Dogs Co Ltd* (1916), rights to photograph were purportedly sold to a dog show. A photographer who had a ticket of admission entered and took photographs but there was no trespass. Horridge J stated: 'In my judgment, no one possesses a right of preventing another person photographing him any more than he has a right of preventing another person giving a description of him, providing the description is not libellous or otherwise wrongful'. In *Correlli v Wall* (1906), the plaintiff sought an injunction to restrain a publication of postcards of imaginary scenes. Swinfen Eady J held that a person could be libelled by a picture or by an effigy, but the facts were not clear enough to justify an injunction.

The authority which offers most support to Peter is *Tolley v J S Fry & Sons Ltd* (1931), where the defendants published a caricature of the plaintiff, a well-known amateur golfer, in an advertisement for their chocolate. A successful action for libel was brought on the basis that the advertisement carried an implication that he had sold his amateur status in advertising the defendant's goods. However, the Court of Appeal took the view that 'unless a man's photograph, caricature, or name be published in such a context that the publication can be said to be defamatory within the law of libel, it cannot be made the subject matter of complaint by action at law' (*per* Greer LJ).

Passing off

Cases involving real personalities have frequently been unsuccessful. In *McCulloch v Lewis A May (Produce Distributors) Ltd* (1947), an entertainer who broadcast as 'Uncle Mac' could not prove passing off of a cereal advertised with the name of his character. In *Sim v HJ Co Ltd* (1959), the actor Alistair Sim failed in his claim of passing off where his voice had been impersonated on the radio.

It is likely that Peter will be in a similar position. Difficulties will certainly be encountered in claiming passing off as it is a prerequisite that every element of the tort must be proved. The essence of the action is to be able to show a misrepresentation and damage.

Other examples may be cited in relation to passing off. In *Shaw Brothers (Hong Kong) v Golden Harvest* (1972), the plaintiffs claimed successfully with regard to their character 'Fang Kang' the 'one-armed swordsman' but the reasoning in this case is not clear. Again the problem is that unless the TV company can be persuaded to bring an action, Peter is not the owner of the 'get up', merely a servant associated with it.

A further bar to an action in passing off is that there is no common field of activity, Peter being an actor and celebrity while

Ollie is a restauranter. Although in *Lego v Lemelstrich* (1983) the plaintiff was able to obtain an injunction to restrain a defendant in a different field, the Court of Appeal has recently moved away from this approach, declaring that to be known to everyone is not the same as to be known for everything.

The question of licensing may have a bearing on Peter's position in another respect. In *Children's Television Workshop v Woolworths (NSW) Ltd* (1981), the Australian High Court accepted that image-bearing merchandise is produced under licence from or with the approval of the image owner and this could amount to a misrepresentation. In *Hogan v Koala Dundee Pty Ltd* (1988), the tort of passing off was held to cover an intentional misappropriation of personality.

Malicious falsehood

In English law, there is no presumption that a person suffers damage from being identified as having endorsed the goods or business of another. Although the law is not entirely clear, it would seem that if the plaintiff is in the business of granting licences under his name, then an unauthorised use will be taken to have deprived him of a royalty he might otherwise attract, even if the plaintiff and defendant are not in direct competition. An alternative claim might be malicious falsehood. The elements of a malicious falsehood which must be proved are a false statement, made maliciously or with a reckless disregard to the truth, resulting in damage. Damage must also be proved.

In *Kaye v Robertson* (1990), the court expressed its distaste at the defendants' who had secretly photographed the plaintiff in his hospital bed and printed a purported interview, and condemned the lack of a remedy to protect privacy. The court upheld a claim that there was a malicious falsehood on the basis that the alleged interview was untrue (the falsehood), the method of acquiring it amounted to bad faith (malice) and the potential damage lay in the fact that the plaintiff's right to sell an exclusive story of his accident and experiences would be reduced in value by virtue of the defendant's publication. Here, Peter might seek to claim that there had been a loss of a licensing opportunity or the chance to sell his 'image' to others.

In this case, it could be difficult to show intention and resulting damage to Peter, unless the court accepts that there has been harm by the diminution of opportunities to license his image to others.

In the circumstances, unless Peter can establish that the publication of the photograph is some way defamatory, he may have difficulties under the current law in obtaining an injunction.

Question 49

Outline the elements of an action for malicious falsehood.

Answer plan

The issues to be considered are:

- Falsehood
- Malice
- *Kaye v Robertson* (1990)
- Damage
- The Defamation Act 1952
- The Defamation Act 1996

Answer

Malicious falsehood is a remedy available to a plaintiff where a party makes statements which are untrue and damaging. The tort is of long standing (being also known as injurious falsehood or trade libel) and may be applied in a wide range of situations. It consists of the making of a false statement, with malice, to a person other than the plaintiff, with the result that the plaintiff suffers damage.

Its origins are to be found in the old action of slander of title involving cases of one person making a false statement about a plaintiff's title to land, causing the plaintiff to find it more difficult to sell it (*Bliss v Stafford* (1573)). The scope of the claim was expanded to encompass slander to goods where the defendant made statements which attacked the plaintiff's goods. A further development was in *Sheperd v Wakeman* (1662) where the plaintiff lost her chance of marriage through the defendant falsely and maliciously alleging she was already married. By the 19th century, it was clear as in *Ratcliffe v Evans* (1892) that an action could lie for written or oral falsehoods, not actionable in themselves, but where maliciously published and calculated in the ordinary course of things to produce or be expected to produce actual damage. In *Ratcliffe v Evans*, the defendant had published a story that the plaintiff firm had ceased to exist. The jury found that the statement had not been published in good faith and that it had caused actual damage. An action will lie for damage wilfully and intentionally done without just cause or excuse.

An action for malicious falsehood may be combined in appropriate cases for an action to restrain trade mark infringement or in a situation where the right lies to restrain threats where these have been made an actionable wrong under statute. The tort of malicious falsehood may therefore be used to restrain comparative advertising campaigns, now also regulated by s 10(6) of the Trade Marks Act 1994. Malicious falsehood has been pleaded in cases of alleged passing off (*Ciba-Geigy plc v Parke Davis & Co Ltd* (1994)).

Essential elements of the action

The essentials of the action were set out by Lord Davey in *Royal Baking Powder Co v Wright Crossley & Co* (1901) as follows: (1) an untrue statement; (2) made maliciously without just cause or excuse; and (3) the plaintiffs had suffered special damage.

These were restated more recently in *Kaye v Robertson* (1990) where the Court of Appeal granted an injunction against the editor of the *Sunday Sport* to prevent publication of an article purporting to be an interview with the actor Gordon Kaye who had been photographed while recovering in hospital from the effects of an accident. The plaintiff did not consent to this course of conduct and an action for malicious falsehood was found to lie. The falsity consisted of the suggestion that consent had been given to the interview and pictures. The photographer and reporter would have known this was untrue when intruding on Kaye in hospital, thus providing the necessary malice. The damage consisted of the undermining of the plaintiff's right to sell his story of his accident as an exclusive to other papers. However, it must be stated that their Lordships were perhaps moved to accept this rather ingenious and constructive approach to establishing a claim of malicious falsehood because of their strong disapproval of the actions of the *Sunday Sport* reporters and the inadequacy of the law in other respects to restrain this invasion of privacy. As a common law tort, it is possible that the action may be open to future development and refinement.

Falsehood

The falsehood in an action must be a false statement of fact as distinguished from an opinion or a mere trade puff. This is as strict a requirement on the plaintiff as in an action for defamation (*Gutsole v Mathers* (1836)). Unlike an action for libel, the onus is on the plaintiff to prove the falsity of the words and the defendant to show the truth of them. There is no presumption of the goodness in a person's title to property or of the quality of merchandise. The need for the plaintiff to prove falsehood has always been vital element in the action. It was stated in *Pater v Baker* (1847) that unless a plaintiff shows falsehood, 'the plaintiff shows no case to go to the jury'. Equally, if a statement is true, no action will lie, no matter how damaging it may be (*Nahmaschinen v Singer* (1893) and *Danish Mercantile v Beaumont* (1950)). The plaintiff must prove that the defendant's statement was made maliciously. It is enough that the statement was made recklessly or with an improper motive.

The authorities were reviewed extensively in *De Beers Products v Electric Co of New York* (1975). Both parties were involved in manufacturing diamond abrasives for cutting concrete. The defendants issued a pamphlet which incorporated an alleged laboratory report comparing the goods manufactured by the plaintiffs with those of the defendants. The plaintiffs' goods were described adversely and those of the defendants were stated to be superior. Walton J held that the test to apply was whether a reasonable man would take the defendants' assertions seriously. For instance, a criticism that a Rolls Royce was useless as an amphibious vehicle would be an example of this category.

Regarding the statements in the brochure, a reasonable man would be likely to take the statement seriously because it was supposed to be a properly conducted scientific report. Walton J held that a trader was entitled to puff his own goods and make statements such as 'our goods are better than these which are produced by the plaintiff' even though the statements may be seen as denigrating the goods of the plaintiff. The defendants were not entitled to say that 'our goods are better than those of the plaintiffs because the plaintiffs' goods are rubbish', unless it could be shown that the goods were indeed rubbish.

In *Greers Ltd v Pearman and Corder Ltd* (1922), Scrutton LJ said that an honest belief in an unfounded claim is not malice but the nature of the unfounded claim may be evidence that there was not an honest belief in it. In some cases, it could be so unfounded that the particular fact that it is put forward may be evidence that it is not honestly believed. The absence of reasonable and probable cause may, but does not always, lead to an inference of malice, but it is clearly evidence of malice where the defendant puts forward a claim which he knows in fact to be unfounded. Malice can be inferred (*British Railway Traffic and Electric Co Ltd v CRC Co Ltd and LCC* (1922)). A reckless indifference to the truth may be inferred with statements of gross falsity and the cavalier way in which they may be published.

In *Atkins v Perrin* (1862), the court was asked to decide as a question of fact: (1) whether the defendant's belief was genuine; and (2) whether, if genuine, it was such as a reasonable man might hold. However, if a defendant seeks to raise a plea of justification the court may not grant interlocutory relief.

In *Easycare Inc and Another v Bryan Lawrence & Co* (1995), a malicious falsehood was alleged arising from the use of 'beware of imitations' in an advertisement. The court refused an interlocutory injunction on the basis that no injunction will be granted in defamation proceedings where the defendant announces his intention of justifying the truth of the statement. This approach follows the practice in libel cases. Only where the statement was obviously untrue on a common sense basis might an injunction be granted.

Damage

As with other torts, proof of damage is necessary to succeed in a claim. Until the enactment of the Defamation Act 1952, a plaintiff had to prove special damage. Possible losses could include diminution in value, loss of particular transaction and general trade losses.

Section 3(1) provides that it shall not be necessary to allege or prove special damage where:

- the words are published in written or permanent form and are calculated (likely) to cause pecuniary damage to the plaintiff;
- the words are calculated to cause pecuniary loss to the plaintiff in respect of any office, trade, profession, calling or business held or carried on by him at the time of publication.

In a case where damage is alleged and proved, it must flow naturally and directly from the use of the words complained of by the plaintiff (*Miller v David* (1874)). If damage is not the natural consequence no action can be sustained.

In *Hatchard v Mege* (1887), an allegation that the plaintiff was injured in his trade was sufficient. In *Dicks v Brooks* (1880), it was held that there must be 'sensible, appreciable damage'. In *Wilkinson v Downton* (1897), the plaintiff sued a defendant who for a practical joke had told her that her husband had been seriously injured. The plaintiff believed the statement and suffered shock. It was held that the costs of medical treatment could be recovered.

The Defamation Act 1996 imposes a limitation period of 12 months for an action under s 5. It also introduces a provision for the maker of the statement to make amends under s 2(1), including suitable correction, apology and compensation. If the offer is accepted it may be enforced through the courts.

Question 50

Kevin's Revolutionary Advanced Phones Ltd is a company set up by Kevin to sell mobile telephones. In the course of trade, Kevin makes a number of statements about models produced by Marples Mobiles, Xerxes's X-Phones and SupaCell Phones Ltd, who are trade competitors, as follows.

'You can try Marples Mobiles, but this won't go wrong. There is no better 'phone.'

'You can call the Moon and other planets on ours. You can't on anyone else's!'

Kevin tells an employee, Clive, to state: 'Xerxes's X-phones are codswallop – mine are genuine. Tests have proved it!'

'SupaCell Phones' mobiles should be called Skull-phones – because of the radiation your head will end up looking like a skull!'

Advise Marples Mobiles, Xerxes and SupaCell Phones on their position.

Also consider the position of Kevin's Revolutionary Advanced Phones Ltd against Kevin himself if he jocularly makes the statement 'Our 'phones are so cheap – they're rubbish, that's why' in a speech. Subsequently, bad publicity results and company profits fall dramatically.

Answer plan

The issues to be considered are:

- Malicious falsehood
- Elements of the tort
- Malice
- Puffs
- Damage
- Defamation Act 1996
- Director's liability

Answer

To make out a cause of action in malicious falsehood, the statements made by Kevin must be both untrue and made maliciously. An action will lie for written or oral falsehoods at common law which were made maliciously and are calculated to produce damage (*Ratcliffe v Evans* (1892)). Each of the parties will have to prove the statements are untrue and that they have resulted in damage. These are the strict requirements which the court will expect to be fulfilled.

Against this, a wider basis for malicious falsehood was suggested in *Kaye v Robertson* (1991), the essentials being the publication of false words maliciously and that special damage has followed as a natural result (s 3(1)). Damage is present if the words are calculated to cause damage to the plaintiff.

Statement mentioning Marples' mobile

Kevin's remark will not be amount to an actionable malicious falsehood against Marples Mobiles. In *De Beer's Abrasive v International GEC* (1975), Walton J held that any trader is entitled to puff his own goods, 'even though such a puff must as a matter of pure logic involve the denigration'.

In *Hubbuck v Wilkinson* (1899), Lord Lindley considered a circular issued by the defendants 'which comes to no more than a statement that the defendants' white zinc is equal to, and indeed somewhat better than the plaintiff's'. Such a statement, even if untrue and a cause of loss to the plaintiff, was not a cause of action. It is not a malicious falsehood for a person to puff his own wares, and to proclaim their superiority over those of his rivals is not actionable. If a statement to the effect that 'my goods are better than yours' or 'mine are better than X's' is made then no actionable misstatement is present (*White v Mellin* (1895)).

The statement about calling the Moon

These statements allege that Kevin's telephone could be used to make calls to the moon and other planets. It is clearly untrue. In *De Beers,* Walton J stated succinctly, 'the courts will do what any ordinary reasonable man would do, namely take it with a large pinch of salt'. In the case, Walton J considered the claim that a specialised diamond cutter was useless for carving into granite. He furnished the example of a defendant describing a Rolls Royce car as inferior because it would sink in water whereas an amphibious vehicle would float.

Whilst it was untrue, the first statement is one which would not be taken seriously. In *Lyne v Nicholls* (1906), it was held the plaintiff must show that there is something which links the two elements. In this statement, what Kevin actually implies about other telephones is true. Whilst there is a false statement, it is about Kevin's goods and not those of the other parties. In an action for malicious falsehood, it is necessary that the defendant must make some false statement concerning the plaintiff's goods (*White v Mellin* (1895)) although statements may be express or implied.

A mere puffing statement, even if inaccurate does not give a cause of action. According to *Balden v Shorter* (1933), an action does not lie without proof of actual malice. A statement false in fact and detrimental to the plaintiff's business, though not defamatory, will therefore not support such an action if it was made in the belief, even a careless belief that it was true.

In practice, the jury may infer malice from all the circumstances. In *Joyce v Sengupta* (1993), the Court of Appeal expressed the view in an application to strike out a plaintiff's statement of claim, that a reckless indifference could be inferred from the gross falsity of the statements and the way in which they were published.

The codswallop statement

If it amounts to a false statement honestly believed to be true but made with an intention to injure a plaintiff, it may be actionable. It would be actionable, however, if the statement was, 'Mine are better than yours because yours are rubbish' expressed in *De Beers*. In *Balden v Shorter* (1933), it was held that no action would lie where false and detrimental statements had been made carelessly without any indirect motive and without any intention of injuring the plaintiff.

Much will depend on Kevin's state of mind when he gave Clive the instruction. If he has a genuine belief in the truth of his statement, it is for the plaintiff to prove the falsity of the words and it will be for Kevin to justify the truth of them and his honest belief in them. If Kevin has not read the report, this could amount to a reckless indifference to the truth. In *Greers Ltd v Pearman* and *Corder Ltd* (1922), it was stated that 'Honest belief in an unfounded claim is not malice; but the nature of the unfounded claim may be evidence that there was not an honest belief in it. It may be so unfounded that the particular fact that it is put forward may be evidence that it is not honestly believed'.

Clive, as an agent, will stand in the same position as the principal (*Watson v Reynolds* (1826)). If he has made a statement in good faith which is unauthorised and untrue, the issue is whether the principal would have been entitled to make the statement. If so, the agent is also protected. Here, Clive has acted on Kevin's instruction but in good faith. Kevin is therefore liable (*Armstrong v Stain* (1951)). However, s 1(4) of the Defamation Act 1996 should also be noted. This puts employees or agents in the same position to the extent that they are responsible for the content of the statement and the decision to publish it.

The skull 'phone remark

In practice, the jury may infer malice from all the circumstances. This is a serious allegation and implies that the mobile phones manufactured by SupaCell are dangerous. There would be no need to prove special damage as the statement is calculated to cause pecuniary damage to the plaintiff in respect of their business being carried on at the time Kevin makes it.

Xerxes and SupaCell would be advised to seek an interlocutory injunction to restrain Kevin from making his remarks and from instructing Clive to do so. The court will apply *American Cyanamid* principles in determining whether to grant an injunction, but if Kevin intends to enter a plea of justification there could be problems.

Kevin's statement about the company's own product

The manner in which an allegation is made, either light heartedly or vituperatively, may render a statement one which a reasonable person would not take seriously (*per* Lord Blanesburgh in *Tolley v Fry* (1931)).

Where a plaintiff is a limited liability company, no less than an individual can maintain an action for slander without proof of special damage, where the words are calculated to injure its reputation in relation to its trade or business. The question is whether a limited liability company can sue without proof of special damage for slander imputing a crime punishable on a corporate basis.

In the case of torts committed against companies, a company may sue for any damage done to it in its corporate capacity by a tort which not of a purely personal nature, such as a libel affecting company property, or a libel reflecting its financial position or attacking its management (*Thorley's Cattle Food Co v Massam* (1880)).

Where the company is a victim of a conspiracy to which directors acting on its behalf are parties, the company will not be considered a co-conspirator, and may recover damages from the directors if it suffers loss (*Belmont Finance Corpn Ltd v Williams Furniture Ltd* (1979)). From these principles, it would therefore appear that potential liability may attach to Kevin in terms of an action against him, but only if any malice can be proved which seems unlikely.

Index

P